Advance Praise for *Countdown*

"For a book written about computers, and the management of technology, and the management of the people who have to manage the technology, Countdown displays unusual clarity and logic. Not only are the array of checklists and 'ask yourself' questions effective, they are also efficient."

—BRUCE CHAPMAN
PRESIDENT
DISCOVERY INSTITUTE

"Peter's insight and knowledge has been invaluable to the Year 2000 team at CIBC. His early advice got us started on the right track and has allowed us to build and execute a Year 2000 program that will assist us in being an early finisher in the race against time. There is always something new to learn from Peter."

—JOHN BURNS
VICE PRESIDENT, PROJECTS
CIBC

"The Millennium crisis has brought together the best project management minds on a global scale in creating solutions in order to minimize its impact. The open and unselfish sharing of ideas, processes, and information within and across all industries has been a key ingredient in mitigating otherwise more disastrous outcomes."

—DAVID M. IACINO
MANAGING DIRECTOR, MILLENNIUM PROJECT
BANKBOSTON

"Is Peter de Jager a Year 2000 prophet, alarmist, or simply a realist? To me it really doesn't matter . . . you've got to read this book!"

—HOWARD RUBIN
CHAIR, DEPARTMENT OF COMPUTER SCIENCE
HUNTER COLLEGE OF THE CITY UNIVERSITY OF NY

Countdown Y2K: Business Survival Planning for the Year 2000

Peter de Jager
and
Richard Bergeon

Wiley Computer Publishing

John Wiley & Sons, Inc.

NEW YORK · CHICHESTER · WEINHEIM · BRISBANE · SINGAPORE · TORONTO

Publisher: Robert Ipsen
Editor: Marjorie Spencer
Assistant Editor: Margaret Hendrey
Managing Editor: Marnie Wielage
Text Design & Composition: North Market Street Graphics

Designations used by companies to distinguish their products are often claimed as trademarks. In all instances where John Wiley & Sons, Inc., is aware of a claim, the product names appear in initial capital or ALL CAPITAL LETTERS. Readers, however, should contact the appropriate companies for more complete information regarding trademarks and registration.

This book is printed on acid-free paper. ∞

Published by John Wiley & Sons, Inc.

Published simultaneously in Canada.

Portions of this book were previously published in *Managing 00: Surviving the Year 2000 Computing Crisis*, ISBN 0-471-17937-X, 1997

This publication is designed to provide accurate and authoritative information in regard to the subject matter covered. It is sold with the understanding that the publisher is not engaged in professional services. If professional advice or other expert assistance is required, the services of a competent professional person should be sought.

Library of Congress Cataloging-in-Publication Data:

De Jager, Peter.
    Countdown Y2K : business survival planning for the year 2000 /
  Peter de Jager, Richard Bergeon.
        p.   cm.
    "Wiley computer publishing".
    Published simultaneously in Canada.
    Includes index.
    ISBN 0-471-32734-4 (pbk. : alk. paper)
    1. Year 2000 date conversion (Computer systems) 2. Software
  maintenance. I. Bergeon, Richard, 1945–   .
  QA76.76.S64D37   1999
  005.1'6—dc21   98-42269
                                          CIP

Printed in the United States of America.

10 9 8 7 6 5 4 3 2 1

This book is dedicated to Chicken Little, who was an optimist, and to the boy who cried wolf and never got the credit he deserved.

CONTENTS

A t the beginning of 1996, I had not heard of the Year 2000 computer problem. By the end of that year, I was hearing of little else. And, since then, it has taken over my life.

Time will tell whether that is a good or bad thing. But I am sure of something: One of the authors of this book, Peter de Jager, bears a heavy responsibility for getting me into this.

The fateful date was 16 April 1996. I was chief executive of the British government's Central Computing and Telecommunications Agency, hired by the government on a short-term contract to sort out the agency—cut costs, introduce a new business plan, reorganize the structure . . . that sort of thing. One of my staff had told me about the Year 2000 problem. I found it hard to believe, but, after some investigation, I decided it was important enough to arrange a conference for the public service. I remember we invited 6,000 and 120 turned up, which seemed pretty bad at the time, although, since then, I've become used to such disappointments. In particular, however, I remember our keynote speaker—Peter de Jager.

As chairman, I opened the conference by saying that, yes, we were facing a genuine problem. But I was unsure of its seriousness—if it was not fixed, where would we be on a scale from some inconvenience to global disaster?

Peter told us we had only 140 weekends left to the real deadline, 31 December 1998. He reminded us of the inaccessibility and fragility of much software. He said that the problem extended far beyond so-called legacy systems. He asked: How many still have all their source code? He warned of staff shortages. He suggested the cost to the United Kingdom could be as high as £20 billion ($33 billion)—an amazing figure then; but not now. He showed how we had trusted the information technology (IT) industry—and how it had betrayed that trust. He reminded us that IT projects are nearly always late—but this one must not be one millisecond late. He illustrated the interdependencies of modern society, how everything was "intertwingled." He spoke of the way one small defect could cause widespread havoc. He made it clear there would be no silver bullet. He told us we could not fix everything—and introduced (at least to me) the concept of *triage*. He emphasized that this was a management, not an IT, problem. This, he concluded, was a matter of survival.

It was a speech that, almost unchanged except for the need to reduce the number of weekends left from 140 to a terrifying 23, many businesspeople and politicians would benefit from hearing today. Far too many—hence the value of this book.

Well, after that speech, I was sure we were nearer the disaster end rather than the inconvenience end of my spectrum. Something had to be done about it.

Now, over two years later—what is the world doing?

Not enough. I have no doubt that the Year 2000 computer crisis will mean, at best, some unpleasantness for much of the world. But, if insufficient action is taken, the outcome will be more than unpleasant. In major Western countries, the action necessary to ensure a satisfactory outcome has been delayed for too long. Elsewhere, far too little is happening. There are only 17 months left until the end of the century—yet there are only the most rudimentary signs of a determined global initiative.

It is hard to exaggerate the seriousness of this extraordinary matter. At the end of the twentieth century, we have allowed computer systems to take over and order much of our lives. Most of those systems are potential victims of this problem. If we get it wrong, the consequences could be appalling: Many of the circumstances of our lives that we take wholly for granted—our jobs, the delivery of infrastructure services, telecommunications, health care, pensions and other financial services, and so on—could be compromised or even fail. And, although the realization of this threat is only a few months away, not enough is being done to overcome it. Survey after survey is unambiguous on this. But such failures are totally unacceptable—the problem has to be resolved.

A few months ago, the British–North American Committee sent a letter to the United States president and the prime ministers of Canada and the United Kingdom. It was signed by about 80 senior businesspeople and academics. They said that they were becoming acutely concerned about government preparedness. They called on governments to deal with the problem as a top priority: "The consequences of failure to act effectively are frightening to contemplate."

Such statements are alarming. Even so, a lot of nonsense is written about what it all means. So perhaps it would be useful to dispel a few of the myths. Or at least so far as those countries that are making progress are concerned—it may be that some of the more worrying predictions cannot be discounted for other parts of the world.

Despite press scares, the following scenarios are most unlikely: planes falling from the sky, elevators crashing to the bottom of their shafts, bank account details being irretrievably lost, microwave ovens and refrigerators failing, cars suddenly coming to a halt, weapon systems going berserk, nuclear plants becoming critical, heart pacemakers ceasing to operate, and so on. Even the much-discussed home PC probably may not have much of a problem. Everything will not grind to a halt at the end of the century.

There is more good news. In March, Tony Blair, the British prime minister, spoke eloquently about the importance of the issue—describing it as an emergency. And, more recently, President Clinton gave an equally strong warning: "This is clearly one of the most complex management challenges in history."

But, although it is encouraging that two world leaders have spoken in such a clear and public manner, that alone is not enough. Is the world listening? There is evidence that it is not. For example, a recent survey—carried out by Cap Gemini, one of the world's largest computer services businesses—indicated that one in six British organizations is unlikely to be ready on time, threatening 38 percent of the country's gross domestic product. Yet the same survey noted that Britain had done more than most other countries—if accurate, that would mean a dismal prospect for much of the rest of the world.

But disaster can be avoided: It is possible for any difficulties occurring after the date-change to be contained within acceptable limits and for total recovery to be effected well within a year. The world's economy is remarkably resilient and is flexible enough to recover. But only if such difficulties are minimized by concerted and effective action being taken now. There is desperately little time left. From now on, every day that passes is precious—none must be wasted.

However, an unexpected difficulty has emerged for those who understand all this and are anxious to see a resolution: Attempts to implement the only practicable solution are being criticized.

The difficulty is easy to explain.

In view of the huge scope of the problem and the extreme shortage of time remaining, a solution is only possible if its nature is widely understood and acted upon. As is clear from this book, it is not a problem that can be left to specialists—the involvement and initiative of ordinary people is essential. Also, because businesses and systems are so interdependent, those tackling the problem need access to accurate and detailed information about what is happening throughout the economy—both nationally and internationally. However, wide communication of what sounds like a major threat itself carries the risk that it could lead to widespread alarm. On the face of it, that would hardly be conducive to a solution.

How can this be resolved? It has to be—doing nothing and watching a mess develop is unacceptable. In any case, the panic and anger that would follow from people learning (probably by rumor and exaggeration) of an impending danger when there was nothing they could do about it would be far worse than anything that might happen if they were involved now.

The alternatives are possible alarm now and certain panic later. And *later* is barely a year from now. So, the answer is clear: A dose of constructive alarm now (albeit with unknown and possibly uncomfortable side effects) is vastly to be preferred to the possibility of an uncontrollable and pernicious panic next year. That must surely be obvious?

Not so, it seems. Those who try to communicate the facts—even with great care, even understatement—are dubbed by some as scaremongers and alarmists. That reaction is the enemy of progress.

So, what's going on? Well, I think it's this—governments are just waking up to the scale of the problem (otherwise they would have done far more by now to fix their own systems), and, understandably, they are worried about how to handle it. A well-proven political instinct is, wherever possible, to buy time—and, in particular, to avoid any unnecessary difficulty today. Therefore, they assert that action is being taken but try to stifle openness until they can come to terms with the issue and decide what to do about it. In normal circumstances, that might be a sensible reaction to an unexpected and threatening problem.

But these are not normal circumstances. In time, governments will realize that they have been getting it wrong. They are, after all, increasingly well advised about the problem. However, it is nearly too late for them to get it right now—so it will certainly be too late then.

Therefore, those who understand the problem and are determined that there has to be a solution have no choice—they have a duty to ignore the critics and look for ways of keeping the spotlight of publicity on the issue. And, at the same time, they must be unrelenting in their efforts to persuade those in authority of the urgent need for total openness.

There are just a few months to get vast numbers of organizations throughout the world to change their approach. For example, few seem to understand how electronics has made the global economy dangerously interdependent—and just how fragile are those interdependencies. In particular, there is the need for the most radical prioritization: There is not nearly enough resources or time to fix it all—less six months for the key systems of most larger organizations.

And, as most businesspeople know, computer projects are nearly always late. Unless there is a new approach, why should this one be any different?

So Tony Blair was right—this is an emergency. And, as he said, in an emergency, things must be done differently. In this case, one of those things is to communicate the facts widely and thereby enlist the energies and imagination of so-called ordinary people. Tell them what this is about and what needs to be done—how to avoid the worst consequences. This book is an excellent example of how to do just that. Get people involved—in finding alternative ways of doing things, in thinking the unthinkable.

In 1982, during the British conflict with Argentina over the Falkland Islands, I ran a medium-sized engineering business producing specialist navigation and communications equipment for the Royal Navy. My colleagues were amazing—they got on with it, focused, cut out bureaucratic nonsense, prioritized. They enjoyed it. We turned around jobs in two weeks that would have taken two months in normal circumstances. And quality improved.

We did the impossible then—and it's possible again now if people really understand the issues and, as a result, can be involved on the widest possible basis.

But this also requires a new approach at the top. And here my organization, Taskforce 2000, has been emphasizing two things: *openness* and *accountability*. Let's find out now what is going on and who is responsible.

We have been calling for a simple approach: Let the people at the top of central and local government departments and agencies, the utilities, listed companies, financial institutions, and so on declare publicly whether they are personally confident that their services or businesses will weather the date-change. If they are unsure, what are their uncertainties? In any case, what are their plans and targets? Let them specify their budgets, their responsible managers, and, not least, their contingency arrangements. And, where appropriate, get regulators and auditors to comment. Above all, tie names to the declarations: Only that way will we get useful information.

But even this will be of little value if some countries act but too little is done elsewhere. So the US, British, and other governments that are aware of the problem should see to it that well-funded, emergency international action is put in place now to minimize the impact of the problem on the global economy.

One other thing is certain: Such global considerations will be worthless unless each organization is tackling its own challenge. Many still need practical non-alarmist help. This book—written by two experienced and respected practitioners—provides just that, an accessible and comprehensive way.

—*Robin Guenier*
Executive Director
Taskforce 2000
July 1998

The following article was published by *Computerworld* magazine as the "In Depth" article in September 1993 and is considered by many as being the opening salvo in the battle against 00. As articles go, it's nothing special. It describes a technical problem everyone in the IT industry was aware of to some degree or other. There's no hype, no exaggeration, no discussion of consequences of failure. It's just a discussion of something we could and should fix.

The annotations are provided by Peter de Jager, the author of the original article. We hope it will serve as a retrospective on the public awareness shortcomings surrounding the Year 2000 problem and give you some perspective of how far we have come and how far we have yet to go.

Doomsday 2000

The title, to the best of my recollection, was chosen by the editor. In retrospect, it was a good choice, since it did eventually get the attention of the press. Understanding of the Year 2000 problem has grown in depth over the years, and *doomsday* seems the most fitting, if admittedly overstated, word to describe the potential consequences of failure to address it in time.

Certainly, for several years, anyone who spoke of this problem was described as a doomsayer.

> Have you ever been in a car accident? Time seems to slow down as you realize you are going to crash into the car ahead of you. It is too late to avoid it . . . you are going to crash . . . all you can do now is watch it happen.

This paragraph summed up my worst fears regarding the problem. Fears which, it turns out, have to a large part come true. The Year 2000 problem was unsolvable, but not from a technical standpoint. I still believe that if we pay adequate attention to the problems, we can still greatly minimize the negative impact we're about to experience.

The real problem, the one which we'll never really fix, is that people still don't believe or understand the nature of the problem. Public disbelief is what kept us from addressing the problem for so long—and now we feel like we're watching a car accident and are powerless to do anything.

> The IS community is heading towards an event more devastating than a mere car crash. We are heading towards the year 2000. We are heading towards a failure of our standard date format DD/MM/YY. Unfortunately, unlike the car crash, time will not slow down for us, if anything, we are accelerating towards disaster.

The problem was always incredibly easy to describe. All you had to do was point to DD/MM/YY and ask, "Do you see the problem as we move from 99 to 00?"

> This is a good news, bad news story. First the bad news . . . there is very little good news.

From the start, it was necessary to inject some humor, no matter how poor, no matter how feeble. Only humor would allow us to maintain our perspective. From the start, everyone aware of the issue knew that we'd be in it for the long haul. There would be no more vacations until this was solved.

> There is no way to avoid the fact that our information systems are based upon a faulty standard. A standard which will cost the worldwide computer community billions of dollars in programming effort. Perhaps more importantly, we are also going to suffer a credibility crisis. We and our computers were supposed to make life easier, this was our promise. What we have delivered is a catastrophe.

And so it came to pass. The question "How could the computer people be so incompetent?" has been repeated in thousands upon thousands of discussions and TV, radio, and press interviews. There's no avoiding it; this is the biggest blunder made by any technology. Nontechnical people still don't understand the reasons we offer up as excuses for leaving off the century.

> The problem is twofold. The date issue itself and, more importantly, our reluctance to address the problem.

It was always a combination of problems. The technical one that we could solve and the human component, which would ultimately force us to procrastinate until time is too short to implement the correct solutions.

> Go to any meeting of the ACM, DPMA, ASM, or any other computing society or association, ask for a show of hands of people addressing the date problem. If you get 1 in 10 respondents, then you are facing an enlightened group. Typically all you get are snickers and comments such as, "I won't be in this position or this company in the year 2000. It's not my problem. Why should I stick my neck out and deliver the bad news?"

The sad fact is the IT industry has been aware of this problem since the very day it created it, but it is too simplistic to suggest that the IT industry be held solely responsible for the resulting mess. Management shares an equal part of the blame. When the two-digit compromise was made, it was made to accommodate budgets. We knew it would not work in the distant future, but in the present, we'd accommodate the quarterly report.

This attitude of the computing community is the real problem. It is very difficult for us to admit that we made a little error which will cost companies millions of dollars. It is also a pay me now or pay me later situation. The problem must be solved or else our applications will produce meaningless results in the new millennium.

We don't have a choice. We must start addressing the problem today (or at the very least tomorrow) or there won't be enough time to solve it.

I'll admit to a bias here. Management has never really understood technology. It has always considered it well taken care of by the folks in the white coats, the high priests of technology. We, the technologists, did understand the consequences; we knew this method of storing dates would not, could not, work properly as we moved from 99 to 00. We had the knowledge and should have stood our ground and refused to compromise on quality.

Placing the blame squarely on the shoulders of the technologists is not a popular view; it's not even one I'm 100 percent comfortable with. However, if we want to avoid similar or worse mistakes in the future, the knowledgeable parties must insist on integrity of the products of their labor, no matter what the penny-pinchers demand.

> What exactly is the "problem"? In order to save storage space, and perhaps to reduce the amount of keystrokes necessary to enter a year, we allocated two digits to the year. 1993 is stored as 93 in our data files, and the year 2000 will be stored as 00. These two-digit dates exist on millions of data files used as input to millions of applications.

It's simple to describe, perhaps too simple. If it were difficult to understand, then perhaps people would be willing to believe the solution was also difficult. As it is, if a six-year-old can understand it, then a six-year-old should be able to fix it. What a delightful catch-22.

> This two-digit date affects data manipulation, primarily subtractions and comparisons. The net results are easy enough to demonstrate.
>
> I was born in 1955 and if I ask the computer how old I am today, it subtracts 55 from 93 and announces I am 38. So far so good, but what happens in the year 2000? The computer will subtract 55 from 00 and will state I am −55 years old. This error will affect any calculations that produce or use time spans. Interest calculations are a good and common example.

In a sound bite, that's the problem. Everything else is commentary. Anyone who knows anything about computing should be able to deduce everything else, including various methods for tackling the problem from this brief description of how such calculations produce incorrect answers.

> If you have some data records and want to sort them by date (e.g., 1965, 1905, 1966), the resulting sequence would be 1905, 1965, and 1966. However if you add in a date record such as 2015, then the computer will return the following sequence: 1905, 2015, 1965, and 1966, which the computer only sees as 05, 15, 65, 66.
>
> These are two types of calculations which are going to produce "garbage," are there others? It depends on your applications. The task facing us is to:

- Identify and correct all the date data.

    Identifying what a date is has proven to be the first major hurdle. It turns out that dates arise in the most peculiar places and are hardly what could be described as "properly labeled" in the hundreds of millions of programs worldwide.

- Check the integrity of all calculations involving date information.

    Once you've identified the dates, you then have to verify that all calculations using those dates are modified where necessary and deliver the same results as would be expected if the dates included the full four-digit year rather than just the last two digits.

    The challenge before us is immense. We must correct the data residing in all data files or write code to handle the problem. How do you identify the problem data and the associated calculations? We have few, if any, standards for labeling data used in date calculations. The only choice we have is to examine each and every line of code and make the necessary changes.

True then, true today, with some minor exceptions. The exceptions have come with the development of tools to assist in most of the detail work. It is not necessary to eyeball every line of code.

    How many lines of code do you have in your organization? How many data files? How many maintenance programmers?

Strange, but true, there are still companies who have as yet to answer these three most basic of questions.

    The problem extends itself beyond mere calculations and into the input/output processes of every application. Can you enter 2000 into your data screen? Or can you enter only two digits, forcing the input of 00? Can your hard copy reports print four digits? Is there enough space on the paper to add two more digits?

This paragraph hints at but poorly addresses the notion that the Year 2000 problem is more than a technical matter of fixing your systems, that it will affect business processes far removed from the actual computers which contain the core of the problem.

    To Gerald Weinberg, author of dozens of books including *Quality Software Management*, this problem is an indication of deeper management malaise. "If software engineering managers cannot manage a change that they've had 1,000 years to prepare for, how can we expect them to manage a change that happens without notice? In other words, if this change causes a crisis in your organization, *everything* will cause a crisis in your organization—and often *nothing* (in the sense of technical content) will cause a crisis."

Weinberg hints at the true cause of this problem. The proper use of technology is poorly understood in most organizations and consequently poorly managed. Ultimately, the Year 2000 problem is a consequence of poor quality of management. Some good will come out of this situation. The use of technology will be questioned in much greater detail than in the past, and technology management will receive more attention.

How big a crisis is it? Ken Orr, principal of the Ken Orr Institute, and Larry Martin, president of Data Dimensions Inc., are working together to get some answers to this question. They state, "An early estimate for Fortune 50 organizations is perhaps $50 to $100 million each to convert all their existing (and under development) systems to accept the change from the year 1999 to 2000."

Early estimates are often wrong. As a rough guess, this was off by a factor of 10. It is not unusual for Fortune 50 companies to have budgets exceeding $500 million. A few in particular have budgets approaching $1 billion.

The mind boggles at a maintenance problem that will cost a company $100,000,000. In fact, this inability to even think of such a project, is the real problem. They continue, "The biggest problem of all is that no one wants to step up to the issue, not data processing management, not the vendors, not the industry gurus. As with all legacy systems, this problem is messy, expensive, and unromantic. No one wants to go in and tell management they have a multimillion dollar requirement just to keep the business running and that they really have no options."

The truth of their statement is evident all around the world. The number one message from companies is that they stepped up to the plate too late. They have not left themselves enough time to complete the entire task.

According to their research, "It looks like it may cost organizations $0.35–$0.40 per line of code to make the conversion, but the truth is, until we work through a complete cycle with some large organization we are not going to really know."

Again, this estimate is proved to be low. The Gartner Group, a research company based in Stamford, Connecticut, estimates that the cost is now in excess of $1.10 per line of code.

All of this leads us back to the crux of the problem. . . . Nothing is being done. Capers Jones, chairman of Software Productivity Research Inc., states, "Long range preventative steps are uncommon in the software industry. I expect that most companies will not start worrying about the problem until 1999. For some, this will be too late."

Not many companies in the United States, Canada, United Kingdom, Australia, New Zealand, or the Netherlands, to name some of the more proactive countries, will be in this state. They may not have done a sufficient job, but a vast majority, greater than 80 percent, have begun the process of fixing their systems.

Gerald Weinberg adds an explanation for this lack of long-range planning, "The point is that we in the IS industry have not been paying our way. We have been building up a 'national debt,' just as surely as the USA has been building up a money debt. It will be paid by our children, our successors, one way or another."

Again, these words have proven themselves true. It is difficult to understand before you examine your reliance on technology, just how reliant you actually are and how much there is of the stuff! Company after company totally underestimates the size of the Year 2000 task.

There is some good news in the midst of all this gloom. Dr. Tom Love, a vice president of IBM's consulting group with worldwide responsibility for object-oriented application development, explains. "There are indications that this problem will result in two changes. The first is a push towards Object Oriented Systems. Rather than undergoing the huge maintenance cost, it will make economic sense to rewrite systems from scratch, using the best software technologies available."

The changes won't be restricted to software. Dr. Love adds, "There will also be a push to explore different hardware platforms. If you are rewriting your systems from scratch, then it might seem a good time to change hardware as well. Changing both software and hardware at the same time will greatly increase the risk of failure. Naturally there are approaches one can take which will moderate these risks. We don't want to exchange one problem with another one."

It turns out that this particular prediction never came to pass. Other than in the development of a handful of the tools created to assist with the Year 2000 problem, perhaps, object-oriented technologies have done nothing to assist in the solution of the problem. In fact, a case could be made that new technologies and the fascination they generate may have distracted us from working on the problem at hand.

Not everyone is ignoring the problem and hoping it will go away. William Goodwin of Brooklyn, New York, publishes a newsletter entitled *Tick, Tick, Tick*, which focuses on the date problem. It is meant to be a forum for people in the IS industry concerned about the impact of the year 2000.

His subscribers are people like Brian Pitts, project manager for the Berry Company in Dayton, Ohio. He states, "Current economic conditions are making this problem more difficult to address. Management is focused on short term results and is placing long term negative consequences on the back burner. I feel like a lone voice crying in the wilderness."

Another subscriber performed an internal survey and came up with the following results. Of 104 systems, 18 would fail in the year 2000. These 18 mission-critical systems were comprised of 8,174 programs and data entry screens as well as some 3,313 databases. With less than 7 years to go, someone is going to be working overtime.

By the way, . . . this initial survey required 10 weeks of effort. Ten weeks just to identify the problem areas. How many systems do you have?

Efforts to share information and make information accessible to the press by people like William Goodwin have been instrumental in creating whatever levels of awareness and activity we've managed to achieve.

Finally, as Nicholas Zvegintzov, publisher of *Software Maintenance News*, writes, "Over the next seven years you are going to become very, very tired of millennium moaners telling you that your software will fail as it enters the new millennium. But be patient with them. There really is something to be said for them."

Another prediction proven true. People are indeed tired of the alarm bells ringing in their ears, especially since they're trying to sleep. It turns out that the millennium moaners were right. There is a problem. And people have ignored it for too long. Now they complain they don't have enough time to fix everything. Sigh.

This article was the "In Depth" article in *Computerworld* September 6, 1993. It was reprinted in the November 1993 issue of *Data Processing Digest* and also in the February 1994 issue of *ASM Systems Journal*.

The authors wish to give credit to Alan (Lanny) Jones, John Munyan, Lisa J. Downey, and Micah Jung of Systemic Solutions, Inc. for their contributions.

A special thanks goes to Larry Rolstad, of Compass Consulting, for the tool knowledge and expertise that was so valuable in constructing those chapters.

Also a thank-you to Frank Taylor and Bill Murphy of Cairncross and Hemplemann P.S., and Dave Kikel of Hogan & Hartson L.L.P., for their help with the discussion of the Year 2000 legal landscape.

The authors owe a profound thank-you to our families, without whose patience and personal effort this book would not have been finished before the year 2000.

Houston, We Have a Problem

It's New Year's Day 2000 and you're headed to your best friend's house to watch football. You're in a hurry because you don't want to miss kickoff, and you have to stop at the nearest cash machine first, because you promised to bring the beer. But instead of cash, the ATM commandeers your card, rudely informing you that it has expired.

Furious, but knowing you won't get much help on a holiday, you head to the nearest 7-11 intending to pay for your refreshments with a credit card. Pulling up to the store, you think a lot of people have the same idea, because there's a long line at the checkout counter. But the problem is not a run on beer; instead, you find out, the cash register is not working. The word, as it reaches you at the end of the line, is that the cash register is computer-based and requires a valid date to start up. And for some reason, it won't. "Some reason" is the Year 2000 problem, Y2K for short.

The preceding hypothetical—but probable—scenario is just the tip of the iceberg, and if collective public denial continues, it is an iceberg that will sink titanic computer systems worldwide. Like the unheeded warnings of disaster on the oceanliner *Titanic*, the alert to the Year 2000 problem has been sounded—on television, in newspapers, magazines, and newsletters, and via the Internet. Often, however, it has been defined simply as the inability of computers to calculate properly with 00—two zeros—signifying the new century. Further, media coverage frequently couches the issue in computer jargon, making it seem irrelevant to anyone other than programmers and information systems managers. The truth is, the Year 2000 problem will affect each of us, personally and professionally.

What is the Year 2000 problem? It is not one, but a series of problems, some involving computer software, some involving computer hardware, some involving data, and *all* involving large amounts of money to fix. The nature of these problems is easily explained. Until 1989, all the standards followed to create computer programs stated that only two digits—the last two—would be used to identify the year, and, to date, this has been an efficient abbreviation. But at the dawn of the millennium—when the year 2000 will be recorded as 00—most computers will regard 2000 as 1900. Thus, computers will treat a driver's license, credit card, passport, or drug prescription that is due to expire in the year 2000 as already having done so.

Happy Birthday

To understand the disruptions this will cause, it is essential to remember that computers were not designed to do arithmetic but to perform operations involving logic. For example, to determine that a person born in 1945 is older than a person born in 1955, a computer calculates ages and then compares them. In 1995, the calculations were simple: $95 - 45 = 50$, $95 - 55 = 40$; 50 compared to 40 is greater. But in the year 2000, these calculations stop working correctly: $00 - 45 = 45$, $00 - 55 = 55$; the computer identifies the older person as being younger. But keep in mind that the last equation should include minus signs, thus: $00 - 45 = -45$, and $00 - 55 = -55$. The calculations *should* still work. And that would be true if all those early programs had been designed to maintain plus and minus signs when doing calculations on dates. But they weren't. Why not? Simply put, these programs weren't intended to run beyond the twentieth century.

Let's take a look at a couple of birthday surprises already caused by the upcoming new year. Brian Hayes, in his article "Waiting for 01-01-00" in *American Scientist* (January/February 1995), gives these two examples of potentially typical, albeit humorous, repercussions of the Year 2000 problem.

In 1992, Mary Bandar of Winona, Minnesota, was invited to join kindergarten classes when her name turned up among others identified in a database search for people born in '88; at the time, Bandar was 104 years old.

C. G. Blodgett's auto insurance premium tripled when he was reclasssified after his 101st birthday as a high-risk youthful driver.

Don't, however, be lulled into thinking that these anecdotes are interesting only as sound bites during the feel-good portion of a nightly newscast. They are symptomatic of potential worldwide disruptions in business, transportation, finance, and much more. Let's get a little more serious.

Say you make a deposit to your personal or business bank account at the end of 1999, then write a check or make a transfer in 2000. If the bank's computer regards 00 in the date field as 1900 (as most do), it will treat the withdrawal as if it were made *before* the deposit, and your personal and/or business accounts will be overdrawn. Now are you beginning to see the problem?

Another dilemma is that back in the good ole days, when people thought 2000 was a long time away, programmers felt safe using the digit pairs *00* and *99* to indicate either *keep forever* or *delete now*. Thus, 99 is commonly used to terminate processing. One organization realized nearly six months into 1994 that its computer was discarding files that were supposed to be stored for the next five years because it was programmed to purge data with 99 in the year field.

Storage space intended for dates has long been used and abused. One retailer, while investigating the possibility of a computer crime, discovered that the year values 94, 95, 96, and 97 were being used to indicate that discounts of various amounts were to be applied. And although some foresighted companies had specified that date fields were to include space for the century, programmers had done nothing to verify that it was done. Worse, in some instances they found that the space had been used to store other data.

Leap of Math

Now consider the following: Shortly after February 29, 1988, a supermarket was fined $1,000 for having meat around one day too long. The problem was traced to a computer that didn't adjust for the leap year. What does this have to do with the year 2000? Read on.

To determine what to do, computer programs refer to internal calendars, most of which were designed to run only through the twentieth century. And while 1900 was not a leap year, 2000 is. If you're as confused as most programmers about how to determine this, here are the three rules for determining a leap year: Rule 1 says that if the year is evenly divisible by 4, it is a leap year. Since 2000 is divisible evenly by 4, it must be a leap year. Not so fast. Rule 2 says it *isn't* a leap year if the year is also divisible by 100. And 2000 is divisible by 100 as well as 4. So it isn't a leap year, right? Wrong again. There's rule 3: When the year is also divisible by 400, it is a leap year and does have a February 29, which includes 2000 (technically, it's a leap-century day). When 2000 arrives, if your computer treats it as 1900, it won't account for February 29, because there wasn't one that year. Needless to say, there are many computer calendars out there in which every month will be off one day following New Year's 2000. Consider the implications of that on computers that are dependent on date data to manipulate security systems, traffic signals, train and airplane arrival and departure information, and surgery schedules at hospitals.

Up from Denial

Make no mistake about it, the Year 2000 problem is starting to generate considerable attention. Nevertheless, Ed Yourdon, editor of *Application Development Strategies* and a widely renowned information systems specialist, conducted an informal survey that convinced him that this attention has not translated into appropriate levels of concern. His impressions were supported in a May 23, 1996, article in *Washington Technology,* which indicated that two-thirds of the "infotech" executives surveyed believed the Year 2000 problem was not a high priority, three-fourths of program officials believed it wasn't a high priority, and one-half of information technology executives planned to wait until 1998 to take action. Finally, a survey in the February 1996 issue of *Information Week* indicated that 50 percent of the U.S. data-processing organizations will not have their software converted by December 31, 1999.

And of those corporations that are actively engaged in solving this problem, most are not speaking out about their efforts. Neil Cooper, a stock analyst with Cruttenden Roth, who is working on the Year 2000 problem, offered the following reasons for this conspiracy of silence:

- Directors and management are fearful of shareholder suits claiming negligence—many employee warnings have gone unheeded for years.

- Acknowledgment of a serious Year 2000 problem within a business unit or across an enterprise may cause clients to flee and competitors to flock.

- The legal ramifications remain unclear for consulting services companies that have provided hardware and software solutions that did not include Year 2000 fixes in the recent past. Generally, both (potential) plaintiffs and defendants will not comment if litigation is being considered.

- Some companies are awaiting the leadership of regulatory agencies and/or financial accounting standards bodies within the federal government for this unique one-time event.

Fortunately, not all organizations are waiting for the ball to drop in Times Square to tackle this issue. A number of companies have completed the initial project-estimating phase, although few have embarked on the fixing stage. Many are still suffering from what car buyers refer to as "sticker shock." Others are trying to determine which computer applications must be saved, which will cost less to replace than fix, and which can be fixed as they break down. Still other companies are so dependent upon computer hardware and software purchased from other companies that they must wait until the vendors address their own internally developed programs.

At Massachusetts Mutual Life Insurance Company, Ron Cote, a Year 2000 project leader, calls his effort a "survival project." "If we don't do this," he says, "it's shut the lights off and go home." So far, the workarounds developed by this organization's information systems people have proved unsatisfactory, and they have 45 million lines of code to change and then to test. Mass Mutual wants to complete its project by the end of 1998, which will provide a one-year cushion. The company has been aware of this problem for more than 10 years.

It is important to realize that many industries have become totally dependent on computers to function. Insurance companies, banks, securities brokers, and many more have become data-processing firms. They get data, send data, and use data to function. Without their computers, they simply would not be able to conduct business. And computers that are not programmed to accept values of 00 in the year field will not run. Don't forget, computer applications are highly integrated. Data from one application often is required for the next to run successfully. If the first one doesn't run because it confronts a value containing 99 or 00, any program dependent on it won't run, either; call it the domino effect.

Complicating the situation is that many programs run in strings, making it difficult to determine which program failed. Finding the problem in the first might only get you to the next in the string, which might subsequently fail. And each failure may take hours to correct. The system failures ultimately overwhelm the people who can correct them. If these problems occur in systems taking orders, paying claims, or issuing paychecks, the companies dependent on them will quickly lose credibility and will be in violation of regulations.

Consider the city of Phoenix, which found out about the Year 2000 problem the hard way. On January 2, 1995, a simple application that calculated five-year payments crashed. When the program tried to subtract 95 from 00, it couldn't handle it. Jack Thomas, the city's information systems deputy director, considers the crash a blessing in disguise, for if the application hadn't failed, the city could have begun calculating inaccurate payment schedules with potentially disastrous results.

An analysis by Viasoft, a tools contractor that began tackling the problem in Phoenix in 1994, found that more than 90 percent of the city's programs use date routines that cause problems. He estimated it would cost that municipality $63 million to fix its Year 2000 problem throughout 14 major applications that support several major city departments.

Financial services companies that know they will be impacted by the Year 2000 problem include Abbey National, Lloyd's of London, Barclays, and NatWest—and that's just in Great Britain. This, naturally, comes at the same time that work must progress for conversion to a single European currency unit—ECU. Other countries in the community, of course, will be facing the same dilemma.

Other institutions and companies that have invested in fixing their Year 2000 problems include many banks: BankBoston, Canadian Imperial Bank of Commerce, Fleet Bank, Nations Bank, and Sun Bank among them. Manufacturers such as Philip Morris, Shell Services, and Texaco (to name just a few) are also engaged in correcting the problem. Some firms, such as Kaiser Permanente and Union Pacific (both of which have participated in important conferences and roundtables on the Year 2000 problem in order to share what they have learned), have already begun, or are close to completing, conversion of their computers to cope with the Year 2000 problem.

In 1991, the northern California division of Kaiser Permanente started setting up a team of about 20 outside contractors and 10 internal staff to begin working through its computer applications. The team expanded date fields to allow for century values, then added the century values to all the current data; it also backtracked into historical data to add the century values. It removed all queries to the hardware manufacturer's date routines and installed its own. Finally, it created a standard set of date-processing routines and replaced all others with them.

In 1995, Union Pacific hired a consulting firm to assess the approximate cost of fixing its computer systems to handle the new century. In 1996, it commenced its project. In some cases, the update team expanded the date fields to support century values and changed the data. In others, it inserted logical date interpretation processes so as not to change the data.

BankBoston set up a special staff to perform date-field expansions. The application support teams send programs to the staff, who expand the fields and replace date routines with standard routines. Any logical processes that must be changed are identified; the altered programs are returned, along with programs to handle data changes, to the application support teams who must change the programs to fix the logic problems and test them.

As always, when someone loses, someone wins. It is easy to imagine that some firms are already building war chests, to acquire companies that fail to survive the countdown to double zero. In fact, more than one company insider has indicated that it is a strategy under discussion. Some companies are already benefiting from their lead in fixing the problem. Kaiser Permanente won a corporate contract for group health coverage when its nearest competitor confessed that it was doing nothing to prepare for the year 2000.

Are you starting to wonder how you and your company or organization will be affected? So far, there are no silver bullet solutions to the Year 2000 problem, although certainly many hope for such an easy way out, exemplified in this statement in the August 3, 1996, issue of *The Economist:* "This is doubtless a technical feat that Microsoft or some other firm will shortly master." Microsoft was having enough trouble dealing with the most recent fallback to daylight savings. As reported in *PC Week* on November 4, 1996, in Spencer Katt's "Rumor Central," at 2:00 A.M. on the morning of daylight savings' Sunday, those who turned their computer clocks back (as prompted on-screen) discovered that one hour later, it was 1:00 A.M. again. Fortunately, few people were up working at that hour. The point is, it would be foolhardy to wait for anyone to deliver a quick fix to the Year 2000 problem.

But it can be solved—today. Like a genetic disorder, the solution lies in finding each mistake in the code—in this case, program code—and fixing it. The bad news is the code is often difficult to find and thus to correct. The good news is enterprises that are well into the millennium update are already reaping significant benefits. Some have won new contracts simply because they can demonstrate preparations are in process. In some situations, budgets that have been restricted over the last few years are being relaxed, allowing organizations to upgrade systems software and hardware. Fixing the Year 2000 problem will enable growth of new functions and potentially decrease support costs.

Our goal in this book is twofold: (1) to convince you that a problem does exist that will affect you and your business, and (2) to give you the insight into how to start doing something about it.

CHAPTER 1

Ground Double-Zero

So much anthropomorphic terminology has found its way into the computer technology lexicon that we forget computers are machines: They can't really "think" or "see," and they don't really "know" anything. When *we* see the date 01/01/00, we *know* it refers to January 1, 2000; when the computer "sees" 01/01/00, it "knows" it is January 1, 1900; or it might "know" to delete the information accompanying the double-zero number string. The looming dawn of the millennium is going to require that we stop trusting our computer systems to know anything other than what we have programmed them to know. It is time to take responsibility for not being farsighted enough to plan for their future use beyond the year 1999.

Programming began on punch cards known as Hollerith cards, named for the man who invented them in the late 1800s in order to get the U.S. Census done on time. Each Hollerith card had only 80 columns, and all information for each record had to fit into those 80 columns. How could early programmers have guessed that one of the shortcuts they developed to accommodate that 80-column restriction would one day result in a data nightmare? To save space for more important information, early on, the year designation was reduced to two digits. The assumption—then rightfully—was that everyone knew the century prefix was 19.

Over the last 50 years, we have gone through countless upgrades of computer technology. At some point, you or your enterprise wanted or needed some feature that required a new computer. The decision was made, the budget was secured, and you bought the new model. The old one was sent to some computer equivalent of an elephant burial ground. You remember what came next: conversion, the process during which you tried to get old programs to run on new equipment. Code was written on the fly, often without documentation, to keep the system up and running.

Through all these years and all these conversions and upgrades, we have been stuffing an ever increasing amount of data into computers. We have tons of it stored on disks and tapes, in huge vaults, and in closets and caves. We also have duplicate data, because most key files are duplicated daily. There are even copies of copies. And for the most part, we have stored this data in large files in date sequence according to when it was collected. Many of the structural programs—the ones that handle physical resources such as tape and disk management, scheduling, and communications—can't manage a four-digit year at all. Business applications depend on these structural systems. If they can't figure out how old you are, how long an invoice has gone unpaid, which transaction should be processed first, or how much interest they owe, the companies that depend on them are in big trouble.

Out of the Closet

These closets full of old data complicate the challenge of making the programs and computers in daily use Year 2000–compliant. Few companies have maintained conscientious code documentation; fewer still can boast that the programmer who wrote it is still on staff. Without documentation, without the programmer(s), the solution is easy to describe, but mind-boggling to implement: Examine and correct each and every line of code and then fix the digit-deficient data residing in all data files, or write new systems able to handle the problem. A single program could have from 10 (a 4GL program) to 100,000 lines of code, and 1 in 20 lines of code have something to do with defining or processing date data. In terms of functions performed, this means that nearly 5 percent of all data-processing operations are impacted by dates. If you look at a medium-size organization with 4 million lines of code, it will have to visually scan, one by one, every line to find 200,000 instances of date usage. It will then have to make approximately 20,000 changes, requiring not less than 13 hours (based on the authors' prior experience in making a similar enterprisewide update) to design test data, create a program to build the test data, and run the tests for each group of about 10 changes. This means that it will require, without some form of automated assistance, 26,000 hours (roughly 13 person-years of uninterrupted attention—no coffee breaks, training time, waiting for equipment, or downtime) to make and test all changes. Then you have to factor in the misses: Every time a change is missed, it will take four to six hours to find and patch the code. And don't forget, the changes must be scheduled in the proper sequence. At any one point in time, it may be necessary to have 60 people making changes so that all interrelated programs are altered simultaneously. Conversely, at another time, only one person may be able to make a change so that 60 others can start working together.

The cost of accommodating all that old data is staggering. Worldwide, the estimate commonly used is $600 billion with up to $300 billion borne by the United States. While U.S. government estimates currently amount to only $50 billion for business and $50 billion for the federal government, there is extreme skepticism on the part of reviewers. Reports of expenses have been highly diluted by failures to account for work not directly associated with program repairs. The major banks each are dedicating hundreds of programming personnel to convert all existing and developing systems to accept the change from 1999 to 2000. All that old data either must be changed or someone must go into every program and put in some code that essentially says, "If the year is greater than 49, pretend that there is a 19 in front of it, otherwise pretend there is a 20 in front of it." Easier said than done. Some dates are not so easy to expand, which brings us to the issue of embedded dates and date stamping. Whatever the actual cost, this we can be sure of, the problem must be fixed. Cost is not the issue; time is now the only important factor.

Getting Embed with Dates

Embedded systems are everywhere. Computers with wide ranges of capabilities have been installed into more and more of the equipment used daily. A lot of people are wearing fancy watches that do all kinds of nifty things with calendars; some of those will stop working when the date rolls over on December 31, 1999. Those in your VCR may cause minimal problems, as there's nothing to record between midnight and 8 A.M. on January 1 anyway. If you plan to set your recorder to record a game, though, you should check it to see if it works (assuming you know how to program your VCR in the first place).

Embedded business systems control lights, elevators, security systems, time clocks, and heating and cooling systems. They are in the scales in receiving, in conveyors on the shop floor, and in emissions-monitoring and waste-removal systems. They control cutters, molders, and pressers. They turn lights on and off in your parking garages and lots. They are in the monitoring equipment in hospital operating rooms. In short, embedded systems control the conditions in which you work; sometimes they even determine *whether* you work.

The problem with embedded systems is that they run in the background, and currently most are running in obsolete equipment. This means that you can rarely just reprogram them; you have to replace processors, circuit boards, and sometimes the whole unit—major expenses, needless to say. Banks, for example, have been finding that not only do some of their ATMs have to be replaced, but also the kiosks in which they are mounted, because the new units are smaller than the older, bulkier ones.

Embedded systems are one problem; embedded dates are another. An embedded date is one that is used as a component of a longer character string to uniquely identify a particular item or event. Embedded dates are commonly found in invoice numbers, such as 94090013, where 9409 is the year and month of issue. They also appear as parts of policy numbers, license numbers, merchandise sales tags, storage bin tags, transaction numbers, and date stamps.

These dates are built into the data that you retain and use daily. The worst of these appear in the key fields you use to determine where and in what order you store data. Others appear in date stamps you use to track data and processing actions. Embedded dates typically appear in four formats:

TYPE	FORMAT	COMMON USAGE
Prefix	YYMMXXXX	Invoice number
Suffix	XXXXYYMM	Policy number
Encapsulated	XXYYMMXX	License number
Date/time stamp	XXX-YYMMDD-HHMMSS.SS or YYMMDD-HHMMSS.SS-XXX	Transaction identification

When dates appear at the beginning or end of the field, they are often used for *intelligence*—to provide the observer with status information. When a field contains an embedded date, the following questions must be answered:

Is it used to determine item aging or age?

Is it used to sort the item into sequence?

Is there a calculation being made?

Dates appearing at the beginning of the identifier create another difficulty. Some application software automatically suppresses leading zeros in numeric fields, causing miscalculations because 00 may be treated as null data and thus be rejected or result in a miscalculation or zero-divide errors.

For example, one apparel retailer that uses dates as a prefix to its stock item numbers spent several millions of dollars on encoding and scanning equipment that could read the garment number. But because the scanners had a limitation on the length of the scan, the date field could not be lengthened; the other characters and digits were equally significant and could not be dropped or truncated. So, if the century field could not be added, all this retailer's inventory dated 99 or earlier could not be tracked correctly, meaning they wouldn't be aged for distribution, disposition, or markdown. Unsurprisingly, this retailer prefers to remain nameless.

Another example was reported in *The New York Post* on July 4, 1998. A large retailer was surprised when its computerized inventory management and pricing system put entire shipments of new inventory on the shelf at huge discounts. The problem was traced to the program that discounts items if they are not sold in 21 months. But because 21 months from now falls in the year 2000, the system became confused and, assuming these products had been sitting around since 1900, slashed their prices.

Date Stamping

Date stamping is another intelligent use of embedded dates in records. Date stamps are automatically placed on the record by the system for such things as transaction tracing and backup recovery. However, date stamps often create problems as the formats change; for example, old data is not recognized by the new recovery routines. If changes are not made, the transactions or records may be processed out of sequence. The results could be as described by Brian Hayes in *American Scientist* (January/February 1995):

> At the local dairy, the oldest milk on hand is supposed to be shipped first, but in the early weeks of the new millennium milk from year 00 is given precedence. Indeed, any milk remaining from December 1999 will not be scheduled for shipment until the end of 2099. Meanwhile, at the bakery across town a computer calculates the bread dated 01-01-00 must be a century old, and sends it to the landfill.
>
> The next example actually happened. A British retail food chain was found dumping loads of cans of tomatoes due to be sold by '05 because the automated system designated them to be expired.

Extend these examples to blood donations, medicine prescriptions, and medical records and you have genuine disasters in the making once 00 makes its way into the data stream.

Certainly code can be fixed for applications created in standard languages, which are well understood by a sizable number of programmers. However, when some unique language such as JOVIAL or APL is involved, costs increase dramatically because of competition for rare resources (those who know the language). Which brings us to one of the key issues in the Year 2000 problem.

No Comprendo COBOL

By some estimates, the number of computer languages in use totals more than 300, including various coding dialects. A few major languages, such as COBOL, BASIC, FORTRAN, and C, probably account for 80 percent of the programs running today, but each has several dialects and versions. Fortunately, most of these are relatively easy to understand, and if a programmer knows one dialect, he or she can learn the others.

Other languages, however, are more obscure, either because so few programmers ever learned the language, or the language enabled the programmer to write in a way that kept the code inaccessible and thereby tamperproof. Thus, in one such program you might see the letter *A* used to signify a storage location for a person's name and *B* used to identify date of birth. In the next program, you might find the same letters used to identify totally different things. (One programmer actually bragged that his efficiency was due to the reduction in keystrokes it required for him to write programs. Imagine a system in which the programmer keeps the whole system's data mapping in his head.)

Other update complications are based on original attempts to save space, while still others relate to the attempt to reduce the costs of data storage and communications. Compression of numeric data and zero suppression on computer terminals are examples. It is hard to imagine that not long ago, less than 15 years, a 2400 bits per second transmission speed was a performance target in data communications. The cost of memory was so high that 32MB of memory (that of a typical PC today) cost about $256 million.

A few attempts to save costs have resulted in imaginative data-storage strategies. People have confronted situations where the dates *look* encrypted: A year may be assigned the value of *A*, the next year *B*, and so on. These date formats are referred to as *interpreted*. The format of the field may appear as YDDD, where Y has an alphanumeric, or even symbolic, value. In other formats of YMDD, both year and month appear with values of 0 to 9 or A through Z. This is, by some measures, very efficient. The single digit gives the system a date range of up to 36 years. Surely every program should have been replaced by then?

Where different versions of the same language exist, the issue is one of effort. Old versions of compilers are not maintained. For example, IBM mainframe COBOL has been changed only in the two most recent releases to accommodate century information. This means that all older releases are not able to read the new dates using the IBM-supplied routines. Upgrading those older releases means that the companies have to go through many thousands of additional hours of work (which is why they weren't changed in the first place). IBM is not alone in requiring licensees of language compilers and assemblers to upgrade to the latest version. Hewlett-Packard, Unisys, Digital Equipment, Oracle, and others have all released upgrades of languages containing date-related changes to allow programmers to handle the Year 2000 problem. Then there's the problem of language obsolescence. Many languages are literally dead. They continue to work, but nobody knows how to change them—and even if you could find someone to change them, there may be no compiler or interpreter still available to turn them into functional code that the computer can understand. Example: IBM created a product called ADF in Europe in the early 1980s. Several million lines of code were written in the language. In 1989, IBM abandoned ADF. Consequently, Big Blue won't (can't) fix it to handle four-digit year designations, and running the programs requires having an active interpreter on the computer at the same time. The interpreter doesn't handle century dates. What does a company still using ADF do? Its choices: Completely rewrite the code (assuming someone knows what it does); figure a way to fool the interpreter and insert that logic everywhere it is required (assuming you can find enough programmers and train them); find a way to convert the code to COBOL (one does exist, supposedly) and then convert it (assuming you can afford the time to find the vendor, learn how to use the tool, convert the programs, and make the changes before the system collapses).

There are approximately 200 other obsolete and/or unsupported languages. The list includes older and widely used versions of COBOL, RPG, Natural, and FORTRAN. Many organizations are facing stiff requirements in updating programs in languages such as RAMIS, Easytrieve, Lisp, Prologue, and so forth where there are few people with the language skills available. Such languages as APL, Dibol, Metacobol, and Total were widely used and some programs are still being run in these languages.

Counting the Costs

Computers have worked astoundingly well in the past. They will do so again in the future. But between now and then users will all be in for a wild, rocky, and expensive ride.

It may seem inconceivable that a couple of zeros in a date could multiply so dramatically into some very large repair bills, but that is what will happen as you prepare to fix the Year 2000 problem. To ease you into this awareness, consider controllable costs, which fall into two subcategories: (1) internally developed computer systems and (2) business practices and operations.

Application Software

Most large organizations have a large number of internally developed programs. John Pasqua, AT&T's Year 2000 head, in public testimony indicated AT&T has over 3,000 applications and will spend $500 million by December 1998. Midsized firms are more reliant on commercial systems, depending on packaged hardware and software for processing or subcontracting their data processing. The latter are expected to incur heavy costs associated with updates to new versions of software or replacement of systems. It is the very large companies that will experience most of the code-fix problems.

In addition, with old programs, the large firms have the challenge of locating the source code. And assuming the source code can be found, there is the problem of verifying it is the same version of the programs that is currently running on the computer. Many of the large firms and agencies could be forced to re-create programs whose functions are no longer understood by anyone in their organizations.

In many cases, no one in any given organization knows where all the programs are located. Many organizations report finding applications two years after the original inventory was taken. The U.S. Social Security Administration announced that it had overlooked nearly 30 million lines of code when it set its programs three years earlier. It is not unusual for programmers' original code to be stored in public and private libraries or in archive files that are not even on the computer. Programmers actually keep tapes in their desk drawers. With programs now being created by accountants, engineers, scientists, and general managers, it can take years to discover programs that are in daily use. Thus, it is also not unusual for even a well-organized programming department to require three months or longer to find the code it owns. If and when it does find it, often it is not sure what it is that's been found.

You will learn, if you don't already know it, that the program versions running on your computer are not always the same ones that match the code you found. It is not unusual for companies to lose source code of programs that have not been changed for a long time. Up to 40 percent of a company's portfolio is not touched for five years or more, and many programmers lose track of code that is often obscurely named and not well managed. Consequently, you will have to hire or delegate someone (perhaps several people) to find these missing program versions and match up the running programs with the programmer-created code. To a noncomputer person, all this talk of code, source, and compilers may be confusing, so please allow a minor digression.

Programs are written in a language relatively friendly to humans. It can be expressed in letters, numbers, words. Values may require special forms, wherein the form translates into directions. Which gets us to the point: The language in which a program is written is *not* actionable by a computer. Action requires that the code (which is why it is called *source code*) be assembled, compiled, or interpreted into machine language (*machine code*). The machine code is put into production libraries. The source code used to create the machine code is *supposed* to be filed away so that the machine code can be replaced if it gets accidentally destroyed or corrupted. In an ideal situation, the source and machine code are kept at the same level. Needless to say, however, the ideal situation is rare indeed. The older the machine code, the more likely that its source code will become corrupted (resulting from changes made but not put into production, source code that is lost and an old version brought up from archives, or source code that is simply misplaced and nobody realizes it). Unless you can recompile (assemble or interpret) the code and fully test it, it is unlikely that you can spot any obvious problems until it is run in production. And because changes are incremental, the differences can be very subtle.

If there are inconsistencies between what is being run today and the versions that were saved in 1992, for example, your designated troubleshooter is going to have to spend time re-creating the changes that have taken place between the versions. In addition, lost programs and code will have to be re-created or restored—if possible. At this late date, you may have to buy software packages to replace lost code—another expense.

The Cost of the Update

The first order of business in estimating your code update/reconstruction cost is to determine how many lines of code you must account for. If you are able to locate all your code, you will be relieved to know that it is possible to obtain line counts using the computer. Source code is usually stored in libraries on the computer. Production versions of the machine language are in *runtime* or *object libraries*. The names of these programs can be matched to the names on the members of the source libraries. This allows you to determine which source code modules are in use. Other modules are not shown in the object libraries because they are *linked* or included during compilation, assembly, or interpretation. To find which of these are in use, it is possible to match the source library names found to the *link libraries*. A similar operation is used to find modules brought together by interpreters, but the method varies by product.

While you will see forecasts of costs from $.60 to $1.70 per line of code, this is an aggregate estimate for the entire code portfolio, including vendor-supplied code and control language code. Industry estimates for the cost of updating individual programs and *applications* (a group of programs with a single business purpose) of course vary significantly—from absolutely nothing to as much as $4.50 per line of code. Individual programs may not require any changes since they do not involve date processes. Many manufacturing companies use an artificial date that cycles every 20 or 30 years. These systems do not require many changes. Remember, we are talking about the wide variability in the cost of changing individual programs and applications—not the entire portfolio. The Department of Defense, for example, estimates that some of its code will cost up to $8.05 per line to change. The industrywide average is probably somewhere around $1.50 per line. Naturally, there is economy in scale of operation, so smaller enterprises will probably have to pay as little as $.50 or as much as $2.50 per line. Complexity is a critical factor: Those applications that interact with a lot of other applications or that were written in arcane languages are more difficult to change (the Department of Defense estimate reflects costs for JOVIAL, hardly a popular computer language). If you want a rule of thumb to determine where you stand in these ranges, consider the following six attributes in the order presented:

1. Available staff knowledge of the application

2. Amount of planning prior to update

3. Capability of project management and level of enterprise awareness

4. Tools and methods that can be employed

5. Complexity of the applications

6. Visibility and risk associated with the applications

The ability of companies to accurately forecast costs has declined over the last two years. The advent of new tools, conversion factories, and the rapidly escalating wages of technical staff have complicated the estimating process. Remediation tools, software products that automate coding changes, often perform some testing for major programming languages (e.g., COBOL, PL/I, Natural, RPG, even MS Excel) in addition to performing program changes.

Many companies have created factories where a firm can send its code and have it altered using tools. The cost of the process is often impacted by the site of the factory. Many have been established in India, the Philippines, Canada, Ireland, Barbados, and other locations where telecommunications links them to their customers and lower wages of local workforces can offset some of the manual labor costs.

Wages are increasing dramatically for programmers of many skills. The salaries of COBOL programmers are said to be increasing 7 percent per quarter in the United States as of the beginning of 1998. The average is no doubt influenced substantially by the New York job market where programmers' salaries are said to be rising by 6 percent each month. This is not limited to COBOL programmers. Many companies are taking a replacement solution.

They are competing for programmers who are skilled in applications such as SAP's R3, Oracle, PeopleSoft, C++, and Java. Even in India, there are shortages of COBOL programmers because those that know the language would much rather be working on new systems or with new languages promising career growth after the Year 2000 problem is resolved.

Because many enterprises have several hundred million lines of code, their costs to fix this problem will run into millions of dollars—most will be spent in 1999. If, for instance, your programming department staff consists of 40 people, they are probably supporting about 4 to 6 million lines of code. Using an increasing average cost of $100,000 per person-year, those 4 to 6 million lines of code will take about 40 to 60 person-years and $2 to $3 million in expenses to fix. In other words, the Year 2000 problem is your first, second, third, fourth, and fifth priority.

Let's suppose your company or agency has 10 million lines of code on your computer system (this is not an uncommon amount for a large firm or governmental institution). The cost may rise 20 to 30 percent over that of the firm in the previous example. The more code you have, the more money per line you're probably going to spend, because all of it no doubt interacts with everything else. Thus, when somebody changes one line, it will impact many more something elses, and more changes will have to be made to make it work (and don't forget, you still have to keep your customers happy while this repair work is going on).

What will the repair cost be? It is not easy to get reliable estimates. The Nuclear Regulatory Commission estimated that the 55 utilities operating 105 reactors in the United States would spend $3 million to $10 million each on the Year 2000 problem. This was promptly disputed by the Edison Electric Institute who estimated that the cost to a utility would range from $10 million to $100 million each. These costs include everything from code repair to replacing security and process control systems.

Counting Other Costs

Don't be misled by the preceding discussion into thinking, as so many have, that the Year 2000 problem is only a budget issue and that you will deal with it when you can finesse the dollars to do so. It is not only a budget issue; it is a scheduling problem, a skill problem, a resource problem, a testing problem, a management problem, and, most important, a time problem. Simply put, we are out of time.

Many applications will not wait until January 1, 2000, to fail. Already systems have failed as their look-ahead requirement has asked them to process date data in the year 2000. At the end of 1998, many more systems are likely to fail as they encounter processes that treat the year 99 as a special situation. These applications may start to reject valid data or treat the data as expired.

Not only are users concerned with the number of working days left between now and the year 2000, but they are also concerned with the number of weekends. Applications are typically installed over weekends to allow time to change data and program linkages and verify that everything was installed as planned. With the number of weekends decreasing, the complexity of implementing changed applications increases. This increases the probability of errors. It is more likely that mistakes will occur that will not be discovered until later—much later. Some of those mistakes may have catastrophic results.

The costs of fixing embedded systems may add appreciably to the total Year 2000 outlay. On May 21, 1998, the *Seattle Post Intelligencer* reported that the Seattle Port Authority approved a budget of $4.7 million to fix code and embedded systems. The article went on to explain that an additional $12.5 million was required to replace a security system that was also subject to failure, but was too old to fix. The *Kansas City Star* reported on June 8, 1998, that Johnson County expected to spend $17.2 million on the Year 2000 problem of which $8.2 million would be spent on the sewer system which has automated controls at critical points.

The embedded chip problem is a problem of numbers. While the percentage of these chips that process date and time data is small, only 2–3 percent, the numbers are huge. With an estimated 6 billion chips produced in the United States alone in 1997, it means that there were nearly 100 million chips with possible date problems created in one year. These types of chips have been created in large quantities since 1975. Since it is prudent to test them all, it creates a problem of enormous magnitude for any organization.

Again, your computer-related costs are controllable. You decide what and when you are going to change. You may decide to replace the system instead of updating it. You can buy hardware as well as software and qualify for capitalizing the cost, stretching the impact on profits over the coming years. You have choices to make, but the decisions are yours.

The uncontrollable business practices costs will depend on the nature of your enterprise. For example:

- Banks that lend money to businesses want to know what those businesses have done to prepare for the year 2000. Loan officers need to know what information to look for.

- Manufacturers of devices that incorporate computers in their products will have to determine if they are going to help their customers reprogram those units that are obsolete or make them buy new equipment.

- Businesses with critical supplier relationships will have to ascertain the readiness of those suppliers. Are they business partners? Is it management's responsibility to help these suppliers survive through the year 2000?

- Businesses with too many noncompliant suppliers will be forced to take some action. Companies that buy computer hardware and software should not purchase products that are not 2000-ready. Consider policy that forces vendors to prove their products will not have date-handling problems.

- Processes that are computer-controlled should be tested for date-sensitivity.

- Enterprises should create a single coordination point—assign a project manager—to ensure that all changes are planned and scheduled to achieve efficiency and avoid system breakdowns between subunits.

- Vendors of perishable products (prescription drugs, etc.) dated 00 will have to design workarounds to ensure safety—and to prevent potential lawsuits.

- Service providers will need to determine the extent of their liability if their systems fail.

If you have not yet started addressing Year 2000 issues, your choices will have to be hard-lined and costs will be more difficult to control. You will probably be limited to fixing only what *must* be fixed, not everything that needs to be fixed.

Tick, Tick, Tock

The longer you wait, the greater the risk to your enterprise and the greater the cost to alleviate that risk. Programmer repair costs mount daily with the ticking of the millennial clock. The competition for qualified people in this area is already fierce. Many consulting firms engaged in the Year 2000 update are already raiding each other for experienced technicians and managers. Many of the larger firms are limiting the number of jobs they are taking on. Some will only take contracts with businesses that promise continuing work after the year 2000. Some accounting firms and large consulting companies, afraid of litigation risks, are curtailing their Year 2000 programs. This trend will continue to drive up costs. Reports of the number of firms who charge to make a sales call are increasing.

Most organizations are already unable to finish the work with available staff. Following is a review of a typical case of an organization with 15 million lines of mainframe code and 2 million lines of code on other platforms. Assume that the planning started on January 2, 1997, and the final system is to be migrated by December 31, 1998. Here's a breakdown of the process:

TIME	PHASE	RESOURCES
January–March 1997	Sizing	12 staff months
January–June 1997	Planning	12 staff months
April–July 1997	Pilots	50 staff months
July 1997–December 1998	Update	1,800 staff months

Beginning in 1997, the overlapping of phase activities becomes necessary. It is important to be finished by the end of 1998 to allow the changes made to be run in production through daily, weekly, monthly, quarterly, and year-end cycles during 1999. The crucial period of this plan is the update. During those 18 months, the enterprise will have to commit 100 people to the task. Not only does it not have the people, but even if it found them, it does not have the facilities and equipment to allow them to perform the work.

If the organization was not already into the update process by July 1997, the time line is reduced significantly, and the resource requirement changes dramatically. A delay of three months requires the addition of 20 people. For every process that is delayed, the impact may be the loss of several precious months. If the enterprise cannot find or devote those resources, its price may be the collapse of many applications. Bottom line: If you don't meet the deadline, the deadline will meet you. The enterprise is already in jeopardy.

Many desperate managers who realize that they won't be able to fix their applications in time decide to perform wholesale replacements using one of the enterprise resource-planning systems. Those that haven't started with systems replacements by July 1998 will find themselves working against industry experience that indicates a one-and-a-half to two-year implementation cycle once the product is selected. The shortage of skilled people to assist with that implementation is also increasing as companies already engaged in implementation find their schedules slipping and their risks mounting.

What is required is a rethinking of what applications and process control equipment is necessary to the survival of the enterprise. This process is called *triage* and is discussed later. The principal mode of operation whether the fix process has or has not been started is *risk management*. The focus is on short-term workarounds or temporary fixes, abandoning some work, using people to make up for equipment that doesn't run, and creating liaisons with companies that will be able to help. For some it means finding a buyer while the business still has value.

Costs You Can't Control

Now it's time to tackle costs outside your immediate domain; those outside factors can bring down your enterprise, even if you do have all your internal applications upgraded and 2000-ready. Few companies are publishing the expenses they are incurring trying to manage the external factors that must be identified, contacted, tracked, and managed. There are no guidelines and no measurements that can be used to estimate these costs.

Look at these recent examples of what may happen because of society's technology dependence when 2000 comes:

- Sabre, the world's largest travel reservations service, has gone down twice since June 24. One shutdown was due to a software glitch, the other an electrical problem. This inconvenienced thousands of travelers, travel agencies, and airlines. American Airlines says about 200 flights were delayed.

- A satellite spun out of control this year and 90 percent of the 50 million pagers in the United States were unable to send or receive messages for the day.

- AT&T was incapacitated on April 13, 1998, due to software flaws, putting thousands of credit card transactions, banks, retailers, and other business deals out of commission. This was in addition to inconveniencing millions of consumers for up to 26 hours and costing AT&T up to $30 million in lost revenues.

Vendors

It has become a practice in the Year 2000 industry to refer to computer-related suppliers and service organizations as *vendors,* and the balance as *suppliers.* The problem with vendors is that they are in the critical path to getting computer systems fixed for the year 2000. The first order of business is to alert your vendors to your needs. Begin by getting answers to the following questions immediately:

- Have my vendors recognized the millennium date problem?

- Will my vendors fix their problems before my business processes require century dates?

- Can my vendors afford to fix their products, or will they abandon them?

- What approaches will my vendors take, and will they be consistent with my standards or will they force me to customize my processes?

- What will be the cost, resource requirements, and time available when I get their solutions?

- Are my vendors dependent on other suppliers that may not perform or may not perform in time?

- How much are my vendors' solutions going to cost me, and when will we have to pay for them?

Vendors requiring management include suppliers of computers and computer-based devices that contain software, operating systems, applications software, data management, utilities, and tools, as well as suppliers of information on electronic media—data importers.

The following steps are recommended to establish control of the vendors (courtesy of Data Dimensions as reported in the *Millennium Journal*, volume II.I):

1. Centralize vendor management responsibility.
2. Set vendor policies for new acquisitions.
3. Determine whether changes are required for each purchased product.
4. Establish the event horizons for each product.
5. Identify the current vendor for each product.
6. Build a vendor database.
7. Determine contractual responsibility.
8. Contact the vendor for plans.
9. Plan implementation steps.
10. Communicate the vendor's and your own implementation plans to others who need to know.

One proactive manager of a testing laboratory in a client/server environment found that he had 14 vendors of hardware and software products. Once he defined his needs for each vendor, it took him about two and a half years to achieve compliance. Specifically, it required individual meetings with each vendor to explain the problem. Then each vendor was asked to test its products and schedule the necessary changes. In some cases, the fix required reprogramming application software; in others, it also meant changing the data output. The biggest problem was in scheduling which changes would be implemented. Certain vendors finished before others, and in some cases the changes didn't work and the vendors had to repair them.

Unfortunately, if you are a large corporation you might have 10,000 vendors for which to define requirements and track for compliance. But regardless of the size of your enterprise, there are four categories of suppliers that you must be concerned about:

- Application software
- Computer hardware and system software
- Embedded systems
- Service providers

Application Software

Application software packages and programs you bought from vendors present several potential problems.

Closed for business. The nature of the fast-paced, ever changing computer industry has resulted in companies going in and out of business before you have a chance to add their cards to your Rolodex. Others will bite the dust as a result of the Year 2000 problem. Thus, you may find that the vendor from whom you bought your software is no longer in business or available to help with your transition.

Maintenance contract issues. If you stopped paying for maintenance for a number of the products you are still running, you may have to reinstate the contract to obtain the upgrades. And be aware that some vendors will charge several years' maintenance fees. You may also have difficulty integrating new features or functions that were added. And even if you kept your maintenance contract current, you may find that your vendor does not have the knowledge or staff to fix your code.

Not my problem. Expect a number of vendors to simply declare your products as unsupported and stop charging maintenance fees. Of course, this leaves you holding nothing. If you are lucky, the vendor may be able to provide the source code so your staff can fix it.

When is soon enough? If your vendors tell you they plan to fix the code, the first question to ask is, "When?" The second question is, "Will it coincide with my needs?" That second question will most likely have two answers, one determined by how much internally developed code must be changed because of the vendor's revisions. The second answer depends on how you're using dates within the system. You may need the changes earlier than the vendor can provide them.

Computer Hardware and Systems Software

Hardware vendors provide the systems software that the computer uses to run, and this software is full of dates. You will be relieved to know that most systems software is either already compliant or in the process of being made so, although some of these fixes are not scheduled to be implemented until 1999.

Unfortunately, as with some application software vendors, some equipment vendors, too, may declare their software as unsupported, meaning that the vendor will not make the changes. Usually this is the case when a vendor does not have enough customers to justify the expense.

In many cases, the hardware issue is complicated because companies have chosen to stay with an older system to avoid the cost of upgrading, and therefore any Year 2000 changes will be to a version that they are unequipped to install. According to the Portland *Oregonian,* in early August 1996, an untested computer system went into service during the Department of Motor Vehicles' busiest season. The manager resigned amid an uproar following her estimate that it would cost $75 million for the new computer system (estimates are now running closer to $123 million), which was originally estimated at $48 million. Ironically, one of the reasons testing may have been put on the back burner by the agency was because of workforce reductions that were made in anticipation of labor savings from the new computer system.

The most well known problem to date, which is widely regarded as the first of many anticipated lawsuits, happened in August 1997. The owners of the Warren, Michigan, Produce Palace International filed suits against TEC America (the makers of the cash machines) and a local vendor, All American Cash Register (the installers of the machines), when the entire network of cash registers failed. This was due to credit cards reading 00. Although customers were able to pay with checks and cash, many left irritated by the long lines and constant failure of the registers. A spokesperson for TEC America blamed the problem on the credit card companies and filed a cross suit against All American Cash Registers.

Another example is from the June 1998 issue of the *ABA Banking Journal* about a Y2K problem that BankBoston experienced. According to BankBoston's senior manager for the Millennium project, David Iacino, the bank experienced Y2K problems in 1998 planning loans for their auto dealer clients. The clients were working with the bank's lenders to negotiate deals based on cars that would carry the 1999 model dates. Floor-planning loans must be tracked carefully to ensure the car is paid at a certain point in its life in the face of rapid depreciation of auto collateral (so the outstanding balance of the car will not get behind the recoverable value of the auto collateral). The challenge came when the floor-planning software took the 1999 model year, evaluated it, and ran the clock forward to the year 2000 when the point of concern for a 1999 car will be sometime in mid-2000. A lesser-known problem of the year 2000 is anything involving a long series of 9s, which is often used for exception items or signaling end of input in many programs. The computer printer began printing out bills for many dealers who just started the floor planning for the 1999 year, far ahead of schedule. The bank faced a potential customer-relations problem, but someone caught the problem and the bank's data-processing staff made fixes. The floor-planning software contained a variation of the millennium bug problem that had not yet been fixed.

Embedded Systems

As we've already mentioned, embedded systems are everywhere, and most are running in obsolete equipment. You won't be able to reprogram them; you may have to replace them. The costs of replacement can be enormous. Banks discovered that old ATMs were physically much larger than the new ones, thus necessitating reconstruction of kiosks when they were replaced. Factory managers have to allow for production delays as old equipment is removed, new foundations are laid, and the replacement is installed and tested. New equipment often requires retraining that adds instruction, time in class, and learning curve expenses to the cost quotient.

Be prepared for unexpected failures in systems you thought were free of this problem. Testing is hit and miss. Some systems are very hard to test. Project leaders in the telecommunications industry report that some systems cannot be tested because they are always on-line. The electric utility industry is trying to figure a way to test the entire grid. Since any one fault by a grid participant can bring the entire grid down, it is of major concern.

As explained later, systems thought to be fixed aren't necessarily. Many systems that were able to handle the date rollover to year 2000 have been found to fail to recognize the day of the week or the fact that year 2000 is a leap year. Leap year date recognition problems are not new. The New Zealand Aluminum Smelter had such a problem when some of its 660 computers simultaneously hung up as the date turned to March 1, 1996, while the others went to February 29, 1996. This confusion on the computers' part damaged the smelter to a tune of millions of dollars. Many AS/400 computer users in the United States also reported leap year–processing problems in 1996.

Service Providers

Obviously, you need supplies to keep your business going. Retail stores, for example, are concerned about whether the bank credit approval systems will be working, whether their lights will go on, and whether the cash registers will work. Lack of supplies will stop them cold. McDonald's, for one, is so concerned that it created a project and hired outside help to assist its suppliers and franchise operators to get their systems ready. It recognizes that its franchisees and suppliers are essential to maintaining its income stream. McDonald's began by investigating the food preparation and order-taking equipment used by the outlets. It then put its franchisees and store operators on notice about the options available. It also began to contact all its suppliers to determine to what extent each might encounter Year 2000 computing problems. Currently, McDonald's is proceeding to make recommendations as to what each supplier should do and is setting up a process to track progress.

Recently, Sears, Roebuck and Co., the nation's second largest retailer with $30 billion a year in sales, sent out letters from top management to all 50,000 of its suppliers. There are no ifs, ands, or buts about it. There will be no special dispensations allowed. Their suppliers and vendors must be Year 2000–compliant the same time Sears is compliant (which is the end of 1998) or they will be replaced. Sears also compiled a list of 500 key suppliers and plans on visiting each supplier/vendor personally to see if it is compliant.

You should have already contacted your service providers to determine which ones you can count on. If you haven't yet, contact them *now.* And get verification—proof. Don't take anyone's word about being 2000-ready.

CHAPTER 2

Behind Every Great Machine

B y now, the enormity of the Year 2000 or Y2K (*Y* for *year* and the programmer's shorthand for two thousand—2K) problem should be obvious to you. Some of you may have your calculators out, trying to do the math for your enterprise—figuring how many programs and how much data you have on what kind of machines and how much it will cost to fix or replace it all. At this point, however, stop adding up the numbers and start evaluating this problem first as one of management, because although Y2K is obviously a costly technical problem, until you get the people together who can take you into 2000 with champagne in hand, you're nowhere. This chapter talks management—finding, forming, and coordinating a Year 2000 management team. It also covers important information related to determining where your 2000-resistant machines are hiding.

Creating management awareness of the Year 2000 problem means launching people into a proactive stance, thus empowering them. The following are several areas you will need to consider before you set up your team:

Staff to locate lost processes and products.   For years companies have been purchasing software, computers, and other equipment that contain computers as integrated components. All of these now have to be identified and studied to determine if they will require repair, reprogramming, or replacement. Some of the companies producing these products have changed their name, moved, sold out, and/or shut down. You will have to determine where they have gone and make decisions about what to do about the products. In some cases the warranty limitations may have expired. In others, you may have chosen to let maintenance contracts expire. In still others, the confidence in the new supplier may not be high. In each of these cases, you may need to involve many in management to get decisions made.

Staff to maintain customer relations, including implementing customer awareness.   Unless everyone understands the importance of the date problem, they will try to waylay preparation efforts in an attempt to get their immediate business requirements met. Make sure everyone knows that the Year 2000 problem has a deadline that can't be extended and that they will feel the impact if you're late in delivering a solution. Involvement and understanding is required of everyone.

The number of companies asking their suppliers to provide status information is growing. Many of these requests are not asking for relavent data and demand to know if a company is compliant or when they will be compliant. Some firms have already learned that inappropriate responses (e.g., "Sure we are!") have opened up the possibility of lawsuits. Education of what to say and what not to say is important. What is right to say may be surprising. Many firms have begun posting corporate Y2K plans and schedules on their corporate Web pages to expand public awareness of the companies' Y2K policies. This reduces the number of supplier and customer queries that must be handled by staff. It also allows the company to point to a single source of answers.

At the other end of the spectrum, employee awareness could minimize future problems. It may, for instance, be wise to make sure that form orders don't continue to include forms that have 19 preprinted on them, and it may be necessary to have some forms redesigned to allow space for four-digit years. In some instances legal requirements force some forms to be redesigned to stipulate field content of month, day, and year. Ambiguity may lead to some of the most serious liability and claims litigation in the next century. Forms are at the basis of all data capture and validation processes.

Support from executives and stockholders.   This is a cross-organizational project. Without senior backing, any efforts to coordinate "the fix" will fail. Competition for increasingly scarce resources and the desire to minimize the impact of making Year 2000 changes will delay decisions past the deadline. The complexity of the decision making that is created by possible failures by the organization, its customers, and suppliers necessitates rethinking many policies affecting personnel, financing, accounting, purchasing, and public and supplier relations, to name just a few.

Personnel to take emergency measures.   Few organizations are expected to become completely compliant leading to some systems that will not function correctly. This will create a chain reaction of system failures affecting other companies in supply and customer channels. The situation demands that every organization develop a risk management posture. Risk management will consist of contingency plans defining risk mitigation actions. It is also necessary to implement practices to keep the problem from growing. Stop purchasing products that are not going to handle dates correctly. Believe it or not, there are products still being sold that are not capable of processing correctly beyond the year 2000. Many companies that once believed their products to be Year 2000–compliant have drawn back from that position following investigation and testing.

Team Spirit

First and foremost, you will need a project manager. This should not be just a task assigned to the first person who volunteers. Project management is a profession that requires a distinct set of skills. Project managers sent us to the moon. They built the Boeing 777 and Microsoft Windows 98. They coordinate, cajole, wheedle, and demand cooperation. They know how to manage people on important and stressful projects.

You will need several people to support your project manager. A small company may require only a project manager, someone to handle supplier and customer communications, and another to handle the technical requirements of computing hardware, embedded systems, facilities, and so forth. Other tasks will be distributed across the organization with the project manager bringing the plans and decisions together.

Larger organizations may require very large core project team members. One large bank assembled a team consisting of the following players:

Applications development representatives (five sites). Determine the impact of the year 2000 on in-house-developed application systems, purchased computer applications, data purchased from other firms, and purchased software development tools.

Operations representatives (two sites). Study the impact on systems administration software, hardware usage, data storage, work scheduling, and define new resource requirements.

Technical programming representative. Analyzes the impact on operating systems software, compilers, utilities, processes performance, and works on design of special tools to handle unique enterprise needs.

Database administration. Investigates the use of dates in the data, handling by database management systems, storage of dates, and passing of date data between applications and to others outside the enterprise.

Production planners (two). Design high-level plans for repairing and replacing applications, systems software, computer hardware, and other equipment.

Forms development. Reviews forms and forms design to determine the location of the printed century, the space to enter the century on forms, and replacement of forms throughout the enterprise.

Facilities engineer. Locates embedded systems within the enterprise and determines what to do about them.

Purchasing. Reviews all supplier contracts and ascertains the status of work of suppliers to fix the problem; change contracts to include stipulations that protect the enterprise.

Security. Studies the impact of the year 2000 on security and surveillance equipment and systems.

Legal. Evaluates the impact on financial statements, develops contract wording, assesses enterprise and management liability, and so on.

Audit. Determines what is needed to meet regulatory changes, develops a process to monitor changes to data, and puts a process in place to review the progress of the enterprise toward Year 2000 compliance.

Vendor representatives from key computer providers (three). Coordinate ordering and replacement of hardware, perform systems software correction and updates, and provide advice on dealing with performance and capacity issues.

The bank organized this team loosely, with dotted-line authority assigned to the project manager. This team reflects the decentralized development and implementation of computer applications. It takes into account the need to coordinate change across a country where the bank has hundreds of offices. The presence of legal, audit, and purchasing reflects its concern not only for the dependency on others, but the effect it will have on others as it begins to fix its problem.

In the case of this team, the enterprise's chief executive officer was convinced of the need for such a team by *another* team that was commissioned to study the problem. The managing directors acted in unison to fund the project and commit resources.

Another organization put in place a smaller team, but a team nonetheless. It contained the following:

Technical coordinator. Works with technical services and operations to obtain computing resources and coordinate changes to systems software.

Administrator. Assembles and coordinates plans of each of the organizations within the enterprise so that human resources could be found and allocated to help them.

Personnel coordinator. Works with organizations to acquire staff for the project from within and outside the enterprise.

Planner. Develops detailed plans for changing computer software and data.

Technical liaison. Works with systems programmers and database administrators on making changes and building tools and support programs.

Quality assurance. Provides an independent assessment of the changes made and assesses the risk of implementing those changes.

Process developer. Develops a factorylike process for making changes to software and data, determines where improvements can be made, and finds tools for automating routine tasks to free up skilled staff to do more complex work.

This team setup reflects limiting the scope to software and data repair and that this enterprise's business focus is on providing services. This is a centralized organization with all services located and directed out of a single site. In this situation, responsibility was spread to each of the functional areas, with applications development providing coordination and direction. The titles they assigned to team members were unique within the enterprise.

Of course, you can call the team members point guards or small forwards or quarterbacks or goalies. The point is, titles don't matter as long as the team accomplishes what you need it to. And make sure that they are the best people you can find.

To help you understand what you're up against, let's review the possible Y2K scenarios if you do nothing or do too little too late. Nearly every computing process is time-sensitive, including safes, phone systems, cooling and heating systems and thermostats, elevators, engines, security and sprinkler systems, video cameras, and much more. Dates enable scheduling processes, determine the sequence of events, record and control events, limit retention, and set and limit values. In short, accurate dating *makes things happen.* Calendars were created to make life predictable and planning possible.

Just after "Auld Lang Syne" is sung on December 31, 1999, chances are that any computer system not 2000-ready will react in one of these two ways:

Dates will roll over to 01/01/00, but the computer will treat the year as 1900. This scenario will result in expired credit cards, licenses, and the like, miscalculations of interest, mishandling of dated perishable products, and so on.

Or else, simply and without fanfare, your system will crash. Transactions won't be mishandled; they won't be handled at all: total shutdown.

Wake-up Call

People can't be involved in something they know nothing about, so one of the first steps is to create awareness of the Year 2000 situation throughout your enterprise. One organization realized the importance of an awareness program when it found its 2000 team recruitment efforts going nowhere because of companywide insouciance. There are many reasons for this inability to recruit. One is that nobody wants to be associated with a job that is expected to terminate at a fixed point in time, especially one in which recruits will not be learning any new skills that will prepare them for the next job. The second is that the job is similar to picking up the trash. If you do it well, nobody notices; if you do it ineffectively, everybody notices. Chances of recognition and reward or promotion are seen as poor. In short, there is no perceived incentive to take on this job.

Some companies have already blazed the recruitment trail by including ongoing articles in their company newsletters or papers that highlight the Y2K team and the program; others have put out brochures signed by the CEO. Another program tied itself to an internal employee suggestion award program. At least one energetic person designed a screen saver, with some version of the warning, "The millennium is coming. This computer is not ready!"

Achieving visibility is important. Making sure that you have a team in place to exploit it is even more important. Some companies produce newsletters to bring the Y2K issue to the attention of employees to solicit coordinated effort. Unfortunately, newsletters often go unread. While work is going on to fix the problem, it has not yet reached the imperative level. It is not even clear to most that fixing the problem is important. This is not unusual. The more decentralized an enterprise becomes, the less able it will be to put together project teams with real authority to make things happen. The people from "corporate" have been declawed and defanged. In decentralized enterprises (federal and state governments fall into this category), each of the computing entities compete for resources and budget. A real leader will have to emerge to get these groups to work together.

One oblique way of getting the message across is to use an estimating survey. Questions like, "When will your application fail?" should be followed by others that help to determine the answer:

- What is the longest forward dating used?
- Do you enter dates in the future? If so how far?
- How long do you expect data in the master file to be kept?
- What is the oldest date stored in each master file?

- What is the maximum retention cycle of any master file in the application?
- How long does the system retain each transaction?
- Are there regulatory or legal retention requirements?

Other awareness mechanisms include the following:

- Training programs for programmers and users to instruct them on standards, policies, and what to look for
- E-mail and voice mail to highlight costs and policy issues, provide instruction, and ensure cooperation
- Management briefings to kick off the 2000 recovery project, review budget issues, facilitate project progress and participation, and minimize business impact

One enterprising group within the U.S. Department of Defense has established a bulletin board on which employees can share questions, information, and experiences.

Reading Is Fundamental

Many organizations support their internal communications with information from outside sources. This book is one of several published that are aimed at awareness. Other worthwhile books are listed in Appendix D. The Internet has provided all kinds of links that provide everything from newspaper articles to forms and guidance. See Appendix C for lists of some of the many that have proven invaluable. The beginner may want to start at the authors' Web sites which include the Year 2000 Information Center located on the Internet at www.year2000.com and www.systemicsolutions.com. Many consulting companies and year tool manufacturers have a presence on the Internet. This book contains an appendix listing many of the most responsible tool and services vendors and their products.

The Year 2000 Information Center has provided many with a forum for sharing problems and obtaining advice. Some have used the site to start looking for employees. If you decide to join the Year 2000 forum, be aware that you may get buried in messages. E-mail is voluminous, and there are now around 600,000 accesses to this site per month.

If you're running out of time or just feeling lost, use the frequently asked questions (FAQs), available from the Year 2000 Information Center, for assistance in sorting the wheat from the chaff.

You will find a similar special-interest group on CompuServe. Most hardware vendors and major software vendors are providing Year 2000 information about their products and what they are doing to solve their problems. And it wouldn't be a bad idea to subscribe to a couple of periodicals that address the Year 2000 issue. Try these:

Tick, Tick, Tick
2000AD, Inc.
P.O. Box 020538
Brooklyn, NY 11202-0012

Year/2000 Journal
9550 Skillman St.—Suite 105
Dallas, TX 75243

Team against Machine

It's game time, time to pit your Team 2000 against the millennium-defiant equipment in residence at your business. First let's dispel one myth: that only big old computers are susceptible to the Year 2000 date problem. You may think that your computer programs will work just fine because they were created last year or were put into a fancy new data management system that uses four-digit-year formats. Think again. Two tests, one performed in Great Britain, and the other performed in the United States demonstrated that some PCs manufactured in 1997 still contained chips that would not handle year 2000 processing correctly.

After performing a full system backup, perform this PC date change test: Find your PC's internal or system clock. On a PC running DOS, you can do this by typing DATE. Change the date to December 31, 1999. Change the time by setting TIME to 11:58 P.M. Then turn off the computer and wait three minutes. When you turn it back on, does it read January 1, 2000? If so, congratulations. Your hardware would seem to be okay.

Hardware and Software

Some Apple Macintoshes, Gateway 2000 PCs, recently manufactured IBM PCs, PCs with OS/2 WARP, Windows 95/98/NT, and a few others will pass the PC date change test. (However, you still need to check your own spreadsheets and make sure you're using software that handles two-digit years correctly.) Most of you undoubtedly found some bizarre number, possibly January 4, 1980. The simple explanation is that the computer's internal clock is set using counters from a previously selected date. These counters have only so many digits and can hold only so many seconds. When they are full, they reset themselves back to the original date.

Of course, you're going to have to check all your programs, too. Microsoft's position is that all programs written prior to 1997 should be replaced with software written for Windows 98 or NT 4. New products use the operating system clock rather than the hardware clock. In order for your current software to work with the new operating systems, it may be necessary to update your applications. For some, this may mean a substantial learning curve. The organizational education and administrative costs involved in moving from DOS to Windows 98 or NT often prove to be greater than the cost of the hardware replacement.

Ashes to Ashes, DOS to Dust

Microsoft has taken steps to correct date problems. The program interfaces for Windows 95 and Windows NT are capable of storing dates for 119 years, starting from 1980, so applications that rely on those formats will work until 2099. Although these particular Microsoft operating systems handle dates well into the next century, mainframe operating system dates historically have not. Programs designed to run in these environments (as well as OS/2, UNIX, and Mac) generally use the operating system clock and not the computer clock. If you are running DOS, you are more likely to find problems with dates.

Many computers can't tell the difference between a day in 1905 and one in 2005 with a two-digit-year date format. Microsoft products that assume the year from two-digit dates have now been updated to make it easier for the computer to assume a 2000-based year. As a result, Microsoft recommends that by the end of the century all PC software be upgraded to post-1997 versions. (Is that your checkbook you hear whimpering?) Even in 1998, Microsoft is still engaged in strenuous testing of its products to handle not only the Year 2000 problem, but also the new European currency.

According to a company paper on the implications of the year 2000, Microsoft warns developers—including those using macrolanguages or building custom databases using such products as Microsoft Access—to use date formats that accommodate the transition to the year 2000. Recommendations include the following:

1. Use the operating system's runtime library's date format as much as possible.

2. Use long dates (four-digit years) rather than short ones whenever creating a custom application.

3. Buy computer hardware and software built in 1997 or later and hope for the best.

Some Microsoft Windows systems don't use the same 32-bit platform as Windows 95, 98, or Windows NT. Windows for Workgroups 3.11, Windows 3.1, and any earlier versions still in use come to mind. The following table shows Microsoft's current products and the life expectancy of the date formats for each. Unless otherwise noted, the products rely on the system-supplied date formats. As you can see, some of these products won't make it much past the year 2000 before running into problems. This does not include the many products that won't make it there at all, so you probably should examine all your current Microsoft programs with the same diligence that you do the rest of your software portfolio.

PRODUCT NAME	DATE LIMIT	DATE FORMAT
Microsoft Access 95 assumed date	1999	Assumed yy dates
Microsoft Access 95 explicit date	9999	Long dates (yyyy)
Microsoft Access (next major version)	2039	Assumed yy dates
Microsoft Excel 95	2019	Assumed yy dates
Microsoft Excel 95	2078	Long dates
Microsoft Excel (next major version)	2029	Assumed yy dates
Microsoft Excel (next major version)	9999	Long dates
Microsoft Project 95 (and older versions)	2049	32 bits
Microsoft SQL Serve	9999	"Datetime"
MS-DOS file system (FAT16)	2108	16 bits
Visual C++ (4.x) runtime library	2036	32 bits
Visual FoxPro	9999	Long dates
Windows 3.x file system (FAT16)	2108	16 bits
Windows 95 file system (FAT16)	2108	16 bits
Windows 95/98 file system (FAT32)	2108	32 bits
Windows 95/98 runtime library (WIN32)	2099	16 bits
Windows for Workgroups (FAT16)	2108	16 bits
Windows NT file system (FAT16)	2108	16 bits
Windows NT file system (NTFS)	future	64 bits centuries
Windows NT runtime library (WIN32)	2099	16 bits

Courtesy of Microsoft and available via the Internet.

Of course, this table assumes that the owner of the PC has up-to-date software, up-to-date hardware, and no trouble with the BIOS clock. Smart PC owners will not make these assumptions, but will check for themselves.

DOS is expected to die, even though a new version will be released. While there are some Year 2000–compliant DOS applications, most developers have abandoned DOS products and concentrated on supporting only the Windows versions. Remember, Microsoft recommends that all Windows programs should be replaced after the WIN 98 release. Windows 3.x will also probably disappear. Vendors do not like to spend money providing fixes for products designed for old operating systems.

PC Inventory

Some PC computer manufacturers have addressed the date rollover problem. IBM is used to illustrate the point, which is that there are a lot of PC products, and it will take someone trained to identify which ones you have and then to determine what it will take to fix them. The inventory will take a lot of time, except for the smallest businesses, especially to do it right. You will be locating job streams, databases, files, applications, and shared code. (You will need this information later.)

According to an IBM publication titled "The Year 2000 and 2-Digit Dates: A Guide for Planning and Implementation," all new models of IBM PCs shipped in 1996 and later will automatically update the century. They have confirmed that the following older models of PC will be affected by date problems:

- All XT286, all ATs, all PS/1s, all PS/2s, all PS/55s.
- All Aptivas before 1996.
- Most 2144 systems.
- Most 2168 systems, although they will update the century byte automatically after you install the flash BIOS available from IBM's Bulletin Board service.
- Commercial desktop PC systems such as the PS/V (models 2405/2410), the PS/V Vision (model 2408), the PS/V Entry (model 2406), the PS/V MASTER (model 2411), the PC 750 (model 6885), the PC 330 (model 6571), and so forth must have the century byte set manually.

Check with IBM if you discover you have any of its PC hardware in house.

The hardware timers on RS/6000 servers, as well as personal systems using PowerPC technology, will not be affected by the turning of the millennium, but it's probably a good idea to test them anyway. IBM PC servers introduced in 1996 handle the century rollover automatically, which says all you need to know about those introduced prior to that date.

Some current and earlier IBM PCs will handle the change quite well, but testing should be conducted to determine which ones will be Y2K-ready. The tests involve taking the PC off any network it might be attached to and then running the test given earlier, where the date is set to just prior to the rollover to the year 2000—12:59:00 on December 31, 1999—and then the PC is turned off for a couple of minutes. Check the date on the system clock and the clock in the operating system to see what date, day, and time appear. They should register as a Saturday, a few minutes after 12 A.M. on January 1, 2000. Remember to do full backups of all your systems before you start date testing.

Commands and utilities are available to help some models weather the changeover. If you are running DOS, which is unlikely at the millennium since it will be necessary to upgrade to versions of products that only run on Windows NT or Windows 95/98, it is possible to enter the correct date using the DATE command. Contact IBM to find out which models need help, and which might have to be abandoned.

It is likely you also have computers from another manufacturer—clones. If so, find out if the manufacturer has a Year 2000 plan in place. If it doesn't—which is usually the case—it is better to know now than to be surprised later. Vendor Web sites for the primary manufacturers list models that are known to be compliant, or refer to the Web site of the BIOS manufacturer that they use.

Hardware and the PC BIOS Dilemma

To determine your PC status, start by taking an inventory. It will probably take from 10 to 15 minutes to register each PC. Collect the following information:

Manufacturer

Model

BIOS manufacturer

BIOS version number

The *BIOS* (stands for *Basic Input Output System*) is a built-in operating system that comes with a computer. It contains the code that tells the computer how to control the screen, disk drives, ports for communications and mouse, and even the keyboard. It also performs such things as keeping track of the date and time.

All computers were originally designed with BIOSs that were *hard-wired* or permanently, and unalterably, programmed on a chip on the PC motherboard. Later, the manufacturer learned that copying the BIOS program to the computer's regular memory could increase speed. More recently, some manufacturers switched to Plug-and-Play (PnP) devices that are stored on a chip that can be reprogrammed. The hard-wired versions may or may not be fixed at all, and in some cases (where the programs being run are not reliant on dates), it may not be necessary to worry at all. Flash BIOS programs can be repaired with upgrade software.

Is Your BIOS Y2K-Compliant?

The initial problem is in trying to determine what type of BIOS a PC uses. There are several different ways to determine whether a BIOS is Year 2000–compliant and several ways that it might be repaired if it isn't.

The easiest way, for some people, is to find out from the manufacturer if their PC model is compliant or not. Apple, Compaq, Dell, Digital, Gateway, HP, IBM, Micron, and NEC are all examples of firms that post compliance status information on the Internet. To reach them try the following Web site: www.mitre.org/research/cots/COMPLIANT_BIOS.html, which can be used for an easy link to the BIOS vendors plus it provides other valuable information on PC compliance.

Compaq (at www.compaq.com/year2000/) indicates that products purchased after October 7, 1997 are Year 2000–compliant. If the product was purchased before that date, the purchaser can download or order an update. Upgrades are not available for all older products. The authors remind readers that Tandem and Digital, both Compaq-owned companies, have their own Year 2000 problems that do not have anything to do with Compaq BIOS processors.

Another way to tell if your computer needs attention is to watch the screen very carefully when it is first turned on. The first message that appears tells the user what BIOS is being used. AMI, Award, MR, and Phoenix produced the BIOS chips most commonly used. Following are some statistics from these BIOS manufacturers that are easy to locate on the Internet.

Award (at www.award.com/tech/biosfaqs.html) indicates the following actions are available:

1. If the BIOSs were released prior to April 26, 1994, the clocks will only have to be reset once. Award advises turning off the computer prior to midnight on December 31, 1999, and turning it back on sometime after 12:01 A.M. on the 1st. The system date can be reset through the system setup program.

2. If the BIOS was manufactured between April 26, 1994, and May 31, 1995, you will have to obtain a BIOS update program (see the following) or reset the clock every day!

3. If the BIOSs were released after May 31, 1995, nothing has to be done.

AMI (American Megatrends, Inc., at www.amibios.com) says that all its versions after July 15, 1995 are Year 2000–compliant. It suggests contacting the equipment manufacturer to obtain any possible upgrades.

Phoenix (at www.Phoenix.com/techsupp/biosfaq.html) claims that all BIOS produced after February 1995 are Year 2000–compliant, but there is no version-number guarantees that the system will work properly in the year 2000. Phoenix doesn't provide BIOS upgrades directly to end customers and advises buyers to contact their equipment manufacturer.

You can obtain a software package to perform hardware tests on your PC. NSTL provides YMARK2000 free to requestors. Other popular BIOS test programs include DOSCHK.EXE, the Millennium Bug Toolkit, Survive 2000, and Test2000.Com. Many of the BIOS manufacturers caveat the use of such programs. Award, for instance, says that passing the test doesn't necessarily mean compliance because some other equipment or software installed may make the computer noncompliant.

You may be able to determine if your BIOS is on flash memory by looking to see if the computer came with a utility such as FLASH.EXE that allows the BIOS to be updated.

The last and most adventurous way to determine the kind of BIOS requires opening the computer case and looking for a 28- or 32-pin integrated circuit chip with a BIOS brand sticker on it. Peeling the sticker will reveal a code with letters and numbers. If the first numbers are 28 or 29, breathe a sigh of relief. The chip is most likely flash memory–based and can be upgraded by a program obtainable from the computer or motherboard manufacturer. If it starts with 27C, the computer can be reprogrammed, but it requires a specialist and special equipment.

It Isn't! Now What?

Fixing the BIOS to recognize year 2000 dates on flash memory–based chips is obviously easier than for those based on hard-wired BIOS. The fix can be accomplished programmatically on computers with flash memory. The original manufacturer is the best source of upgrades for flash BIOS. A company called Micro Firmware sells upgrades for many PCs. It can be reached at 800-767-5465 or at www.firmware.com. Updating your flash BIOS is not a simple process; you may want to seek help if you have not done it before.

If the computer is one that copies its program to regular memory before it is executed, there are software programs that can be used to intercept BIOS date requests before or immediately after it runs to correct any date problems. Some may find it easier to acquire and install a small utility that stays in the computer and overrides the clock on many Intel-based computers. There are many on the market. DATE-A-FIX, HOLMESFX.COM, Millennium Toolkit, Survive 2000, and Test2000.Com are examples.

Software

Don't stop at the hardware. You also need to know how many software program updates you will have to buy. PC software is not exempt from the issue of old release versus the century-compliant release. Older DOS releases and even some Windows versions of popular software such as Sidekick, Quicken, Excel, and Lotus 1-2-3 do not all handle dates in 2000 in the same way. These inconsistencies will cause problems. Older programs and the Windows 3.x calendar function do not handle the century rollover properly, and date problems abound in interpackage data sharing because dates are assumed to be prefixed by either 19 or 20.

Fortunately, software packages are available to help you complete your software inventory. Greenwich Mean Time Inc. (56 Oyster Quay, Port Solent, Portsmouth, Hampshire, UK P06 4TE) provides a package to do this inventory (their URL is www.GMT-2000.com). The following are some generic steps that will help you to complete this inventory.

Task every organization with completing a PC inventory.

Be sure the inventory contains the following information:

- Whether the PC is a client, server, or stand-alone model
- Model number
- Processor type (e.g., Intel 486 100 MHz)
- BIOS date
- Software operating system and version number
- Vendor packages loaded on the hard drive (product name, vendor, version)
- Internally developed software packages
- All spreadsheets that are used routinely
- All databases that are used routinely
- LAN ID number and address; name of LAN

Consolidate the list in a database or spreadsheet.

This information will enable you to determine licenses that need upgrades and training requirements. The processor type will tell you whether you are faced with hardware replacement. Vendor packages and versions will tell you how many and which products have to be upgraded. Greenwich Mean Time's Check 2000 also provides Year 2000 compliance information on the products it inventories.

Don't be surprised to discover that many of your PCs are running software with duplicate serial numbers. Often, people reload with the first set of disks at hand. Any system or program can be affected if it uses only two digits for the year. Old habits die hard: Recently developed desktop software often has the same problem because it is easier for programmers to reuse old chunks of code and plug them in than to write each program from scratch. One of the ongoing problems for firms that have updated their applications to handle the year 2000 is that programmers trying to fix bugs occasionally use code from their personal libraries that does not process dates correctly. This reintroduces problems that are found out only later after much damage has been done.

Be aware that you may experience trouble well in advance of the year 2000, if you haven't already. Application programs working with time-sensitive data are likely to produce incorrect results today. Prescriptions, subscriptions, inventory aging, scheduling, depreciation schedules, expiration dates, renewal dates, effective dates, and birth dates are the common examples of time-sensitive data.

The PC BIOS dilemma covered in this chapter is only one example of an integrated component of your computer system that may be affected by the Y2K date problem. The next chapter, "The Monster in the Closet," looks at other *embedded systems* affected by dates and helps you determine the impact of these components on your computer or network.

CHAPTER 3

The Monster in the Closet

Embedded Systems

An *embedded system* is hardware or software that is a component of a larger system. The embedded system can be a computer, or just a computer-like component that performs a specific function. Say you have a beer factory with a conveyor system run by a computer. While the computer is visible as a separate component mounted in a rack, it is an embedded system, because it is wholly integrated into the conveyor system.

On the other end of the scale, a VCR is a small appliance and has nothing that resembles a computer, in the familiar sense. It does have complicated and often confusing *functions* which control timed recording of a program, speed of a recording or playback, and which can reject a tape when it is inserted backward or upside down. The VCR actually contains a number of embedded systems each of which is a microprocessor chip which is soldered to an integrated circuit board. Each takes its input from a sensing device (i.e., remote controller, pressure gauge, light receptor, and switches), and its output is a switch that turns parts on or off, or an activator that controls things that act like valves. Each embedded system is integral, and without it the VCR would not function. In general, embedded systems are either not reprogrammable or are programmable only with professional assistance.

A computer itself is not much more than a collection of embedded systems. The discussion of the PC BIOS problem in Chapter 2, "Behind Every Great Machine," introduces one of many embedded system components that exist within a PC. A typical PC contains many embedded systems which include the following:

CPU (central processing unit)

Core logic

Super I/O cards

Peripheral controllers

Video and audio cards

Networking cards

PCMCIA cards

PCI bridges

Modems

Motion controllers

Power converters

Power supervisors

Embedded systems perform two types of functions—process control and process monitoring. A *process control system* uses a predefined menu of instructions which perform certain functions when something happens. The simplest process control systems are like those in a clock/radio. When the clock detects that the time set on the alarm has been reached, it either turns on the buzzing of the alarm or the radio, depending on how the sleeper has set the selector. Oil refineries and manufacturing plants use very sophisticated versions to control manufacturing processes. A *process-monitoring system* doesn't perform any specific production function but records, stores, and compares information giving a warning if things are not working the way they should. The oil pressure warning light in a car is an example of a simple process-monitoring activity that only warns. In elevators, the process-monitoring system keeps track of how much time has passed since the elevator was last serviced. In the process control function, the embedded system(s) feeds instructions to the primary system to initiate some action. In monitoring mode, systems collect data and generally pass it along to some other computer.

Neither process control nor process monitoring becomes a Year 2000 concern until an additional time-related function is required. When the embedded system is called upon to say when something happens or how frequently it must happen, it accesses a built-in clock which tracks both time and date. The internal clock tells the embedded system to perform a function, such as get data from a sensor, or tells it to stop doing a function.

"Watson, My Magnifying Glass, Please!"

For this discussion, ignore embedded systems that are based on computers. Embedded systems in computers are relatively easy to find, and the fixes for them are fully discussed elsewhere. There are several kinds of embedded systems or *microprocessors.* The next two sections explain what they are, what they do, and products in which they might be found.

Sensors and Detectors

Sensors and detectors sample the environment where they are installed with a relatively high degree of frequency. They are found in temperature gauges, pressure sensors, gas detectors, and circuit breakers. They operate on the basis of keeping track of clock cycles. The cycles could be very fast—microseconds—or slow—days. For example, video controller chips in VCRs use the time and date to trigger recording of a televised program. Elevators may determine that they haven't been serviced for more than the one year allowed, and shutdown. In a chemical plant, the clock on a valve may mistakenly determine that it is time to allow a chemical to flow through a pipe that already has another product in it, thus destroying the product being manufactured.

Many sensor/detector microprocessors do not have timing functions. In devices that are connected to actuators, such as float valves and strain gauges, the device simply sends a signal that an event has occurred. For example, the water level in a boat's bilge tank is measured by a float valve. When the water gets too high, the float trips a switch telling a microprocessor to turn the bilge pump on. Another example is the standard home thermostat, which contains a mercury vial that reacts to the temperature in the room. The mercury trips a switch that sends a signal to a microprocessor in the furnace to turn it on or off.

Nontimed sensor devices are unlikely to cause much of a problem, but their microprocessors' internal functions may depend upon the clock in ways that are not easily detected. A gas detector used on an oil rig may seem to have no reliance on date processing, but it may use the clock to send signals to a computer far away from the site. Bad dating may not allow the two computers to synchronize communications and they will either shut down the sensor or initiate a false alarm. A microprocessor that acts on short cycles may not *directly* contribute to a Year 2000 fault since there is no date checking. The clock is rarely reset and eventually rolls over, returning to a value of zero.

On August 21–22, 1999, this zeroing out of dates will occur in many land-based Global Positioning Systems (GPSs). The microprocessor will feed a value less than the last registered value used by the system. This will upset the timing and sampling systems and interfere with reception of the satellite signals. It could also send false data about the location of the GPS, saying it is far from where it actually is. An autopilot system slaved to the GPS may shift course and much distance may be covered before an error is detected. This could send a boat upon a reef. Most larger vessels contain redundant systems and owners are aware of the problem, so this is unlikely to occur, but small vessel owners are not as well informed and may become lost at sea for a while.

Will this type of fault occur in other devices that day or on another date? The probability exists, but no testing of other devices for this fault has been reported. The problem is real. Other systems dependent on microprocessors have reportedly failed. One story circulated in the industry suggests that a military satellite left orbit and burned up in the late 1980s because of a clock that rolled over.

The microprocessor is typically a chip installed in a piece of equipment—and is totally inseparable from the device. In such a situation, it may be necessary to replace the entire piece of equipment to solve the Year 2000 problem. Microprocessors are commonly found in just about any type of equipment that has to provide a sensed response including those in the following:

Environment control systems (temperature monitors)

Energy management systems (power-level monitors)

Oil and gas pipelines (flow monitors)

Automotive systems (emission control monitors, engine speed monitors, antilock braking systems)

Newer stoves and refrigerators (temperature monitors)

Microprocessor assemblies

Microprocessors are typically part of a circuit board that plugs into a piece of equipment or is soldered in place. They are found in traffic controllers, data-acquisition devices such as testing equipment, monitoring devices such as effluent samplers, and real-time control systems such as robots and conveyors. Many of these devices consist of a small computer or even a PC board installed as part of the device. The Year 2000 problem may affect application software that controls data gathering, data storage, data retrieval, and reporting. Data transmission is often controlled by such microprocessor assemblies. The clocks in these devices may send information too early or too late to another device which simply loses contact, causing lost transactions.

Lost transaction problems have already occurred in situations not related to Year 2000 problems. In Washington state, a person at a grocery store attempted to pay for groceries using a debit card. The transaction failed to get approval twice, so the person wrote a check. Later the person received notice that the check had been returned for insufficient funds. It turns out that the two debit card transactions had each gotten as far as withdrawing the funds from the account, but the confirmation had not been sent to the grocery store because the system had timed out. There was no audit trail indicating where the money had gone. In this case, witnesses and logic prevailed and the bank reinstated the lost funds. If there were massive failures, witnesses may not be available and logic might be wasted on overworked bank managers.

Other stories about bad timing exist, including the shutdown of telephone exchanges and the halt of transactions on the Belgian Stock Exchange. On February 29, 1996, a little-known event occurred when computers were adjusted for a *leap second* to get them realigned with the International Standard Time. The programs were written to perform the function, but there was no way to test them prior to the event. A failure misaligned several systems, halting communications for hours until it could be fixed and the communication resynchronized. Some large monetary transactions allow funds to be loaned for short periods of time, sometimes just overnight. Such transactions, if not executed, prevent business from being executed, costing the intended borrower late fees or penalties and the loaner interest. These lost interest amounts can reach well over $100,000. Failed stock sales and purchase transactions can create confusion. If a person needs to buy stock to satisfy a short sale or fails to sell stock to satisfy a long sale, the costs can be large. Windows on stock sales may be very short. Imagine how it would feel to a shareholder who wanted a stock sold at an available price, but whose order was not able to be executed until the stock had dropped several points lower.

Many are concerned that air traffic control systems could fail on December 31, 1999, and January 1, 2000. A loss of air traffic control would ground many flights because safety would be at risk. Planes in the air would be hard to identify, making it necessary to spread them out miles apart until it was possible to determine which flight was which. Some planes would be landed at airports far from their destinations, stranding passengers.

In cities, traffic light systems could malfunction, turning off traffic lights or rescheduling traffic intervals. The major effect could be gridlock in our cities. (Drivers in San Francisco, Los Angeles, Seattle, New York, and some other cities might dismiss this as "what's new?") The major impact might be interference with deliveries. The costs could amount to millions of dollars in spoilage of food; delays in delivering medicine to patients; and obstruction of ambulances, police, and firefighters.

Computer Subsystems

Another type of embedded system is that which stands out as an easily recognized computer that is part of a large system. These are found in security systems, environmental control systems, energy management systems, and manufacturing process control. These computers are connected to other microprocessor systems through a facility to determine what is going on and what to do next.

The largest number of obsolete computers are found in computer subsystems. These systems are highly susceptible at both the hardware and application software level. The potential Year 2000 problems can relate to retrieving the wrong set of instructions, sending the wrong instructions, storing and retrieving data incorrectly, losing data, failing to transmit data, and reporting incorrect data. Computer operators could be locked out of their computer rooms because their passwords have expired. Robots could suddenly reposition themselves, dropping material. Power could be shut off in the middle of a medical operation.

As mentioned in Chapter 1, "Ground Double-Zero," obsolete systems use operating systems no longer supported, and most are not Year 2000–compliant. Many of the process control computers and their applications were developed for computers like DEC's PDP-11 or IBM's Series One. Many are written in languages which are now obsolete. This means that, like their bigger brothers, language support is not offered, and the programmers able to fix the systems are difficult to find.

Obsolete computer systems and subsystems are the most expensive to replace. Airports around the United States are replacing security systems purchased only 8 to 10 years ago with newer ones at a cost of $12.8 million not only because the new ones are better, but because they are also Year 2000–compliant. Failing to maintain these systems means that the security levels necessary in this age of international terrorism cannot be achieved.

How Serious Can It Be?

Nobody really knows what could occur as a result of problems with embedded systems. The Institution of Electrical Engineers (IEE Technical Guidelines 9:1997) suggests users may not be able to access the extent of Y2K-related problems with embedded systems until the year 2002. Several levels of problems could be due to failures of embedded systems including the following:

Annoyance and temporary inconvenience

Confusion over sequence of actions

Long-term loss of effectiveness

Serious production problems and loss of profitability

Injury or death to individuals

Damages to fortunes, businesses, and governments

If our morning coffee is cut off because the embedded system fails, or the VCR fails to record when programmed, it is a minor inconvenience. (Well, not getting coffee first thing in the morning may contribute to road rage and have consequences beyond inconvenience.)

Companies that don't uncover embedded-systems problems could face lawsuits, regulatory actions such as supervision, or loss of quality accreditation. Certainly replacement of the offending systems entails significant expenses. In the United Kingdom, there is a 25 percent tax provision for the writing-off of machinery and plant costs associated with Year 2000 problems. In Canada, a similar tax allowance has been granted to small companies that may face replacement costs well ahead of typical schedules.

Production problems could result from failures of embedded systems that either manage elements of the environment or control the production process, or systems that may interfere with distribution of the product or inhibit production when supplies fail to arrive or cannot be off-loaded even after they are received. Try to imagine working in an office without telephones or electricity, in a fish-processing plant without water or waste handling, at a dock where the cranes do not function.

As mentioned earlier, on February 29, 1996, in New Zealand, an aluminum plant began to run amok because its computer was not programmed to recognize the leap year. No injuries occurred, but they could have. Imagine a chemical plant suddenly routing chemicals down a pipe from the wrong tank because the computer thinks it's Thursday not Saturday.

Perhaps the most costly problems that may result from embedded systems failures are the potentials for death, injury, and damage to the plant. Consider the control embedded systems have in energy generation. Computers are involved in the creation of electricity by hydroelectric dams, gas-fired turbines, and oil- and coal-fired turbines (where they control the scrubbers that must be used or the generators would have to be shut down according to antipollution laws). An embedded system might strike one or more systems, causing a brown-out. In the United States, nuclear plants that are not proven to be compliant will be shutdown. Nuclear energy is the source of 30 percent of the power on the eastern seaboard. Not only may they be faced with loss of power, but a plant shutdown can cost power customers millions of dollars to restart. The energy industry is very concerned and working hard to avoid such problems.

These embedded systems often do not act alone. Similar to a PC, there are many embedded systems that obtain data and pass it along to other embedded systems. Because an environmental system will think it's Thursday and turn the heat up, another may determine that the heat has risen too much and start the cooling process. A system in a plant may start running equipment while another may detect the operation startup and initiate a security alert. Literally chains of reactions could result from a combination of embedded systems reacting incorrectly to date-related information.

Catching Small Bugs with a Net

A common belief is that manufacturers afraid of Y2K-related warranty claims by irate owners will notify their clients and volunteer to fix the equipment. Experience says that the equipment owners will receive a general warning saying that all equipment has the potential for breaking down due to a Year 2000 problem. The notice may also say that the equipment could also cause external problems so the equipment should be turned off during the date rollover to prevent unnecessary damage. They will probably issue these warnings to everyone during the last quarter of 1999 to avoid impacting sales.

Tracking down the embedded chips or components may prove to be very difficult: The original chip manufacturer may change the programming used on the chips being manufactured without making any change to the chip model or version numbers, which are usually based on engineering specifications, not programming ones. The manufacturer then sells large quantities to a distributor or other large system manufacturer. The distributor may then retail some chips and wholesale others without keeping track of the model and revision information required to trace the components. The wholesaler sells in quantity to a manufacturer, who is not concerned with anything more than the chip or component model. These components or chips are then placed in bins from which assemblers select a part and install them on circuit boards or in larger systems. All information about what chip version the product contains is lost. It becomes impossible for the original manufacturer to notify the end customer of possible Year 2000 problems.

Only a small portion of embedded systems have date processing associated with them. Hospitals have lots of equipment with embedded processors, but only 0.5 to 2.5 percent have date functions. Generally, the older the enterprise, the fewer embedded systems it owns. Chevron reports that a tanker built in 1982 has 1,800 subassemblies of which 122 are suspected to contain date-processing activity. An older tanker built in 1972 has only 239 subassemblies containing only 24 suspect systems ("Industry warned of millennium bug disaster," Marcus Hand; *Shipping Times Singapore;* June 10, 1998).

How Do I Find and Test Them?

Finding a microprocessor is a project best left to engineers. In general, anything that has a wire going into it or a battery could contain a microprocessor.

One firm used the novel approach of issuing strips of red dots to everyone on the staff with the instructions to put a dot on any device that they suspected might contain a microprocessor. The engineers followed, examining each device and putting blue dots on those devices determined not to be Year 2000 risks. The rest were inventoried for follow-up and the red dots were left in place.

Where should you look? The following list contains examples of common equipment that could be affected:

Office and retail systems:

- Answering machines
- Cash registers
- Copiers
- Computers (desktops, laptops, networks)
- Email services
- Faxes
- Inventory scanners and labelers
- Personal data assistants (PDAs) and personal organizers
- Point-of-sale devices, scanners, registers, card readers
- Postage meters
- Printers
- Telephones (cellular, mobile, and system controllers)
- Timed recording systems
- Voice mail
- Voice response units

Building systems:

- Air-conditioning and filtering
- Backup lighting and generators
- Building management systems
- Burglar and fire alarm systems
- Closed-circuit television (CCTV) systems
- Door locks
- Energy switching systems
- Fire control systems
- Heating and ventilating systems

- Elevators, escalators, lifts, pneumatics
- Lighting systems
- Safes and vaults
- Security access control systems
- Surveillance systems (monitoring and recording)
- Sprinkler systems

Production floor:

- Computer-Aided Design/Computer-Aided Manufacturing (CAD/CAM) systems
- Conveyor systems
- Emergency response systems
- Emissions control systems
- Energy control systems
- Environment management systems (heat, cooling, circulation, venting)
- Production monitors (scanners, flow meters, cooling)
- Power grid systems
- Process-controlled tools (cutters, borers, stampers, molders, injectors)
- Robots
- Scales
- Testing equipment (scanners, infrared, ultraviolet, scales, heat, motion, pressure, sound)
- Time clocks and stamps
- Uninterruptable power systems

Again, the list of equipment presented here serves as a small sample only of embedded systems affected by Y2K. Each industry has its own embedded systems concerns. For example, in the transportation industry, microprocessors are found in most of the following: automobiles (personal and police), trucks (ambulances, concrete misers, delivery, fire engines, tankers), trains, airplanes, ships, engines, drive equipment, navigation, communications, and in a wide variety of other related devices.

The infrastructure for the transportation industry is also dependent on embedded systems. They affect the roads with traffic signals, bridges, scales, and railroad crossing gates. Switches affect our trains, railcar tracking systems, and signaling systems. The airports are dependent on air traffic control, weather-monitoring systems, emergency response systems, radar, baggage handling, security, and ticketing equipment. Shipping is dependent on cranes, pumps, conveyors, and communications. On the way to work, drivers encounter traffic signals, tollgates, and parking lot gates.

Testing microprocessor and process control devices is not easily done and is best left to the manufacturers or other qualified engineers. The product may be date/time-sensitive and be activated or deactivated when a clock is reset. An attempt to handle what the system thinks is an improbable event (e.g., leap year 2000) may not even be possible. Resetting the date/time back to actual may cause data to be deleted or the system to malfunction.

Following are a few things you can do without even touching the suspect system.

- Look at any physical output (paper or screen displays) for date or time representations.
- Review the installation manual for instructions about setting date and time.
- Look at the maintenance manuals for references to frequency or clock settings or adjustments.

Several resources are available to arrange testing of these devices or to gather information about Year 2000 compliance status. Some firms and organizations perform testing, others solicit information from vendors. Some vendors offer free information, while others require payment for reports. The following organizations are just a sampling of those who may provide help.

Engineering Consulting Firms:

- TAVA, Inc. in Englewood, Colorado (www.tavatech.com)

Technology Service Providers:

- Conversant Business Technologies in Joliet, Illinois. Provides information on embedded systems and support providers (www.y2knonit.com)
- Data Dimensions, Inc. in Bellevue, Washington. Provides status information on hardware, application software, and data providers (www.data-dimensions.com)
- DataPro, Inc. in Plainwell, Michigan. Provides information on application packages (www.data-pro.com)

Embedded Systems Information:

- Biomedical Equipment Year 2000 Status Database (www.fda.gov/cdrh/yr2000/y2kintro.html)
- Chip Manufacturers Directory (www.hitex.com/chipdir/c/index.htm)
- Embedded PC Component Suppliers (www.pcengines.com/embchip.htm)

The first products with embedded systems were calculators designed in 1969. The good news is that almost all the embedded chip and component manufacturers still in business are pretty technical and thus have an Internet presence. Phone or e-mail to determine what component risks exist and what solutions are available.

Physical testing by a nonspecialist is not recommended. The average person should absolutely *never* test a microprocessor device attached to a computer. Any testing could destroy record keeping being performed by the computer. Some devices simply cannot be tested because the unit is inaccessible (at the bottom of the ocean or embedded in concrete) or because the microprocessor functions which require testing cannot be interrupted to conduct the test. Some devices are set at the factory, such as Global Positioning Systems (GPS), and cannot be altered. Some GPS devices have a special problem that will appear August 21/22, 1999, when internal clocks roll over, as was mentioned previously.

Testing does not mean just entering 23:58 on December 31, 1999, and waiting to see what happens. Some systems will sail right on without stopping while a similar setting with the equipment turned off (as when power fails) may result in the microprocessor failing to restart (ever!). There are other date tests you must also have performed:

January 9, 1999 (Julian 99009)

April 9, 1999 (Julian 99099)

September 9, 1999 (Gregorian 9999)

December 31, 1999

February 29, 2000 (leap day)

February 30, 2000 (invalid date)

October 10, 2000 (first date to contain 8 positions—10/01/2000)

January 1, 2001

In each case you should test the equipment in both an on and off state. For some devices, it may be necessary to run the unit all day (when testing for nines) to see if the time counters trigger a response or a programmed event during which a computer responds by doing something. Many of the date tests should only be done by factory specialists since a fault could shut the system down permanently.

Soldering Irons and Sledge Hammers

There are four ways to repair an embedded system problem. At the lowest level, you can replace the microprocessor chip. Some microprocessors can be reprogrammed (see Chapter 2, "Behind Every Great Machine," for the PC BIOS discussion). If you can't replace the chip, or reprogram the microprocessor, you may be able to replace the microprocessor board. In the most onerous scenario, you will have to replace the complete system containing the faulty equipment.

The chip replacement and reprogramming solutions are relatively expensive since they require highly skilled technicians and specialized equipment. In many instances simply taking the equipment off-line requires careful scheduling and advanced booking of the technician. In addition, the equipment may have to be disassembled and reassembled. Some repairs require preparation tantamount to open-heart surgery. Backup systems must be in place, and downtime for the device must be scheduled for times of low usage.

Replacing a board-level product is probably the easiest—it requires making an appointment with a service technician from the supplier of the equipment or a supporting organization. Be warned, you may have difficulties getting an appointment. Remember, you will have to compete for resources with other companies that need equipment serviced. Get your order in ASAP.

By far the most costly and frustrating fix is complete equipment replacement. Many embedded system owners may be faced with replacing equipment that has not even been fully amortized because it is already obsolete and the vendor of the equipment no longer supports the model owned. Sometimes the equipment must be removed from service for days. A telephone switch takes four days to replace. For a large company with redundant switches, this doesn't pose a large problem, but what about the small companies with only one switch? Such a company might be forced to sell out to a larger provider rather than take its subscribers out of service. Perhaps it might have to expand or acquire new facilities and install a new switch at the expense of its current subscribers.

Many replacement exercises turn into major projects because the equipment must be removed and changes must be made to the facility before the new unit can be installed. Banks found that they had to rebuild kiosks for ATMs because the old units were much larger than the new ones. Similarly, the power and cooling requirements for old telephone exchanges differ from the new ones. A third example: Security systems often require extensive alterations of floors, walls, and ceilings because the new systems can't be installed in the same way as the old systems.

Replacing computer boards/systems and whole systems may carry more unforeseen baggage, including transfer of old data to new formats. The equipment you have in place often communicates with other systems and provides output to people. You may need to reprogram other existing systems to accept the new data formats. You may also have a human resources issue—operators and data users will have to be retrained before the new equipment can be fully utilized.

One last sobering thought. Replacement of equipment becomes a more risky proposition as the year 2000 approaches. This is not because the new equipment won't work or that it requires a lot of work and scheduling to put the new equipment in place. It is because there is limited manufacturing capacity to replace the old equipment. Most of the equipment in place now was purchased over many years. Plant capacity to build new equipment is limited to what sales in the past dictated. It is hardly likely that the excess capacity exists to build all the replacement equipment required in only the time left—which, at the second edition of this book, is very short!

But take heart, sometimes the problem is easily rectified by obtaining new software from vendors. Lucent Technologies, one of the prime manufacturers, believes that software fixes should be available for all of its most extensively used products before the end of 1998. The other big switch manufacturers are also on schedule for 1999. Some systems can be fooled by simply resetting the clock back 28 years (*time warping*, a technique discussed later). The next chapter, "Avoiding Future Shock," gives you some action points to ready your mission-critical systems for the year 2000.

CHAPTER 4

Avoiding Future Shock

These days, the Social Security Administration seems anything but secure, as government spending threatens its very existence. It may then seem surprising that in the United States, the SSA has been at the forefront of efforts to deal with the Year 2000 problem, working since 1989 to rewrite its code to be 2000-ready. With an 11-year head start, the Social Security Administration set its sights on the end of 1998 to complete its task—a clear indication of the enormity of this problem. (See www.ssa.gov/facts/y2knotic.html)

Action Hero

Is there still time if you have not yet begun to address your Year 2000 problem? If you have very little computer automation, your job may be relatively easy. It may require only testing and replacing obsolete hardware, upgrading existing hardware, and bringing in an upgraded or replacement software package. These steps may take a while if vendors must be selected, products tested, data converted, and staff retrained. If you are extensively automated, you may be restricted to fixing only those systems which are most critical to your operations and letting the rest just fail if they can't handle the year changes.

The point is, if you haven't started, you need to take action quickly but methodically, because seat-of-the-pants tactics will result in wasted effort.

Before you take on the biggest project of your life, be sure you are forearmed with a plan. Your ability to correct the Y2K problem will depend upon the following:

- Understanding that the scope of the problem encompasses more than computers.

- Estimating what it will cost to fix and finding the money to do so.

- Identifying and contacting your vendors and suppliers to find out their awareness/readiness.

- Setting up a project team.

- Building awareness to obtain cooperation.

- Inventorying your computers—determining where and how old they are and what is running on them. Which are your critical systems? Perhaps more importantly, which are your mission-critical services? Which will be impacted first by threshold dates? In what sequence will changes have to be made so that you can keep your enterprise up and running?

A typical enterprise software portfolio includes all systems that manage the products and/or services provided by the company. It typically includes human resource systems, e-mail, accounts payable, accounts receivable, actuarial programs, operating systems, and document imaging and/or scanning programs, as well as some word-processing programs, spreadsheets, and databases—and don't forget that little envelope-printing program the mailroom clerk uses because he or she doesn't like the company-supplied one very much. End-user-installed software can be a Year 2000 risk as well.

At this juncture, you should have your enterprise team in place, and all of them should be 2000-aware. If you have not yet determined your level of dependency on others, do it *now*. Even if you are panicking because you have just started your Y2K efforts, keep in mind that your vendors and subcontractors may be in deeper trouble than you.

The Dangers of Codependency

Get out the list you made of all your suppliers and vendors. It is time to determine what recourse you have and what response you can expect from them. Ask yourself the following questions:

- Do your contracts entitle you to fixes?

- Are there performance guarantees?

- Will your suppliers or vendors be willing and/or able to meet those terms?

- If the provider is able to perform, but with some delays, what is the risk to your business if you can't meet commitments for days or weeks? Can you stay in business if suppliers can't operate for a given period—especially if they are your sole source? (You might want to look into finding alternate sources, workarounds, or creating a stockpile in case of emergency.)

- If your ability to perform is diminished by supplier/vendor breakdown, how will this affect your customers, employees, retirees, and your ability to meet regulatory requirements?

Answering these questions will put you in a proactive position. In Chapter 12, "Staying Afloat," we discuss how the answers can be used to develop contingency plans. True, you still won't be able to control some of these elements, but knowing the probability of their occurrence will give you a leg up in dealing with them.

One of the first things you can do is contain the problem to the present: Make sure all your future contracts include statements to relieve you of responsibility should you be unable to perform because of the breakdown of your supply chain or delivery mechanism. This is especially important for service providers.

Dependent and Unsupported

Conducting your hardware and software inventory probably seemed like opening Pandora's box. You no doubt found one or more of these nasty surprises:

- You have programs running that no one seems to know anything about.

- Most applications pass data across system boundaries.

- There is no clear ownership of much of the data.

- In-house staff does not support many programs being run.

- Many programs can't be easily associated because naming standards are not enforced.

- Source code is missing.

- There is a dearth of tools that enable you to track things.

- Some programs, tools, and utilities were purchased from vendors who are no longer in business; some products were sold; or you've let maintenance contracts lapse.

- You may be running vendor software illegally. Certain software may be licensed to a specific computer only; and pricing schedules may be different for certain computer processor sizes. Many organizations overlook these contract points when they acquire new equipment.

Multilingual Madness

Your software survey team will also need to inventory the many different versions of the various products and programming languages used by the company. As mentioned earlier, you may uncover code written in languages that essentially are dead—a serious problem if no one on the current staff knows the language or the product is no longer sold. Many of these have date problems that can't be fixed, and no conversion option exists to translate them to another language.

Other programs you unearth may have been written in languages that, while extant, are so old and have been running untouched for so long that the program converting them to machine-understandable form (a compiler) is no longer available. One of the most common languages used in business applications is COBOL, which comes in about 30 different versions. Some companies have several different versions of COBOL on the same computer at the same time, each of which reacts to the year 2000 in different, though equally ugly, ways. Many companies are faced not only with a Year 2000 problem, but also the requirement to upgrade programs so that they can be compiled by the latest version of the language.

The only version officially supported by IBM is COBOL for OS 390 and VM. Many companies are upgrading to a revised version of COBOL as part of their Year 2000 effort. This upgrade may make sense in your situation, too, especially since you are already investing considerable sums to make your system Y2K-ready.

An Arm and a Leg

Pull out your hardware survey and put it on top of the pile. Did you identify which outdated machines you are relying on and which version of the operating system they are running on? Determine whether the operating system can process dates past December 31, 1999, without going into red alert. If it can't, it may be time to place an equipment order. Find out if there are conversion programs to move your applications. And don't forget to make sure that the new software will be Year 2000–compliant. You probably will want to order extra data storage, too, because conversions and the update and testing processes are bound to eat it up more quickly.

Using the inventory you compiled in the previous chapter, you will next estimate the cost. At the same time you are doing this, try also to determine how much time it's going to take to fix and test everything. You can purchase scanning programs to look for the incidence of dates in your code and estimating packages that will forecast the staffing requirements, duration, and cost of making the code changes.

You will have to take the time to acquire estimating products, learn how to use them, and then get set up to run them. Most consulting companies can offer services and tools to provide this information more efficiently than you can. There are few, however, that have retained the support staff to perform estimates. Frankly, at this stage of the game, it becomes a matter of what you can do in the time available, and how much support you can afford.

Some organizations prefer to skip the estimating step, and they calculate a simple amount advocated by some consulting organizations. At various times, the amounts $.60, $1.00, $1.10, and $1.50 have been applied to the *total* number of code lines in your inventory—not just the number of lines to be changed.

The problem with using these amounts is that they are broad-stroke industry averages that may have little application in your environment. If you have many embedded systems, missing source code, a lot of real-time processing code, and code using obsolete compilers, expect your costs to be much higher. If much or most of your code has been purchased from vendors who are working on making their products compliant, expect your costs to be lower. If you have a good count of the lines of proprietary code (including spreadsheets, JCL) that you have in your portfolio, you might save time and money by multiplying the number of lines by $1.50 and asking for that amount as a budget to fix the source. Chances are that escalating wages and tool costs will increase the amount by 8 percent a quarter through 2002, so you may want to prepare management for escalation of costs.

Many of these industry estimates are based on work done by enterprises that have been successful in managing their own application conversions. They have typically been working on the problem for four to six years. Their costs are sometimes best guesses because other work (e.g., upgrading compilers or moving to new databases) is being performed simultaneously. There has yet to be a scientific study of the true cost of performing the Year 2000 changes. Even companies forced to reveal their expenditures have evaded revealing the true costs by reporting only the costs directly traceable to code repair efforts. This overlooks the management costs, facilities costs, supplier tracking expenses, embedded systems repair costs, equipment replacement expenses, and so forth.

The question of whether to capitalize or expense Year 2000 repair costs keeps arising. Fact is, when you spend your money, it's gone. You can continue to hide the Year 2000 burden by buying capital equipment with software or buying expensive software that can be counted as a capital purchase. Capital depreciation allows you to spread the cost reporting over several years, but does not change the real impact on your wallet.

Trouble on the Horizon

Once you have established a budget, it is best to get ahead of the problem. You will want to determine the event horizon for every software application and embedded system. *Event horizon* is a term used by Year 2000 consultants to express the point in time when applications will cease to function correctly or cease to function at all. The concept of the event horizon is critical in developing a plan to resolve the Year 2000 problem. You must first determine the earliest potential failure date and make sure the application is converted or replaced before that time. The event horizon for an application is fairly easy to calculate:

- Determine how far into the future stored files are dated.
- Identify the oldest dates in the application.

Knowing the event horizon and the duration of the project will tell you if there is enough time to make the change. The following sections first look at a Year 2000 project started in 1997, and then look at another company who waited until October of 1998 to start.

A Magazine Publisher's Y2K Project

You are a magazine publisher and you sell two-year subscriptions. In order to enter two-year subscriptions you must have changed your systems prior to January 1, 1998. Actually, you had to start entering subscriptions that expire in 2000 by October 1997 because you are planning a Christmas offer. Your event horizon was, therefore, October 1, 1997. Your estimates indicated, based on the factors you entered, you needed five people working on the package for eight months. This meant that in order to get the job done by October of 1997, the process should have started on February 1, 1997. Let's say you discovered this in March 1997, so you were already behind. To make up for lost time, you decided to hire three more people to work on the Y2K project instead of dropping the two-year subscription from the Christmas offer.

You found out quickly that the billing system uses the expiration date in the subscription system. It had to be changed in time to produce the bills that go along with the two-year subscriptions. However, the billing system does not actually have to be compliant until the magazines are shipped. If shipping is a month ahead, December 1, 1997, was the event horizon for the billing system. If the magazine is bimonthly, the billing system event horizon was in November. You really needed to have both subscription and billing systems done at the same time to meet the Christmas offering. Because of this unforeseen complication, you decided to patch the billing system to handle the offering and make billing system changes later. That meant you went into the same system twice to make the Year 2000 updates, and you also had to retest. And guess what? The extra effort added up to extra costs, which the extra Christmas revenue failed to offset. (Yes, even if you've already started, the process is complicated and snag-ridden. Welcome to Year 2000 project planning.)

You've Waited until Now?!

Let's say you are a procrastinator, and you've just started your Y2K assessment. All right, let's give you some credit. You've done your inventory of hardware and software and services and determined the extent of your problem. With your event horizon in hand, your next concern is how much time it will take to convert or replace the system.

If you, like many, will not have enough time to make all your systems 2000-compliant, you will have to make the following decisions:

- Which computer-dependent services are mission-critical; that is, which business services must be available at all times to keep your company alive?

- Which of these services can make the transition successfully without modification?

- Which ones will have to be abandoned because you won't have time to correct them and must find some alternative, non-computer-dependent method, to deliver these services?

Only you can decide which services are the most important to your company. Pareto's rule applies here, because 80 percent of your benefit is derived from 20 percent of your effort.

Now determine your staff and computer resources. Previously, we mentioned the project planning and coordinating teams, which are part of the corporate date solution. Here, we're talking about those who actually get into the code or the equipment. Fortune 100 corporations may need thousands of employees working on the problem to get it fixed in time. If, say, you have a staff of 20 and one and a half years left, then you have 30 years' worth of effort to allocate to this project. If the findings from your assessment phase indicate you actually need 45 years' worth of effort, some systems will have to fend for themselves, by which we mean that they will have to be run without attention. In fact, someone on the user side will have to check constantly to verify that these systems are running correctly; if a problem occurs, the staff will have to request a fix. But that is far preferable to having the whole enterprise go down. And now's the time to get tough, because the sooner you decide which systems must be fixed, the greater are your chances of delivering them on time.

Triage: Business Style

You should come away from the exercises in the previous sections with the knowledge of which parts of your company are the most important and, thus, valuable. (If you're tempted to think the answer's obvious, remember that threats to normal business processes have a way of casting operating assumptions in a whole new light.) Once you determine which systems you have, what needs to be fixed, and the resources you have with which to fix them, you are able to perform *triage*—business style.

Triage is used mainly in battlefield situations where the casualties outnumber the available medical resources. At such times, the on-site medical experts must allocate their available resources, their time and supplies, to victims according to an objective and emotionless system of priorities designed with only a single goal in mind: to maximize the number of survivors. Setting these types of priorities involves difficult decisions.

Applied to the Year 2000 situation, this concept requires slight modification. We're not trying to save the individual systems; we're trying to save the organization relying on those systems. To be even more precise, we must attempt to make sure that the services we depend upon to run our businesses are available when we need them. This means that the computer systems themselves are no longer the priority. If you can devise a way to provide a service manually and this can be done more efficiently than fixing the system, then that's what must be done.

We begin the process by examining our organization and identifying which services and/or processes make it possible for our organization to operate. Once we have a list of these dependencies, then we can zero in on the most important.

1. We first identify mission-critical services: those services that define what our organization does for a living. Mission-critical services are the handful of processes that must operate at all times in order for us to continue to do what we are paid to do.

2. The next group of services are those we could live without for a while, and perhaps, forever. Their loss would affect our ability to conduct business . . . but we could continue shipping product and providing basic services, however slowly, expensively, and inefficiently.

3. Finally, identify those services you provide or depend upon, but don't really need and wouldn't really miss. At first you might respond, "We need to continue doing everything we do! Otherwise we wouldn't be doing it!" Remember that Pareto's rule applies to organizations as much as any other human endeavor. Looked at from the hind end, 80 percent of what you do generates less than 20 percent of the benefit.

If we look at a courier service for a moment, perhaps we can provide some examples to clarify these three categories. A courier service is in business to perform a single service. It delivers packages from point A to point B in a guaranteed amount of time at the request of a client, without losing track of the packages.

The mission-critical services include:

The ability to receive an order

The ability to dispatch a truck to pick up the package

The ability to track the location of the package

The ability to transport the package reliably

The ability to route the package to its destination

The ability to ultimately charge for the service

The ability to pay its staff

The important but nonessential services include:

The electronic capturing of orders; instead this could be done manually.

The electronic communication of pickup orders to the trucks; instead cell phones could be used.

Creation of bar codes to aid in tracking; instead manual processes could be used.

Automatic monthly billing; instead handwritten invoices could be used.

The nonessential services include the following:

Automatic discounts for volume users

Interoffice e-mail

Computer-generated optimal shipping routes

Obviously, as you examine this list, it will generate some emotional responses. You might agree with everything in the first category, but disagree with items in the second and the third. Remember that the basic premise is this: You have not left yourself enough time to do everything you'd like to do, so choose. If you could only do seven things, which seven do you do? The choice is yours, and the fate of your organization rests upon your decision.

Looking Out for Number One

Needless to say, you're going to ignore everything but those items you decide to place in the first group. Simply put again, if you don't have the resources to save everything, what you do have must be focused on maintaining the availability of the mission-critical services. Doing anything else is poor project management and bad judgment.

Doing triage in any organization is an extremely difficult task. It is not easy to choose between two services and the underlying systems which make these services possible. The only time you would even consider such drastic pruning is when you finally understand that you really have no choice. You don't have the resources/time available to do everything—what do you chose to do?

Reducing the Options

The reality is, mission-critical systems contain more functionality than they need. We were once told there are 50,000 ways to purchase an airline ticket: using discounts, charter programs, group rates; staying over Saturday; bringing your own food, bringing food for the pilot; flying on a day that doesn't have a Y in it . . . well, you get the picture. Are all these options necessary? Not when it comes down to choosing between having a system with everything on it or no system at all.

Sometimes the underlying system will be too complicated, too labor-intensive to fix. You'll be forced into finding alternative ways to deliver the service. Could you deliver the service manually? Could you write a skeleton system, one which delivers the bare bones of the vital service until you manage to fix the full system? Remember the final goal is to still be able to provide service on January 1, 2000.

Another alternative, although not without its own associated risks of on-time delivery, is to purchase a stand-alone package which does 100 percent of what you need, even if it only delivers 10 percent of what you want. Keep in mind, though, that the goal of triage is to decrease the amount of work necessary to continue delivering critical services.

You will have to make tough decisions if you intend to greet 2000 with a smile. You may have to revert to bare-bones programming in order to survive. (Naturally, not all systems can be slimmed down without involving an entire rewrite. And this is *not* the right time for that, but you might be forced to follow that route.) Systems that obviously have to be fixed are those involved with product or service delivery (manufacturing, shipping/receiving, inventory, bill of materials, etc.), selling, and billing for the product or services. Accounting systems that handle crediting for payments, systems that pay for services (including payroll), and general ledger are also essential.

The typical event horizon for a budgeting system is five years. This, unfortunately, is no longer feasible, since 2000 is little more than a year away. Some credit card companies that renew clients for a period of two years or more have already discovered that their systems will not accept dates past 1999. The question is, will your applications continue to operate properly for 1999, 2000, and 2001? An application that processes future dates may already have an undiscovered failure (this is called a *soft* or *hidden* failure).

Several types of hidden failures occur. The following are representative.

A transaction is created for the year 2000 and filed. The system interprets the date as 1900 and stores the record under that date. Queries to find the records for year 2000 return no responses. Queries for records written in 1900 are rejected because the validation routine catches it. The user thinks the transaction is lost and reenters it. Only a physical search of the database can locate the record. In some cases, the normal processes continue showing the correct number of records and processing against the transaction as if it were open and normal.

A transaction is processed as dated in 1900. An interest calculation is performed, but the field is not large enough to hold the value, so the amount is truncated. The values may be larger or smaller than they should be, but because everything appears to be working, this error is not recognized until monthly or quarterly summaries are generated.

A transaction is processed as dated in year 2000 and everything appears normal. During the month, the number-of-days calculation is performed on an overdue payment routine. It looks at only the last two digits of the date, indicates that the account is overdue, and issues an overdue notice. The calculation of the overdue amount uses a different routine and prints zero amount overdue. A dunning notice is sent to the customer. After receiving several increasingly demanding dunning notices, the angry customer calls. There is no record of a problem, so the call is dismissed. The customer keeps getting the notices, and finally bill collectors are given the account. They bring the problem to the attention of accounts receivable, but by that time the client has terminated his or her account.

Beg, Borrow, Steal

We don't really recommend that you beg, borrow, or steal to keep your systems up and running into 2000; our recommendation is to *buy, trade up,* or *transform.* Obviously, the most important consideration is getting all your changes done on time, so use whatever will work for you and your company.

Buy

Those systems (accounting systems come to mind) you determine to be candidates for reduction may be eligible for help from a commercial diet plan. If you realize that, on your own, you can't fix your entire system in time, perhaps you should consider an off-the-shelf product. Dun and Bradstreet and Great Plains Software both have announced their products will be Year 2000–compliant. Perhaps they or some other vendors offer a way out.

But don't expect vendor packages to meet 100 percent of your requirements. Only custom software can do that, though not as well as you would hope. However, you can usually adapt the business to fit the package. Keep in mind that each change you make to the packaged software will increase the installation time.

Trade Up

Another alternative is to trade in your application for a better model. Many programs are still in place because they work. They may be old; they may be ugly; but they're paid for. And some enterprises run more than one version of the programs because one department or division wanted features another did not. Now's the time to standardize. It will save time. Replace an older version with the latest version—but be sure to find out if it's 2000-compliant before you do so.

Resist, though, the temptation you may feel with this option to throw the old application into the trash, then spend too much valuable time developing a new in-house version complete with bells and whistles. Remember, time is running short. Your priority now is to be ready for the year 2000. A new and glorious program would be great, but not at the expense of company survival. You don't have time for everyone to learn a new system. If you'd started on this project five years ago, it might have been possible, but you're way too close to the deadline to risk the company on it now.

Transform

And then there's *transform*. The focus of this effort is to coax your programs past the year 2000 using a number of different methods that will enable them to perform their normal functions. Automated tools can help your programmers find most of the dates, though they will still have to hunt for some hidden ones. Other tools can help them change the hidden dates so the program can deal with the year 2000, though they will have to use other techniques as well.

Only you can decide whether to do all this in-house, hire some of it out, or hire all of it out. Some companies prefer not to have others know their business, while others feel that they are better off concentrating on their products or services, letting the computer experts handle the technological problems.

But be aware, if you decide to seek outside help, you will run into computer contractors who promise you the proverbial moon. According to research done by Capers Jones, a pioneer in software measurement, the likelihood of any programming effort being delivered on time is less than 62 percent. When Jones analyzed large projects involving more than 12.5 million lines of code, the percentage plummeted to less than 14 percent. If you hire a contractor, examine his or her delivery record, especially on large projects.

Also, keep in mind that by now, with little more than a year left, many consulting firms are not taking on new projects because of the risk of litigation. In other words, if they sign a contract to fix your problem by December 31, 1999, and they miss the deadline, they risk a lawsuit with you. Many are now offering code remediation through factories. It is incumbent on the contractor to determine what to send and what to change, and then to provide detailed testing before the code is put into production. Those who use factories often find much of the work is still their responsibility and the service provider does not have any tangible responsibility for success. For many consulting companies, the financial gain is no longer worth the gamble. They are simply refusing any additional work. See Chapter 13, "The Price of Failure," for information on the legal costs of the Year 2000 problem.

Calling in the Cavalry

If and when you decide to hire outside help (and you can find it), your first order of business is to ascertain the organization's track record. Then find out if it can do the following:

- Meet the deadline of January 1, 2000.
- Work with internal and external interfaces.
- Insert the code changes for both procedural and data structure. (Not only will they have to change nearly all your procedures, but also the way your company stores the information.)
- Perform file and database conversions. (Being able to access information compiled from past years may be important.)
- Coordinate internal and external staff. Helping people work well together under these circumstances is going to be difficult, but necessary.
- Commit to an extensive work effort, which now means dedicating extra work power, since time is so short.
- Perform phased implementations. Changing over all at once could easily throw things into chaos. Trying to track a problem is made more complicated by the size of the implemented code.
- Plan, track, and control all programs in an organization.

Secondary functions you may want or expect an outside service to perform include the following:

- Updating the language your computer uses and standardizing it so all of your programs speak one language.

- Expanding financial fields or implementing other changes in how your company stores information.

- Eliminating dead code, which will give you more computer space to work with.

- Rationalizing data names—if you have to examine your system again in the future, you will want to be able to figure out what you've got.

- Reverse engineering data structures and procedure code into a central repository—giving future managers and workers necessary information they'll need the next time something goes wrong.

- Upgrading applications and user documentation.

- Adding tools to enable you to determine how well your programs are working and how well the conversion progress is going, and to make testing easier.

Extras should be considered only if they will not delay the delivery of the Year 2000–ready product. At this point, you should concentrate on mission-critical tasks.

In Charge of the Light Brigade

The checklists may have encouraged you to believe that someone is going to save you and your company from ruin. And that may still be so, but only if you stay involved, which means you have to know how to manage any outside help you hire. Do not let them manage you.

The planning activities outlined in this chapter will give you the best chance for success in the year 2000. You will tackle only meaningful work. You will have a team in place to do the work. You will have the cooperation and support of both management and the rest of the company. Are you ready to run?

CHAPTER 5

Ready to Run

The planning activities outlined so far are only the first steps toward solving the Year 2000 problem. To reiterate: You will tackle only meaningful work. You will put a team in place to do the work and enlist the cooperation and support of both executive management and other departments. While you are engaged in these activities, your computer people should be taking other actions, defined in this chapter, which will lead you through the steps involved in creating a process. This is not a trivial or simple activity. It involves defining and reducing the work to a routine so that it may be completed as expeditiously as possible, with as much automation as can be brought to bear.

The process-building activities involve the following:

1. Setting standards
2. Defining a working update process
3. Creating a controlled change environment
4. Establishing a testing environment
5. Selecting tools
6. Choosing and executing a process pilot

The problem that must now be faced is that time is running out. It is necessary to overlap these steps as much as you can. The typical company is now relegated to using the tools at hand. The problem of determining what available tools will help the most remains.

Those companies lucky enough to not be concerned with proprietary code developed inside may still be required to test the code provided by software vendors. Converting data to new formats is not a task to be taken lightly. Many a company has already found that users have figured out ways to pervert a product's original intent to create data which does not fit a product's profile. When such data is converted blindly and fed into another application, the results are often chaotic.

Setting Standards

Smart businesspeople realize that creating standards is a way to avoid having to make the same decisions over and over again. In addressing the Year 2000 problem, some standards are obvious, and therefore easy to set:

- Buy only products that are Year 2000–compliant.
- Design new software programs so that they are Year 2000–compliant.
- Define Year 2000 compliance (unfortunately no one definition has yet found global acceptance).
- Look for programs that were designed to fail when the year becomes 99 or 00.
- Define minimum requirements for date testing prior to Year 2000 changes. (Remember, many programs already don't process dates correctly.)
- Define minimum requirements for Year 2000 testing.

The one standards decision that often causes dissension is whether to standardize on two-digit or four-digit years. The first option usually is greeted with dismay by noncomputing people. After all, isn't that the problem? No. The problem is not in using a two-digit year designation; the problem is that the *programs* were not designed to use two-digit years across millennium boundaries. In Chapter 1, "Ground Double Zero," we suggested this was a *design* problem.

In the first edition of this book, we advised that the decision to standardize on four-digit versus two-digit years was actually very simple: *Use the one that will get you standardized the fastest with the least risk.* That said, however, the most cost-effective solution over the long term *is* to move to four digits. This means fewer program design changes, but it requires data changes. Making changes to handle two-digit years means the reverse. Thus, the question of which to do depends on the data and the processing required to process two-digit-year data in a four-digit environment. Suffice it to say that every organization currently engaged in the Year 2000 redesign has taken one path or the other and compromised when necessary.

Our advice is to set the standard for the long term and then define the rules for doing things in the short term. Employ four-digit years whenever and wherever possible. The cost of employing four-digit years in the time remaining has become prohibitive, and the time required to implement data changes is threatened by the ultimate event horizon. We now say *use two-digit years*. When you receive data from another organization, there may be a four-digit date standard, so do not blindly believe that only two-digit dates are the rule.

Year 2000–Compliant

Discussions of the Year 2000 computer problem invariably raise the concept of Year 2000–compliant or –compatible applications. And as usual with concepts, their definitions vary depending on the circumstances of implementation. It doesn't matter what anyone else thinks 2000-compliant means. It is only necessary that you and your organization agree on a working definition before you begin implementing a change process.

Your first attempt at a definition might be based on the obvious assertion that if all years were represented as four digits, then applications would be Year 2000–compliant. It's tempting to declare that any application using fewer than four digits to represent the year be deemed incompatible. While that has a certain simplicity and elegance, you'll quickly find it's too strict a definition, mainly because the standard MMDDYY (*MM* being the space allocated for two numbers representing the month, *DD* for day, and *YY* for year) is almost universal. Some organizations have taken steps to standardize on YYMMDD or YYYYMMDD just because it is less ambiguous to have a single format.

A much simpler definition, sidestepping the entire technical coding requirements debate, is to say that if an application is working correctly today and will continue to work correctly during and following the year 2000, it is compliant. Some organizations have bounded the period of time, which must be considered. GTE, for example, looks at the range of dates from January 1, 1900, to December 31, 2050, as being the key dates. It specifically notes that all years divided evenly by 4, except for 1900, must be correctly handled as leap years.

The challenge is to prove that a program is compliant according to this definition, because it is impossible to test today's complex applications to the point of determining that they are 100 percent error-free. Part of the problem is that many applications have become so complex that nobody really knows what the program is doing, or if it is doing it correctly.

When people delve into their code to determine what to fix, an all too common occurrence is uncovering instances of date calculations that have been performed incorrectly for years—calculations that have been accepted as correct by management, users, and clients. Consequently, you may have to backtrack and rectify errors of past years. Alternatively, you may decide to sustain that error but to make sure that it works correctly from now on; this means getting the program to ignore those past incorrect calculations while performing all future ones correctly. You may ask yourself, "If errors of past years can be 'lived with,' how important can those records be to the company?" The problem becomes significant if you are using outside assistance. In this case, it becomes a matter of determining whether the problem was preexistent or was introduced. Faultfinding can slow the correction process to a stop and accomplish nothing.

It is alarming to realize that in the past, testing applications against the year 2000 has been specifically and deliberately avoided. Why? Because programmers and managers knew that if they tested their accounting applications, for example, against a year with a value of 00, the program would fail. They were intentionally designed to stop running because a date of 00 was not supposed to exist. Programs were written to prevent such a date from coming into being.

The consequence of this is that most people have very little experience with these types of temporal tests. Testing dates involves thinking about the possibility of miscalculation or faulty logic. Test cases must involve testing for the correct rollover of dates. Dates frequently tested to assess millennium compliance include 1998-12-31, 1999-09-09, 1999-12-31, 2000-01-01, 2000-02-28, 2000-02-29, 2000-03-01, 2000-12-31, 2001-01-01, 2027-12-31. Of these, there are two that most people find unusual: 1999-09-09 is a legitimate date, but it can be handled incorrectly by programs that test for 9s only; 2027-12-31 represents the limit of many computers' date-storage capacity and often rolls over the storage buffers, giving an invalid result. To completely test the applications, it is necessary to test the handling of invalid dates. Many have found their applications sailing right past 1900-02-29, 1999-99-99, 2000-00-00, 2001-02-29, and 2100-02-29 as if they were perfectly legitimate dates. Testing to see if it is possible to break the system is as important as testing to see if it works correctly.

In addition, to properly test for the year 2000, you have to time-warp all of your systems, hardware, and software into the future, which is difficult to do when many of the underlying applications such as the operating systems themselves are not yet ready to be tested in this manner. The only real test of the year 2000 will come on January 1, 2000, as everything ticks over into the new year, for real, and forever. Finding yourself in situations where your passwords or software licenses have expired when you move the system date forward could be irksome and may cause time-consuming workarounds.

This brings us back full circle to how we go about defining millennium compliance. The following definition for *century compliance* was adopted by Bank-Boston:

- Date fields must have a two-character century field (i.e., CCYY); and processing logic is sound.

- Data input specifies valid century.

- Hard-coding in century fields and date fields has been removed.

- Applications will interface with all date data that is imported or exported.

- Date validation routines must include century.

- No null values in the field are converted to 00.

- No date fields are used for other than date purposes (i.e., no dates are used as logical switches).

- There is a legitimate plan in place to retire or replace the application prior to the event horizon.

GTE has taken a different approach. Its compliance rules are as follows:

- No value of current date will cause interruptions in desired operation.

- All manipulations of time-related data (dates, durations, days of week, etc.) will produce desired results for all valid date values within the application domain.

- Date elements in interfaces and data storage permit specifying century to eliminate date ambiguity.

- All software maintained by and for GTE may contain literals or constants for dates unless required to capture specific business rules.

- Date fields must be initialized with either all zeros or null values (the latter as defined by the development facilities such as the compiler).

- Applications may not use special date values as logical flags.

- For any date element represented without a century, the correct century is unambiguous for all manipulations involving that element.

- All developed and third-party software must permit the use of date formats that explicitly specify century according to American National Standards Institute (ANSI) X3.30 in all data stored or transmitted, unless there is a superior application standard or convention.

- Third-party products must permit formatting data with explicit century in the user interface.

- All developed applications using third-party products must always explicitly supply century and never rely on those products' default value for century.

- Developed and third-party software may imply century in the user interface format, YYMMDD or YYJJJ (as specified in ANSI X3.30).

- In storing or transmitting date data, some applications must conform to domain-specific standards whose requirements for dates may supersede ANSI X3.30, as appropriate.

These century-compliance requirements attempt to safeguard against the possibility of miscalculations made by individual company's standards or customs that allow or require date definitions not fully compliant with ANSI X3.30. However, exceptions allowed within the standards permit certain editing masks to be used "as deemed necessary by standard or custom." Obviously, these expectations are finding their way into contracts for third-party software. To get around these problems, the wording of the contract is becoming very simple, requiring the vendor to define the testing and meet the obligation, something to the effect of, "Process all dates between 1900 and 2100 without error or opportunity for ambiguity." The point, lest it be missed, is that you not only have to protect your organization against third-party practices, but against those that are allowed by standards.

Creating an Update Process

Nothing is more important than *creating the update process.* By doing so, you can find out a number of things:

- What obstacles are being encountered?
- What manual tasks are required?
- What is needed before the output can be passed?
- Where do components need to be kept while being worked on?
- Where is the input to a process exceeding its capacity?
- When does each activity need to begin?
- Who needs to be involved?

You also need to create an *awareness* of the process. Here, rather than project managers, you will need process managers—people who not only look at schedules but also at what determines those schedules. To such a person, the preceding questions are instinctively asked and processed saving enormous amounts of time. Experienced computing people are project-oriented, concerned about when something gets done, not how. That's why the best process managers often come from outside. If you can find someone who always asks *why,* put such a person on your update team. Of course, if you can find a computer person who can do that, even better. He or she might be able to find simple solutions and save time.

Creating a Controlled Change Environment

There are two significant components of this activity. The first requires taking the inventory previously discussed and building a tracking mechanism. The second is to establish a software-change control process. Both steps are essential. Many computer programs are shared by applications; thus, it is necessary to track change progress so that you know what has been done. It is also important to know this before changes are made so that program alterations do not accidentally affect other programs. It is also not uncommon for millennium update changes to be made in parallel with other production changes, requiring a merger of the two types of changes prior to reintroducing the software to the production environment.

Planning and Tracking

To do this, you need to find out what you have on your computers, what needs to be changed, and what you are going to change. Ideally, this should be done at the same time you are establishing the inventory as discussed in Chapter 1, "Ground Double-Zero," and doing the scheduling as suggested in Chapter 4, "Avoiding Future Shock." The best place to put this inventory is on a computer. If your environment is not terribly complex (containing lots of internally developed programs and time-dependent processing), it does not have to be a fancy process. Many organizations have done very well with a PC-based spreadsheet or database application.

If your environment is complex, you will want to track a lot of different items. Programs share tables, file definitions, and common processing modules. Programs are related to data. Programs and data are related to computer job streams or process sequences. It will be helpful if you know, when you schedule one program to be changed, which data or definitional code will have to be changed at the same time and which other production processing actions will be affected. Some of these changes will be affected by, or affect, vendor products—application packages and/or systems software. Large enterprises put this component planning/tracking tool on their biggest computers to make the information available to the whole team rather than just a single administrative person.

There are software products available from vendors (we explore buying vendor tools in Chapter 9, "Taking a Tool Inventory") that do this kind of component relationship mapping, but some are limited to a single platform and do not capture all component relationships such as the systems software components. A good Year 2000 planning/tracking tool not only keeps track of application software, but also of vendor software, external data files, systems software, and hardware. The best of them have been custom-built by the enterprise or, under contract, by consulting organizations that specialize in large-scale conversion projects. These, unfortunately, are not for sale. Commercially available relationship mapping tools will give the moderate to large organization a good footing.

You must give the process team the resources it needs. This requires setting up a documentation system so you know exactly which component changes are going to be made, when they're going to be made, and what the final goal will be, in detail. There are a couple of reasons for this which follow:

You want to protect yourself legally. If you have problems with business operations because of the process, you will be able to show that it was used for a good reason. This will also demonstrate later to any disgruntled parties that you behaved as a prudent business executive.

If something goes wrong with the process, you'll know sooner rather than later. If the process causes some unexpected glitches with computer operations, proper documentation can show the team the most likely cause, or at least the nearest rat hole in which they can start looking. A well-presented, logical explanation of events is also good to have when dealing with angry stockholders. There's nothing like an ignorant spokesperson to incite the people with the pitchforks and torches. Despite extra effort spent on the paperwork, in the long run you'll find it will make the whole procedure go faster and easier. It's always cheaper to do something right the first time.

Control Change

Have you ever felt like your right hand didn't know what your left hand was doing? During the date update process, be prepared to feel that all the right hands don't know what the left hands are doing on the entire process team. Some programmers will be making changes to ready the programs to process the Year 2000 dates, while others will be continuing to meet the demands of day-to-day business.

Many computing organizations face this situation frequently due to program sharing, mentioned earlier. To deal with it, they put into place a process called *change control.* In different organizations, change control takes different forms; and it can be a manual process or an automated one. If your enterprise is dependent on a manual process, you will need to examine it for robustness: Can it handle the change process you will be implementing? If you have an automated software change management process in place, you may be ahead of the game. If you have automated software configuration management that manages shared component usage on a platform, you own the game. There are software change and configuration management systems available, but be aware that some are difficult to implement and may add an unnecessary burden to the date update project. They also add staff overhead to the normal operations of the computing organization and meet with a lot of resistance because they slow down the normal process of change.

Much of the impact of implementing change management is related to the preparedness of the organization. If you are well organized and familiar with the problem, implementing it is simple. If your organization clings to flexibility and individual initiative, you are pushing a large rock uphill. These change control products require meticulous inventorying of components and in-depth knowledge of the applications. Some are adaptive to organizational structure; others require the organization to adapt to them. Determining which is right for you versus which is needed is an exercise for the strong of heart.

Creating a Test Environment

Creating a test environment is not an easy task. Computing people generally test on the same computer on which production programs are running, which essentially runs the testing of year 2000 into a brick wall. As we have indicated, the problem is the *system* date. The dominant procedure for handling all processing is by determining what the current date is, which programmers do by reference to the computer clock. If you change the computer clock to sometime in the future, then the current production processing will be handled incorrectly.

There are several solutions to this problem, none of them ideal:

Buy another computer so that one can run production and the other can run different dates.   Problem: If you are testing different applications simultaneously, you need to have different computer dates for each one. The only answer: Buy several computers (possible only with generous budgets).

Buy a software product that allows the programmers to artificially change the system date.   Such tools have gotten better, but the problem has shifted from tool capability to one of date management so that someone else does not shift the date at the wrong time. The complexity of managing the test environment has bogged down testing in many companies.

Replace all accesses to the system date with calls to a table.   Dates can be stored in a small data file that can be processed like a list. It is possible to select one date from the list or many. This list is called a table. Looking up dates in a table can be achieved under specific instructions that tell the program which date to use. This is often useful for testing many dates in a pre-determined order. In addition, the table can be installed so that when the program is put into production the program will continue to access this table instead of the one provided by the computer manufacturer. Downside: Who will be responsible for maintaining this table? That is the question that was originally answered by having the computer manufacturer supply the date. Besides the computer's system, software still uses that system date. What happens if the two dates get out of synchronization?

Be forewarned: there are no easy answers. But there is another alternative. Some disaster-recovery computer services are providing special testing environments. For a fee, you can transfer your testing processing to their computers. This means you won't have to buy additional machines.

One word of caution: Plan on spending more money on computer storage devices because changing and testing at any level requires more space. You may recover some space by deleting programs that nobody uses, but you will need more. And don't forget, everybody else will need more storage devices, too. Production capacity may not be able to keep up with demand.

Selecting Tools

You need tools; no ifs, ands, or buts about it. Automation will help with all segments of the Year 2000 update process. Costs can be reduced by proper selection of tools and the right plan to implement them. Tools can improve productivity through better quality, speed, and completeness—when properly applied. Our experience indicates that the cost of the conversion can be reduced from 15 to 35 percent, depending on the tools used and the kinds of programming languages they have to work with. Unfortunately, no single tool will do the job by itself.

Take a look at the following table. It is an example of the project automation typically available, if all conditions are optimal, to a typical large computer shop.

ACTIVITY	PERCENT OF TOTAL PROCESS	PERCENT OF TASK AUTOMATED PROCESS	PERCENT SAVED OF TOTAL PROCESS
Inventory (location of date objects)	1	80	0.8
Planning (deciding what to change and when)	3	27	0.8

ACTIVITY	PERCENT OF TOTAL PROCESS	PERCENT OF TASK AUTOMATED PROCESS	PERCENT SAVED OF TOTAL PROCESS
Analysis (specification of design changes)	14	10	1.4
Update (expansion of date fields, data and logic, or insertion of windows)	16	80	12.8
Testing (unit, systems, and integration testing)	42	60	25.2
Migration (production transition, data change, and training)	5	20	1.0
Management (change, project, process, resource)	19	33	6.3
Total saved			48.3

The problem with tools is that the time expended in determining what tools to buy and how to deploy them may absorb much of the potential savings in the time left. It is becoming more efficient to select a well-known tool than embark on a search for a tool. It is important to note that this example indicates this shop *could*, not necessarily *will*, achieve nearly a 50 percent productivity improvement for the entire project. The caveat springs from the *if* statement preceding: "*if* properly applied." Most computer programmers and managers typically know how to use only about two-thirds of the tools they own, for very understandable reasons: Not all of these tools have been useful to them in the past. It takes time to learn how to use tools; knowledge of how to use tools is lost when the tools are not used on a regular basis; and knowledge becomes obsolete as the vendor updates the tools. Here are some interesting observations:

- It takes an average of three months for a person to be trained and become proficient in the use of a given tool.

- The average person can learn no more than two tools of different categories at one time and achieve competency in the same period.

- Achieving an optimal Year 2000 update process may require as many as 30 or 40 different tools, depending on the operating system and the number of computers and computer languages.

Assuming no tools are currently in place, an individual on your Year 2000 team would not become proficient using all the update tools for three years. But consider the following observations to counterbalance the preceding:

- It is a rare organization that does not have some tools already.
- Some computers are sold with many tools that support the process.
- COBOL, the most prevalent computer language, is supported by many tools.
- Many tools work on PCs, meaning they are easier to use and make less of a demand on the mainframe computer. (However, there is a steep learning curve if the staff is unfamiliar with PCs.)
- Optimal automation may achieve a 48 percent performance improvement with a total investment of less than 7 percent of the equivalent wage investment.

Code-Change Tools

Code-change tools can be used to alter computer code, create file conversion programs, and build database bridges. But it is essential to be aware before investing in these tools that, at best, they can be implemented to automate an activity that amounts to a maximum of 24 percent of the total project effort. Generally speaking, we have found they work best for straightforward changes and in support of the most common programming languages. Most work only with COBOL written for IBM—370 architecture or later—mainframe platforms. They are designed to work with expanding two-digit date fields to four-digit fields. Few attempt to make changes to the process instructions. Nearly all require the customer to define date *seeds* identifying date fields. Many lists of seeds miss a lot of dates because the staff does not recognize the dates, or the application cannot trace them through redefinition, levels of definitions, introduction of aliases, or levels of shared code modules.

Some insert logic to *window* the dates, allowing the program to interpret the century as 19 or 20 based on parameters defined by you. This has already gotten many organizations into trouble because the window can change depending on the data. Such window changes may occur as many as five times within a single program. Automatic insertion of logical century assignment is the most dangerous practice known. It, and the dates used to set the window, requires careful management.

Silver bullet tools are being announced weekly, and everyone claims to have the "solution of the century." The problem with silver bullets is that even they would take years to test and would still leave problems that could only be found with line-by-line analysis. Remember, some dates were intended to be processed in a specific way (e.g., when zero was always meant to mean zero, not 1900 or 2000), and users sometimes create dates where they weren't planned to be by the programmer (e.g., when a clever clerk decides it is quicker and more informative to store the year in the policy status field rather than type in "closed").

Some vendors of these change tools will offer to take your code, date-field seeds (rules for identifying date fields), and window requirements, make the changes, and give the modified code back to you, compiled or ready to compile. These tools have increased in accuracy over time since the first edition of this book. Accuracy of the locating process has gotten to be very good, reaching 95 to 98 percent. However, none of these tools has reached the state of perfection. Even a small failure at detection can mean critical dates are not located and the program will not process correctly. The burden of accuracy remains with the program owner.

Whenever sending programs through a rule-based update process, you must know which rules the process employs to change the code and how it makes those changes; that way you can anticipate things it doesn't change and prepare for errors when it changes things it shouldn't. In general, use these code change tools, but don't expect too much and you will not be disappointed. The advantage is that these programs are good at imposing standards; but there is yet to be a tool of this sort that can provide an average accuracy of better than 95 percent (some applications that employ unusual constructs may achieve only half that accuracy), which means that a programmer must still go through all the code and identify sections that the automated process missed.

The reason these tools are limited in their effectiveness is that they can't anticipate the creativity of programmers. For example, on computers that don't have the space or the ability to process four-digit years, programmers have been forced to use several single-digit century options. A common solution is to store the century as a single-digit logic flag: A century indicator is set for $0 = 19$ and $1 = 20$. (Even IBM isn't consistent. In some equipment, 0 is used before the years 1940 through 1999, while 1 is used for the years 2000 through 2039.) Some enterprises use $0 = 1800$, $1 = 1900$, and $2 = 2000$. Another variation uses signed values, where 1900 has the value of 0, 1 or +1 represents 2000, and −1 represents 1800.

Systems programmers frequently use elapsed time. The first step in this method is to choose a starting or base date. IBM talks about using Lilian dates, which start at October 15, 1582 (the date the Gregorian calendar was adopted). Dates of January 1, 1600, and January 3, 1980, are also often used as base dates. The date values stored are not true dates, but the number of days elapsed from the base date to the date intended. If the base date is January 3, 1980, and the date to be represented is March 1, 1980, the value stored is 58. Since the date itself is not stored, anytime the data is to be treated as a real date, it must be converted by a program routine.

Other techniques that change dates for storage include displacement, modulo, and nines complement. The *displacement* technique subtracts the year from 2000 so that 1995 is stored as the value 5, while the value for 2005 is −5. The *modulo* technique uses a base year (e.g., 1964) and stores the difference so that for 1995, the value 31 is stored, and for 2005, 41 is stored. The *nines complement* technique subtracts the two-digit value of the year from 99 so that for 1995 the value stored is 04, and for 2005 it is 94. All these techniques require an arithmetic step in each place the date is validated, stored, retrieved, and displayed. Sorting can be tricky, too; using the nines complement, values for dates 1998 through 2002 are 01, 00, 99, 98, and 97.

An alternative programming method assigns century values by adding 30 to the year and comparing the two-digit result to 30. Any calculated value of less than 30 is assigned a century value of 19, and any value equal to or greater is assigned a century value of 20. For example, 1995 plus 30 results in 25, so the century is 19. Likewise, for the year 2000, the calculated value is 30, so the century is 20. Sorting is simplified by this method, but other complications arise. For a date prior to 1970, you will need to use a value greater than 30. When date ranges span a wide time frame within a set of dates, different incremental values are required within the same program.

Confused? That's understandable, and the preceding is just a small sample. There are more than 40 different typical date formats with which to store dates. As you can imagine, finding a tool that handles all the common and the uncommon routines will be difficult, if not impossible. The bottom line, then, when using these tools is to know what they do and don't do, and you will achieve some effective help.

Choosing and Executing a Process Pilot

Time for the dress rehearsal. You have established standards, determined an update process, and selected tools that you can reasonably use on your computer programming date problem. It is time to decide where to start. It is imperative to perform a pilot process in order to identify problems and to establish a reliable time frame for the real thing—beware, the first application through the process typically takes three times longer than you planned.

Plan your first project around some small system that you believe could be updated in a month. Make sure that it is *typical of the applications in the environment*; that is, it uses the primary programming and operating platforms (computer, operating system, programming languages, data management system, and communications process). Then do the following:

1. Employ the tools that you already own and plan to use throughout.

2. Enforce the standards.

3. Rewrite any process step that doesn't work.

4. Design alternative processes. (It may take more than one process to do a single activity due to languages, criticality of the component, the fact that it is shared, and so forth.)

When you are done, review your results against expectations. You are bound to find justification for automating some additional tasks.

The following are a few additional suggestions gleaned from the experience of others in regard to staffing the update process: Do not leave it up to the computer people who normally support the applications. They will try to fix things that are technologically imperfect. They will try to fold in changes that the computer users have been requesting for years. They will generally delegate the changes downward to the least-experienced person on the team. In general, they will not be efficient.

After you complete your first pilot process and make the necessary corrections, we suggest that you do another cycle in which you measure the results. These measurements can be used to adjust the estimates for your budget. Note that the pilot is a demonstration of the process and produces tangible results. Whether you treat the first execution of a process as a pilot may determine if you improve your process over time.

The next chapter, "Managing the Fix," reiterates the issues facing Year 2000 project managers and helps you develop a management strategy for your Year 2000 efforts.

CHAPTER 6

Managing the Fix

The purpose of this chapter is twofold: (1) to consolidate and reiterate the lessons learned in the first five chapters, and (2) to prime you for the nuts and bolts of Chapters 7 through 12, which tell you how to get the most from your staff, how to approach the workload, how to automate, how to choose the right tools, where to get help, how to manage your risks, and how to avoid the dangers of litigation. In addition, a related problem is discussed which throws a monkey wrench into the already complicated fix process—the EMU.

Too Late?

In the first edition, the opening section for this chapter was called, *They Who Hesitate Are Lost*. Now, with little more than a year left, is it too late to address your Year 2000 problem if you have not yet begun? One estimation is that an enterprise that started in 1997 is likely to get through only about 80 percent of its applications; if it waits until 1999, only 30 percent. And even conceding that only 30 percent of the applications may be critical to the business of the enterprise, that 30 percent is probably attached by data to another 40 percent of the other applications that won't make the transition in time. At best, the organization will be crippled; at worst, it will no longer exist.

Probably the most knowledgeable organization in the world on computer statistics is Software Productivity Research, headed by Capers Jones. He maintains that October of 1997 was the latest time at which Year 2000 repairs could have started with a reasonable probability of them being finished before 2000. His estimates (published in the white paper, "The Global Economic Impact of the Year 2000 Software Problem," at www.spr.com, which is *must* reading) state that there are about 1.92 million professional software personnel in the United States, including managers, operations staff, and other nonprogrammers; and there are 32.4 million applications—*not counting* spreadsheets, which are produced primarily by noncomputing professionals. With less than 50 percent of the estimated total still needing to be repaired, this means that each professional still has more than 20 applications to update between now and the year 2000. Can it be done? It took from 1988 until now to do the first half!

Arthur C. Clarke, in his book *The Ghost from the Grand Banks* (Bantam Spectra, 1990), writes:

> During the closing years of the century, most of the world's star-class programmers were engaged in the race to develop a "Vaccine '99"; it had become a kind of Holy Grail. Several faulty versions were issued as early as 1997—and wiped out any purchasers who hastened to test them before making adequate backups. The lawyers did very well out of the ensuing suits and countersuits.

No Year 2000 "vaccine" has been developed, although there are some tools which can help automate the process. (Chapters 9 and 10, "Taking a Tool Inventory" and "2000: A Tool Odyssey," talk more about tools.) Remember, a silver bullet would have to find all the dates; redesign data-handling processes; change the code; test the old date processes; test the new date processes; migrate code from old versions to new; and make decisions about when and how to change things *without* tripping over decisions it makes about other applications, external data sharing, and spontaneous vendor solutions. It is very unlikely such a silver bullet will be invented between now and the new millennium.

With that in mind, if you haven't yet started, it is time to begin—*now.* The days and weeks are ebbing away even as you read this. The sooner you begin this project, the better your chances of protecting your business from Year 2000 fallout. Delay, and you put everything at risk. One issue only mentioned in passing thus far is litigation. This very real risk is covered in detail in Chapter 12, "The Price of Failure." For now, here are some points to keep in mind.

In the aforementioned white paper, Caper Jones says: "For every dollar not spent on repairing the Year 2000 problem, the anticipated costs of litigation and potential damages will probably amount to more than $10." He notes that in the United States, where people are quick to take things to court, costs and damage awards could mount to 20 times larger than the actual cost of making the code changes. At the very least, he cautions that senior corporate executives who do not exercise "fiduciary responsibility to act in the best interests of the shareholders" will see their careers damaged, if not ended.

Many cases will go to trial before the year 2000 when systems fail because of dates such as 98 and 99 having special significance. These court cases will place an additional drain on management and on programming personnel as they are subjected to court appearances. Still other programmers may find new careers as expert witnesses.

But don't forget: Risk and opportunity go hand in hand. There really are silver linings in these clouds. Here are a few of them:

- Consolidating these libraries and eliminating just-in-case data storage enables some companies to recover up to 40 percent of their program storage space. Eliminating dead files certainly can't hurt, and it may well help, because using four-digit years, along with other methods to assure the computer knows what day it is, will take up more room; you will have more room once you clean closets.

- You will realize that not all reports have to go to all the people in your organization. In a documented instance, one department didn't realize after being accidentally cut off for three months that it wasn't getting its reports, and a couple of offices never noticed.

- You will have the opportunity to purchase or consolidate other enterprises as they are overwhelmed by the effort required to make changes and repair failing applications.

- Standardized date systems throughout the whole company will benefit staff, too, not just the computers. And, as a bonus, people may even develop a more professional attitude toward their own machines.

- Getting a handle on your software inventory will turn out to be just as important as tracking your inventory of supplies and work—and just as profitable, too. You'll eliminate marginal functions that serve little purpose.

- At the end of the process, you will know precisely which of your computer applications are important, and this will help you determine how to prioritize future investments.

- Working with your suppliers, vendors, and customers will go a long way toward reducing your own future data exchange problems. Ensuring they don't have Year 2000 problems will net long-term goodwill rewards, as all of you realize your mutual business dependency.

- Budgets that have been tight for years will be relaxed, which will allow some organizations to update software that hasn't been fixed since the first episode of the original *Star Trek* series. The same goes for hardware. Eliminating ancient hardware will mean eliminating personnel headaches—trying to train someone to work on those antiques.

- Just finding what's there may uncover hidden treasure. Many employees have squirreled away programs and data that nobody else knows exist.

Some enterprises have had to keep two versions of the same software for years and spend money on maintenance and version management. That savings can help pay for this work.

- Applying configuration management techniques to oversee your systems software, tools, and vendor application packages will cut down on labor costs (and frankly, after this conversion process, employees will just want to go home anyway).

Instant Replay

The title of Chapter 5, "Ready to Run," is borrowed from Michelle Callow of IBM, who used it as the title of her speech at the Central Computer and Telecommunications Agency Conference Forum in Norwich, England, in April 1996, where she mentioned the following factors as critical for success in solving the Year 2000 problem:

Management commitment

Definition and redefinition

Scheduling and resources

Monitoring and feedback

Communication

Exception handling

User consultation and acceptance

Determination to succeed

The following section outlines the points you should take away from the first part of the book so the information will be fresh in your mind.

Although the Year 2000 problem is directly related to dates, it is an indirect outcome of the following:

- The human desire to save time and effort
- The legacy of the initial high cost of technology
- The legacy of data that was stored in the form that best met the first two reasons

The nature of the problem is manifest in its worst form in computers, which will be unable to do the following:

- Calculate date arithmetic correctly
- Compare dates correctly
- Sort dates in the proper sequence

The problem has not gotten much serious press for the following reasons:

- It's perceived as something too big to be real.
- There are serious implications to the survival of government and financial infrastructures.
- Most large organizations take a long time to get enough data to describe their problems. CIBC, a large, well-managed Canadian bank, experienced 15 months elapsed time to inventory its applications, estimate and analyze what it has, and determine what it wants to do about fixing them. It is not the only one. Other organizations may spend a year looking at tools and conducting pilots with no appreciable movement toward getting the change process started.
- Many organizations are *still* trying to figure out what to do about the problem; nobody wants to appear incapable of dealing with it.

The fact is, the following large sectors of the economy are already working on the problem:

Governments, at all levels

Financial institutions

Public utilities

Transportation providers

The Year 2000 problem is not limited to legacy programs, mainframe computers, or specific programming languages, but also affects the following:

- Embedded systems (computers built into machinery)
- Obsolete computers
- Obsolete languages and programs
- Business processes that employ dates
- Vendors that won't or can't fix their products in time
- Suppliers that can't fix their problems
- Customers who will not understand

To repair the problem will require the following:

- Finding the software
- Identifying and fixing existing, but unrealized, date problems
- Converting old versions of software to new versions that are supported
- Replacing and expanding hardware
- Purchasing computer resources and software tools
- Recovering lost computer code

- Retraining staff
- Redesigning the software

Related and possibly concomitant problems include the following:

- Failure to solve the problem may result in litigation, drawing away money and staff resources, possibly resulting in the loss of executives.
- Operations may be suspended by failures of internal systems.
- Operations may be interrupted by failures of infrastructure systems—heat, power, communications, transportation.
- Coordinating with vendors, suppliers, and customers will involve all management staff.

Costs of the repair will be both controllable and uncontrollable:

CONTROLLABLE

- Internal software fixes and replacement
- Internal hardware fixes and replacement
- Business process changes

UNCONTROLLABLE

- Vendor delays, failures, and noncompliance to standards
- Litigation costs
- Staffing turnover and cost escalation
- Failures of suppliers
- Overlooked problems

The problem resolution is dependent on the following factors:

- Time
- Managing the large numbers
- Management decision making
- An unmovable deadline

Two parallel processes must take place in order to get the problem under control: planning and preparation. *Planning* includes the following component activities:

- Locating software and hardware components
- Testing date processes
- Estimating the repair/replacement costs
- Surveying vendors and scheduling changes

- Performing triage on the applications
- Sequencing the work effort
- Building awareness
- Obtaining resources and forming a team

Preparation includes the following component activities:

- Setting standards
- Creating an update process
- Creating a controlled change environment
- Establishing a testing environment
- Selecting tools
- Choosing and executing a process pilot

The following vehicles will tend to drive the project to failure:

- Doing nothing or getting bogged down in decision making
- Waiting for somebody or some company to develop a silver bullet
- Adding too many other jobs to fixing this problem
- Expecting everything to happen on a schedule
- Expecting to keep all people on board for the entire project
- Trying to accomplish everything all at once
- Working without a plan

The imperatives propelling you to address this problem are (1) staying in business and (2) minimizing litigation costs. The long-term rewards are as follows:

- Cleaning the closet
- Eliminating unnecessary reports and functions
- Getting the leverage to buy out competitors
- Standardizing; improving quality
- Eliminating marginally profitable products
- Building closer relationships with suppliers, vendors, customers
- Finding resources that can save time and money in the future
- Establishing controls over the computing environment

While the problem is complex and may seem overwhelming, it is still manageable. Hopefully, you have already begun the update process, following this book's suggestions. If not, you should still be able to minimize the risks to your business using risk management methods. (See Chapter 11, "When in Doubt, Outsource.")

The European Monetary Unit and the Gamble

In today's global economy, the risk factors associated with the year 2000 are further complicated by the new European monetary unit (EMU). The proposed European common currency involves extensive changes to existing computer systems (estimated by some to cost about £100 billion), and therein lies the challenge and the gamble.

The Bathtub Race

Fixing the Year 2000 problem on time is like running a 4-minute mile. Few organizations will effortlessly accomplish the task and deliver a solution on time. Given the necessary rigorous training and motivation, you can, and hopefully will, deliver a timely solution. However, to ask any company to complete the Year 2000 project and at the same time attempt to complete the changes necessary to accommodate a common currency is like asking it to run a 4-minute mile with a bathtub strapped on its back.

The added burden is unreasonable and, considering the consequences of failure, foolhardy. This fact is not unknown to those who have to do the work. At a conference several years ago in England, Peter de Jager made the blunt statement that we should not attempt the currency conversion because it would place the Year 2000 project at an unacceptable level of risk. A gentleman stood up at the back of the room and stated strongly and loudly that Peter did not understand the "real world," and that when his boss told him to do the currency conversion, he would have to comply.

The authors are too well aware that when our "masters" say "jump!" there is a natural tendency to ask "How high?" And, it takes a tremendous amount of courage to stand your ground and question commands, which by their very nature are questionable.

At the conference, Peter responded with: "Do you realize that by attempting both, you will deliver neither?" The man's response was both shocking and informative; with an absolute certainty evident to everyone in the room, he replied quietly, "Without a shadow of a doubt."

His answer, of course, leaves no room for argument. If someone recognizes a course of action will lead to certain failure, and decides on that course of action regardless, then there is no point trying to use the existence of known consequences to stay that action. The person's mind is made up to fail.

Walk and Chew Gum?

A legitimate question from someone might be, "Do these two projects have to conflict? After all, just because two tasks are large does not mean they necessarily draw upon the same resources."

That's true enough. At any point in time there are many large projects on the go. Countries send rockets to Mars at the same time they are planning for the Olympics, raising bridges, and building tunnels under the ocean. Society is quite good at juggling several huge projects simultaneously and still delivering them on time (within reason) and within spitting distance of the original budget. (Yeah, right)

The projects previously mentioned vary greatly in their demands on available skills and materials, as well as in their impact on everything else around them. However, EMU and Y2K (Year 2000) are unique. While they are indeed separate projects, they draw on similar skill sets and raw materials—the computer applications upon which twentieth-century organizations and society are totally dependent.

Comparing Year 2000 and the European Monetary Unit Project

To understand why it is such a gamble to attempt to accommodate the new European currency and perform Year 2000 fixes, you need to examine how they are related. First, the following discusses how the two projects differ.

Size Differences

EMU is primarily a European phenomenon. While it is true that organizations worldwide will be forced to accommodate EMU, the main effect will be within the European Economic Community (EEC) and its immediate trading partners.

The Y2K project, on the other hand, is worldwide. Every organization that depends on computers (which includes every twentieth-century organization) must undertake a Y2K conversion. There are only isolated exceptions.

Skill Differences

EMU is a significant change to how an organization manages and reports its worldwide financial activities. It is not, as some have suggested, merely the addition of another currency.

The skills required to implement EMU must come from both the financial and computer departments of the organization. The computer skills required are in-depth analysis as well as programming skills.

Y2K, on the other hand, is a relatively simple task compared to EMU: Fix the date calculations using two-digit dates so they produce the expected results. This requires no financial expertise, and with respect to the code changes themselves, little in-depth analysis. A squadron of competent programmers, operating under a fully funded, comprehensive, closely monitored, and well-managed project plan can complete the task.

Given these different skill requirements, tools developed to assist in the EMU conversion will be significantly less efficient than those being used to assist in Y2K conversions. Y2K tools can actually modify code, providing a huge reduction in workpower requirements. EMU tools will be less capable of actually modifying code and will be mainly beneficial in identifying where code should be changed.

Deadline Differences

When all is said and done, the deadlines for EMU, regardless of when they are, are set by people. There is nothing sacred about them. (This statement is, of course, sacrilegious to all the politicians and economists involved in this history-making endeavor.)

Nevertheless, the fact remains, the dates are literally contrived, and if missed, the world will not end, even though there will admittedly be heavy economic costs for any delays in the published time lines.

The Y2K deadline is also, in a manner of speaking, "man-made." There is nothing mystical or ordained about a 2 followed by three zeros. There are many calendars still in use today which do not, at this moment in time, roll over to 2000. Our calendar is arbitrary—but it is fixed, and there is no avoiding the fact that in less than two years it will roll over to a 2 followed by three zeros, at which point our programs will fail and so will companies dependent upon those programs.

Not even Pope Gregory would attempt to change the calendar at this late date; the problems that this would cause would far exceed the cost of 10 Y2K conversions.

The following three points define how the two projects differ:

- EMU is smaller and more complex than Y2K.
- Y2K has a fixed deadline which cannot be missed.

- EMU is a contrived date which will be costly to miss, but which will not bring businesses to a halt.

The following considers how the projects are similar.

Skill Similarities

Both tasks require programming skills. The Y2K project, even though more addressable by automated solutions, is already depleting resources in the United States. A survey (August 26, 1997) by Cap Gemini, a Y2K services company based in New York, reported the following findings:

> Over the past four months, the percentage of Fortune 500 corporations that intend to hire additional Y2K personnel jumped by one third: from 45 to 65%. In addition . . . 19 out of 20 such companies report that acquiring staff with appropriate skills has been difficult. More than 82% of these companies describe the Y2K Labor market as "tight" or "extremely tight."

There is a tendency to discount the findings of any company with a vested interest in the problem to be solved, but it is difficult and, perhaps, foolhardy to ignore this information. South Africa, for example, is losing 30 computer people a month to U.S. recruiters who are willing to travel abroad to find the necessary people at any price.

Adding EMU to the existing demand will merely increase the efforts of recruiters to raid people from existing project teams. The cost in delays due to team rebuilding will make immovable deadlines impossible to achieve.

Application Changes

Many applications are affected by dates; a smaller number will be affected by EMU, but a significantly large subset will be affected by both.

Making two different types of changes to the same application at the same time increases the likelihood of introducing new errors. It will, therefore, greatly increase the size of the absolutely necessary task of testing to make sure these programs will perform in the future as they have in the past.

Bottom line: It's an unavoidable fact that the more you change a program, the more likely you are to introduce errors and delay delivery.

Time Constraints in Common

Many of the proposed changes for EMU are due before 2000. The changes for Y2K must also be implemented during that same time frame. If the world decides EMU must be done on schedule, then it will be done during the same period when programmers are working on Y2K. The demands will fall on the same pool of resources and the activities in the same programs, making this strategy *unwise*.

Some European government officials have decided that EMU should be delivered first and then attention should be turned to Y2K. In other words, start Y2K projects sometime in 1999.

Companies who have been working on the Y2K problem for three years have stated they doubt they will complete everything on time. The notion that a company will delay commencement of the Y2K project until the eleventh hour, and then expect to complete it on time, despite past experience, ignores the most basic of prudent risk management strategies. The risks, even if understated so that management will accept them, would be unacceptable to any competent gambler.

Time To Tell the Truth

There is yet another facet to the preceding argument that computer people are loathe to dwell on; and they are certainly not going out of their way to communicate it to the people (management) who must understand it. The computer industry has proven itself unreliable when it comes to delivering projects on time.

To drive home this point, here is a recap of an audience encounter repeated dozens of times worldwide over the past years:

Question to the audience of IT professionals: *Raise your hand if you have a high degree of confidence in your ability to deliver the Y2K project on time.*

Response from the audience: *A forest of hands raised in affirmation.*

So far, so good. This reflects what they have been communicating to management: "Don't worry, we have this under control, we can handle this, we'll deliver it on time, trust us."

Next question: *Over the past three years, raise your hands if you have delivered 100 percent of your applications on time.*

Response: *A gale of laughter.*

Why? Because the notion of 100 percent on-time delivery is as foreign to the IT industry as is the notion that airlines can deliver 100 percent on-time departures.

Next question: *Raise your hand if your historical record of on-time delivery is 90 percent.*

Response: *At best one hand is raised . . . only to be lowered quickly in response to the laughter and catcalls of "liar!"*

Next question: *Raise your hand if your historical record of on-time delivery is 80 percent.*

Response: *2–3 percent of the audience raise their hands.*

Next question: *Raise your hand if your historical record of on-time delivery is 70 percent.*

Response: *Another 2–5 percent of the audience raise their hands.*

It is not until 60–50 percent is reached that half the audience raises their hands, which means the historical track record of half the audience is below 50 percent for on-time delivery.

Remember when asked if they had a high degree of confidence in their ability to deliver a Y2K project on time, the audience gleefully answered yes!?

A question of intense interest to management is: Why are they so confident about their success in the future, when in the past they have failed so miserably?

The next question is: *Are any gamblers in the room? Would you like to play a little gambling game? The game has three components: the ante, the event, and the payoff.*

Put $1,000 in the speaker's left hand. He flips a coin. If it turns up heads, the $1,000 is returned to you; otherwise, the speaker keeps it. The response is naturally another gale of laughter. It's a sucker's bet.

You are already playing the game, except that the stakes are higher. Much higher.

The *ante* is your organization. The *event* is IT's proven ability, not wishful thinking, for delivering projects on time. The *payoff* is the ability of your organization to function in the year 2000.

Ask yourself if adding EMU to this gamble will increase or decrease your chance of delivering Y2K on time? Do your stakeholders agree with your answer?

Do they agree with the risk you're about to undertake?

Do you?

At this point, you are putting enormous pressure on your IT staff to fix the Year 2000 problem on time. It may not be possible if the process is not already underway. To ask them to accommodate the changes required by the EMU at the same time is foolish. With the demand for skilled Y2K team members increasing exponentially, you risk losing your staff to other companies competing for resources. The next chapter, "Power to the People," examines staffing concerns and good management practices associated with heading a Year 2000 project team.

CHAPTER 7

Power to the People

The single most critical resource you have available for fixing the code-repair part of the Year 2000 problem in your organization is your trained and experienced staff. Twenty percent of the work involves management: resource (people, hardware, tools) management, change management, configuration management, and process management. Even work performed by nonmanagement personnel will require supervision. This includes inventorying and planning (4 percent), analyzing the code to be changed and deciding how to change it (14 percent), changing the code and building data-handling programs (16 percent), testing the changed and developed programs (42 percent), and finally, changing the data and putting the programs into production use (5 percent). These statistics represent industry averages.

Don't ignore the nontechnical aspects of the Year 2000 preparation effort. Management and nonmanagement workers will be involved in tracking down and evaluating suppliers, vendors, service providers. Sales team members may take part in assessing customers. Engineers may invest weeks of effort in locating, assessing, repairing, or replacing equipment containing embedded systems. Scheduling service workers and planning production interruptions to minimize business impact could absorb weeks of staff time.

Manual Labor

The latter efforts are obviously manual. Most people are shocked to find that for implementing changes to computerized systems, most of the work on the

95

Year 2000 update project is manual. The following is how the roles of the managers break out:

Change management requires a person knowledgeable of priorities and schedules to determine what is to be changed and when.

Configuration management uses tools or keeps track of components to coordinate changes to each of the involved sectors to ensure that all parts reach production at the same time, minimizing code-freeze duration.

Process management identifies process difficulties, opportunities for improvements, and work processes that can be handled by less-skilled staff. It also manages personnel turnover which requires recruiting and retraining, and which imposes a heavy burden on the resources you need most—your most knowledgeable staff.

Resource management involves making sure the people and hardware resources are available to make the changes. It requires constant attention to ascertain that decision makers are available to solve problems and determine which design changes will be implemented. It also involves verifying that training happens when and for whom it is needed.

Even after you have minimized decision making by imposing standards and simplifying the process, you will find another 7 to 10 percent of the update effort involves analysis because, although the scanning performed in the estimating process will locate many dates, it will not find them all—meaning they will have to be isolated at analysis time. Remember, every date is suspect, even those that appear to include four-digit designations. Why? Because there are applications in which a century field has been allocated but never used, or ones in which four digits have been moved into the two-digit-year field where the century has been lost in the truncation process. In other situations, a literal *19* has been inserted into the century position of every year. Finally, even processes that involve only day calculations may be in error because routines that determine the day of the week might be using a calendar that rolls to the year 1900, resulting in every day of the week appearing incorrectly.

Although using tools to implement code changes will be helpful, you will find that staffing demands will be high for redesigning the code. And, if you have purchased tools that employ rule-based processing, you will have to spend staff time identifying rule requirements and testing those rules. Or, if you can create your own rules, you will find time requirements to be just as high as making the code changes. Each rule has to be programmed and tested. The more rules that are created, the more difficult it becomes to create a rule that does not conflict with another. The testing has to find every situation where the rule could be applied and then make sure that it works and the code is changed in the intended way. If you are dependent on a vendor to provide those rules, you will still have to manage that process.

Even if you have no computer systems to correct for Year 2000 problems, your key vendors and suppliers may be faced with significant labor demands. Understanding this may encourage you to ask specific questions about client and supplier systems your business depends upon. Those systems may not be fixed in time though the supplier may continue in business and fulfill the requirements necessary for its survival. You may find that you are severely impacted and might suffer decreases in profits due to rising costs. You may be required to add staff to overcome the failure of others' systems.

Surveys performed by Cap Gemini in the first part of 1998 indicated that, coming into the year, the largest organizations had spent an average of only 21 percent of their Year 2000 budgets. Four months later the percentage had risen to only 24 percent. The U.S. government effort also reported slowing as workers were lured away to private industry with offers of much higher wages. President Clinton announced, in an address before the National Science Council on July 14, 1998, that the government was seeking to bring retirees back to assist in the repair work. Further, the American Association of Retired Persons (AARP) had been asked to assist in bringing retirees in to work for the government.

Industry pay averages for programmers and experienced Year 2000 project managers were reportedly rising as fast as 6 percent a quarter in the United States. One reliable source said that he had heard that wages were rising 7 percent a month in New York City. While some people forecast huge layoffs or pay reductions for these high-demand opportunists after the Year 2000 problem passes, indications are that those prognosticators may be in for a surprise.

Many of the people will be engaged in Year 2000 work long after the midnight deadline. A recent true story states that when a publisher tried to book a hotel room to celebrate the arrival of the new millennium, it was shocked to find that a hotel not even built yet has been fully booked through April 2001 to house Year 2000 workers! With the current effort going into short-term fixes, the real repair work remains to be done after the beginning of the century. 38 percent of the Chief Information Officers leaving a DCI Year 2000 conference in January 1998 indicated that they would not get all their applications repaired in time. Even without the Year 2000 problem to create a high demand, the number of programmers required is estimated to be 80,000 greater than the number entering the market. Starting salaries of graduates from college computer-related programs is in the range of $40,000 to $50,000. Caps exist on the number of computer professionals allowed into the United States from other countries.

Bottom line, people, especially skilled computer people, will remain critical to the success of everyone's Year 2000 programs. Retaining them will be a challenge for years to come.

Time in a Bottle

During the Year 2000 update process, most of your technical staff time will be allocated to testing. The typical programming staff will discover that creating test scripts, preparing test data, executing, and validating tests will absorb at least 40 percent of the total project effort. Some applications, because they are highly visible or strategically important, will see testing efforts rise to as high as 80 percent of the total effort. Even those who adopt a replacement strategy will see an equal range of effort invested in testing.

Why the concern about testing in a chapter about retaining people? Testing is brutally tedious and it takes even greater patience. The people who plan the tests and perform them have to be intimate with the operation and functioning of the application. They have to be able to read computer code and build scripts that will test not only date-process changes, but also the continued running of other functions that are not supposed to have been affected by changes. These tests must be run over and over again, a process called *regression testing,* for as many different dates as is shown later in the discussion on testing. Asking skilled people to perform mind-numbing work is a sure way to create disaffection.

Some strategies (which are explained later) can reduce that effort in some situations, but in general, testing is a time-consuming part of the process. Further, keeping track of test data and comparison files will add another burden to your staff if they are unfamiliar with regression testing. You will find regression testing is essential since you will need to retest some programs over and over because of their linkages to many other applications that can't all be changed at the same time.

Heading South

Migration, which includes changing data and file definitions, retraining application users, and moving applications into production, will be significantly complicated in the Year 2000 update process. The typical data-processing organization performs one or two migrations a month and usually schedules them for weekends to minimize impact on the workload and to provide a buffer against glitches. In large organizations, the migration effort may require that multiple applications be moved from testing to production in a single weekend; because of the on-rushing deadline, some migrations may have to be performed during the workweek. The increased complexity and scheduling of the migrations create a greater possibility for systems crashes that will shut down operations for companies. Minimizing the risk will require the utmost in planning and orchestrating if these migrations to production are to be executed successfully. This will challenge even the best of your project managers.

A Project by Any Other Name

So far, the term *project manager* has been used to describe the leader of the Year 2000 update effort. It is probably a misnomer, because a *project* is loosely defined as achievement of a goal by completing a number of predetermined tasks. But with the Year 2000 problem, technically organizations do not have a project, they have a program because all they have is a *plan* to execute a number of projects. This may appear to be an inconsequential distinction, but it is not. Programs are managed differently from projects. A project is achieved by committing the appropriate resources to a predefined set of tasks. The management of a project thus involves getting the right resources assigned to the task, then making sure it is completed as required. The focus is on what you do, not how you do it.

Program management takes into account that you don't have control over all the resources. It focuses on *how* you work to make sure that you achieve the best you can with the resources you do have. Thus, program managers have significantly more latitude for decision making. Project managers can create a plan; present it to management; and negotiate schedules, resources, and authority because all the requirements are known, whereas a program manager lays intentions on the table—an estimate of the sequence of actions that will be taken, a requirement for cooperation. The program manager is given far more power to act than the project manager.

Many organizations already employ one or more project managers. The individuals in these roles often have too little authority and too narrow a scope within the organization to effectively carry out the job of the program manager, which is required on the Year 2000 effort. Those organizations should institute a new title to distinguish the authority vested in the leader of the effort, although this book will continue to use the term *project manager* for consistency's sake.

Centralized Authority

Many enterprises have decentralized data-processing organizations so that responsibility for data processing is divided along functional lines. While this gives the functional organizations more control over data-processing priorities and more direct accountability for the budgets, it has created an environment of parochialism. For example, many applications are duplicated. You may find your organization burdened with a dozen general ledger systems and several payroll systems. During the Year 2000 triage process—determining where to assign increasingly scarce resources first—the cost of this duplication becomes apparent. Because of the desire to retain control and minimize the impact on each organization, users will fight to retain their versions, thereby delaying the start of the work.

At this juncture, you may have to make some tough decisions. Should you

- Recentralize some applications?
- Impose one application solution on all the organizations?
- Undertake simultaneous changes to all the applications at the same time?
- Coordinate the passing of data in different formats?

These decisions cannot be made by a project manager with a reporting relationship to a single-line authority. They must be made by an individual who puts the interests of the enterprise ahead of departmental concerns. This person must be able to do this in an environment divorced from politics; otherwise, the decisions may come too late to prevent widespread problems. The project manager must have the authority to make these decisions with limited accountability, a capability usually found only at the upper layers of the enterprise.

Even those enterprises that have retained strong centralized data-processing organizations discover that some decisions take too long to make. These enterprises have delegated the budgets for data processing to the functional operations groups, usually in organizations where managers compete on the basis of budget management. In such organizations, the cost of the repair may invoke a heavy penalty on an individual manager. The repair bill will be highest in accounting and human resources organizations where date-dependent processing is widespread. Other organizations may have smaller price tags; for example, engineering and manufacturing systems generally have fewer date-dependent processes. In such enterprises, the politics of funding the project often cause delays in initiating fixes.

Internal politics also impose delays on the project, which subsequently increases costs. Where applications are shared by more than one organization, funding must be obtained from each of the organizations in order to perform the work, and usually it is difficult to obtain such approvals. Priorities within one or more of those organizations will delay allocation of people or financial resources.

True, workarounds to delays can be implemented, but this, too, may add to the expense. For example, some portions of an application may have event horizons that are earlier than for others, thus forcing you to build additional data interfaces that later must be removed. This piece of the application may affect one part of the enterprise that has only a minor interest in the whole application, and the primary application owner may not want to fund the work. Again, only a strong centralized authority can cut through the red tape to avoid additional costs and focus the resources in the best interests of the enterprise.

Organize for Success

The need to assign a central program manager/leader has already been discussed. It is time now to talk about the other key players who will work for and with that leader. The number of people required will vary by organization size and the talents of the individuals involved; nevertheless, each of the following roles should be accounted for in one form or another.

Awareness Coordinator

The awareness coordinator performs different functions during the project. At the outset, this person performs the role of publicist, defining and explaining the problem, which is a full-time job. One difficulty for the person filling this role is that outside the data-processing organization there will, no doubt, be significant resistance to the cost of doing work that has no apparent payoff. Later, this job will change to one of coordination.

The awareness coordinator prepares the application support teams to release their applications for changes to the date processes while keeping them consistent with business changes. The person in this role also must ensure that the applications can continue to run while operating-system software is changed and vendor software changes are implemented.

The awareness coordinator also works with end users. A good coordinator will uncover context problems that occur when users do such things as put 00 or 99 in the year fields to force sorting of records in a way that simplifies the use of the data. The coordinator may also identify places where users have discovered weaknesses in the system, such as a failure to adequately validate data entry resulting in nonnumeric data appearing in date fields. This process is called *discovery*. Discovery prevents two problems: (1) the failure of the system when it is put back into production (testers check only for what they expect, not for what they don't know), and (2) the wrath of users who find they have no way to perform a function they have been performing for years.

The awareness coordinator may also double as end-user trainer. When it is necessary for the data-processing staff to change the way an application accepts or presents data, the awareness coordinator will be in the best position to explain the necessity and the reason for the solution being implemented.

Vendor Manager

No one person will be more important than the one who keeps track of all the vendors. As you now realize, changes will be made in hardware, application and system software, and incoming and outgoing data. The latter—data changes—may include requirements imposed by regulatory agencies, suppliers, or clients.

Because software vendors will not be eager to make commitment dates, the vendor manager will have to stay on top of the vendors to track changes in schedules and the way they are addressing the date problem within their products. While standards do exist, survival is the issue for many of these companies, and they will be doing what they can for the least expense. As mentioned previously, do not be surprised if some of these vendors simply give up and go out of business. And even if you have copies of the vendor's code in escrow in a safe-deposit box somewhere, it will probably not prove to be of much use. Undocumented code of any type poses a daunting task for any organization. The vendor manager will have to try to anticipate late or failed deliveries.

Supply-Chain Manager

It's hard to even imagine an enterprise that is not dependent on outside providers. Consequently, utilities, service providers, and commodity vendors will all need to be tracked. Many will be affected by changes to the organization's applications, which may be as minimal as report or form changes or as significant as the requirements for data in formats needed for millennium-compliant applications. The supply-chain manager may have to work with other organizations to coordinate these demands on suppliers.

The supply-chain manager also fills the role of information provider to the suppliers, monitoring them to make sure they take the date problem seriously and assessing the suppliers' responses. If the supplier is not going to meet your deadline, it is the supply-chain manager's responsibility to determine what action to take: to delay schedules, acquire additional reserves, or find a new supplier.

Technical Coordinator

The technical coordinator manages changes to the data-processing environment. As changes are made to the systems software, this person works to minimize the testing and to coordinate changes to the applications. This person also works with the hardware and systems software providers to determine the impact of vendor decisions on the organization's data-processing capability and to coordinate hardware replacement and migrations with the vendors and the staff.

The technical coordinator may also be required to direct replacement of the PCs that cannot be upgraded to function properly beyond December 31, 1999. After the century change, many applications will not be able to run under the current operating system. For example, computers using DOS versions that are no longer supported will require replacement. Many vendors will move to the latest version of MS Windows, which may require more memory or even processor speed changes that will force the organization to replace its hardware. Older PCs that have been put into use as printer servers or in other roles may not be able to perform those menial functions any longer because their internal clocks will not function as required to show the correct date.

Quality Assurance Manager

This role does not exist in most organizations today. It was abandoned when it became popular to make everyone in the data-processing organization accountable for quality. But in this project, the quality assurance manager plays a key role in containing the problem by monitoring the acquisition of software to ensure that it's all 2000-compliant and by monitoring routines to ascertain whether they handle dates according to standards.

Testing is also the responsibility of the quality assurance manager. He or she must ensure that testing goes beyond proving that the application works the way it is supposed to. He or she must guarantee that the applications cannot be broken. This means, for example, in the case of the century change, testing not only for 1999 but for 2099 as well. If dates are stored in binary formats, the quality assurance manager has to test all binary combinations to make sure that they are converted correctly. Finally, he or she has to enforce testing of data coming in from the outside to make sure that internal data is not corrupted.

Purchasing Coordinator

The purchasing coordinator is the liaison with the purchasing department, the one who influences vendors to meet commitments. This person also works with purchasing to assure that new purchases are century-compliant.

Legal Coordinator

One or more people from the enterprise's legal staff may be required on the team. A legal presence is necessary not only to work with purchase and maintenance contracts, but also to make sure that contracts entered into by the enterprise include force majeure clauses, which make nonperformance due to others' inabilities to overcome Year 2000 problems as excusable as any other natural disaster.

Legal staff members play a key role in defining product compliance, risks, and negotiating prices reflective of millennium-compliance benefits and risks. They work with vendors who have changed product names to make sure that the vendors retain responsibility under the terms of any contracts. If you need to make changes to vendor software, they obtain the appropriate releases. They renegotiate services for products whose contracts have lapsed or that have had warranties voided due to unauthorized code changes.

The legal coordinator works with accountants, executive management, and the board of directors to minimize financial liabilities, continuing coverage by director and officer insurance, and business continuation insurance. The legal coordinator also plays a key role in keeping the enterprise out of collateral litigation due to failure to meet regulations, injury or death arising out of supplier failures, or actions based on incorrect data.

Process Manager

Throughout the correction process, it is important to oversee the update team because measurement of daily work may be key to the success of the project overall. To repeat the opening of this chapter: People are your most important resource; you cannot afford to have anyone sitting on his or her hands waiting for others. The process manager will be responsible for finding these problems and identifying the causes and possible solutions.

From time to time, the process manager also defines tool requirements and process changes or makes recommendations for further training or staff alterations. This requires the process manager to constantly search for new tools. He or she may participate in testing and evaluation of tools to see how they perform. The process manager also needs to keep abreast of how well tool vendors are responding to problem reports and difficulties found with the tools owned.

Tools Manager

Software tools will not remain static; they will change as vendors receive additional requirements and make alterations to add functions or fix what does not always work. The tools manager coordinates these changes, provides instruction, communicates requirements, and makes sure that new people receive coaching on the use of the tools.

The tools manager also supervises the internal development of tools to handle unique processes that are not supported by vendor-supplied tools. Internally developed tools may change data, track suppliers, handle special file accesses, alter enterprise calendars, or provide date processes that are unique to the enterprise.

The Others

Obviously, it will be necessary to have on staff those people—analysts and programmers—who actually make the changes to the enterprise's software. But this is not as simple as just assigning everyone to a change team. There will be special demands. You will still have to support applications that have not been made century-compliant as regulatory and data requirement changes are made by other organizations. Some staff may have to write new technical file interface programs or take on PC rescue missions to save end-user-created programs that require changes, but for which the end user lacks resources to implement those changes. This may require learning PC database applications and spreadsheet macrolanguages.

Process Management and Continuous Improvement

Those enterprises that are careful to define the process, measure the workflow through each stage, and then take action to improve that workflow will achieve the best results in managing both costs and cycle time. They also will be best able to adapt to changes in schedules, shifting priorities, and defections in the workforce.

Setting up a process management environment is a three-step activity:

1. Defining the activity
2. Describing the work
3. Measuring the work

Defining the Activity

Activity definition involves identification of all activities required by the organization to update the system, from preparation to change applications through migration to production. Defining the activity can be done by bringing the representatives of the various line organizations together in a design session, which may take from one to three days depending on the complexity of the environment. Do this on the basis of the computing platform because the process differs for each. This first effort will take longer because the processes that follow need only to identify differences, and this can often be completed in hours rather than days.

During this step, identify accountability for each activity. It is also necessary so that activities are delineated. Many people prefer to do this by separating activities into sets of tasks that are related but that report to different people. This method tends to resist change and improvement, however; only by breaking the activity at the lines of authority is it possible for a change to be made, which means the process ends when accountability for the product is transferred to another person. For example, while a contractor may be responsible for building the whole house, he or she makes the plumber accountable for the plumbing, the electrician accountable for wiring, and so on. In IT organizations, different people have specific domains for which they are responsible. Nobody is allowed to cross those lines of authority.

Other activity delimiters include changes in skill requirements and the use of specific hardware or software tools. For example, the knowledge requirements for making changes to a COBOL program are significantly different from those required to make changes to an assembly language program. They use different talents, may employ different tools, and require variable time frames to obtain the same effective throughput. If, for example, the activity is moved from one computer to another, the person will require a different set of skills (e.g., operating the computer) and knowledge (e.g., working with operating systems, job-scheduling languages, and compilers). This is important if the activity is to be improved later.

Describing the Work

Workflow description is done by the people who do the work. Taking the process definition prepared in the first step, they perform a test update project. Try using a small project consisting of not more than 100,000 lines of code. The system selected should be one that will exercise as many of the defined activities as possible. For instance, in an environment that uses database management, communications management, and PC development tools, you will want to select an application in which all of these are encountered and, therefore, subjected to the update procedure.

Throughout the process, the workflow definition team should document each task, the tools it uses, and its knowledge requirements. When problems are encountered, the team should identify them and refer them to the person named accountable for those process activities. During the initial run, you may find that additional process activities are defined. At the end of the test, you should have a set of processes in which the inputs and outputs are clearly defined and the boundaries of responsibility are set.

Measuring the Work

Measurement is key to achieving efficiency. However, do not expect to measure the first use of the process, since that should be regarded as an exercise of documentation and problem resolution. Subsequent exercises of the process will be necessary to determine process timing. Choose small applications with similar attributes to work the bugs out of the process (do not repeat the same application conversion, as familiarity will alter the effort measurements and you want to make progress as quickly as possible).

During a second run, you may wish to ask someone *not involved* in the effort to observe the volume and time attributes of the run. You may wish to establish anticipated time frames based on the skills of the people involved in performing the tasks so that allowances can be made for those with greater or lesser skill. At the end of this second run-through, you should be able to identify where the bottlenecks could occur, where volume could slow the process, and where dependencies on skilled resources exist.

You should have enough information not only to manage the process, but to take a number of actions to improve workflow. You may decide to purchase or build a tool. You may choose to scale the work, creating more pipeline segments to distribute the work to several individuals. You may see the need to provide training in the use of tools or to subdivide the activities. This exercise is key to process management and performance improvement. It does not end with a first or second run-through of a process, but is ongoing. Constant change in the types of code handled, tools used, people skills available, and application knowledge require ongoing adaptations of the process.

Reducing Skill Dependencies

A well-documented process includes the three steps just defined and identifies how to deal with exceptions. At this juncture, decision making should be minimized, and the number of people included in communications should be reduced to a single person—the individual identified as accountable for a particular activity.

As the demands for skilled computer people increase, you will be faced with rising costs and, perhaps, increased defections from your current labor pool. The labor pool of experienced programmers with the knowledge required is finite. It can take a year, for example, to train a person in COBOL, DB2, and CICS, putting a drain on your staff while you train newcomers. The demand for these people will rise and push salaries upward. Since most organizations have rules that limit the size of raises, you may fall behind the competition, thereby forcing your own people to go elsewhere. But having the processes clearly defined will mitigate these defections. A new person with the appropriate skills can be handed the descriptions of the processes they are expected to perform and become proficient in the shortest amount of time.

Once the process descriptions are completely defined, you can also begin distributing work to individuals who may not be fully skilled in all aspects of the work or even familiar with the makeup of the organization. Clerical staff already employed by the company can perform many tedious and redundant tasks currently performed by skilled computer experts. (Many of these less-demanding tasks are now being done by your most highly paid technical staff.) The lack of process descriptions, low volume, and infrequency of the work required have prevented this from happening. You cannot bring a person into an organization and make him or her a part of the process in less than two days. If the work lasts only a day or two, bringing someone in is not practical. The advantage of solving this Year 2000 problem is that it creates new opportunities, as the need to do many of these tasks becomes constant.

Less-skilled workers can be part of an assembly line: finding lines with dates in them, creating test data, changing screens or reports, and more. Key employees may be able to supervise the work of more staff because they won't be as involved in providing orientation, training, or coaching.

Building a Factory

Many organizations have found it productive to build a *factory* to which the code is sent. This factory takes the existing code, makes the changes, compiles the code to make sure that it is error-free, and returns the code. These factory workers must be familiar with all the available date routines, know the tools to identify all the dates, and be able to use code-update and editing tools to make the changes. They also should be able to identify processes that need redesign.

If standards have been established, factory personnel can use them as a guide to implement the changes. Where the standards fail to address the redesign work, they should create exception reports and return them to those who best understand the application and can make the necessary decisions or changes.

Normally, a factory includes a team that works with the application support staff. This team identifies and gathers the components to be changed and creates requirements for bridge programs and data-conversion programs that can be built in the factory. It also defines special testing requirements that will have to be performed after the code is processed by the factory.

At the back end of the factory, where the code has been changed but not tested, the same team that supports the preparation also facilitates processing the exceptions and scheduling tests. These staff members may be skilled at data creation using tools and may manage regression testing for the organization. Normally, the testing, data conversion, and migration are left to the application support teams.

Create Talent Pools

You will want to assess your staffing and perform a skills inventory. It is essential to identify critical talent requirements, which may fall into two distinct groups. The first is technical talent, those people who know the operating system software, the coding languages, and the available productivity and management tools. The second group includes those staff members who know the processes used by the enterprise, the applications, and their users.

The technical talent forms the skill backbone of the staff who change the code and move the code and data into production. This group should consist of programmers fluent in each of the languages employed, database administrators who know the data and file management tools used, communications specialists who have knowledge of the communications management software, and a technical support staff member familiar with the operating system as it was installed and all utilities that are provided to support it.

The second group provides your decision support and usually consists of experienced analysts and management personnel. Few people know more about the organization than the managers. They may be, or may have been, project managers, senior systems analysts, or business analysts. They generally have come up through the ranks and have been involved in the implementation of the systems. For the most part, these people should be familiar with the systems that have been identified as critical to the enterprise during the triage process.

Identifying these two groups has several benefits that will manifest themselves in the following discussions. The primary point here is that these people form the core update team, and thus will be critical to the success or failure of the entire project. These are the people who must be kept on staff at all costs. It is not, however, necessary that these individuals report to the project manager; rather, it is important that they be available to the project manager whenever required to provide training and advice to the teams performing changes.

Tiger Teams

It may not be necessary for anyone in the preceding two groups of critical talent to actually be involved in the changing of application code. Together, they own the context, or the environment, in which the decisions and changes are to be made. Consequently, you still need people experienced with date changes and problems.

Over the last seven years, industry research has found that knowledge of date processing and the way that dates are handled is more important than application knowledge. People familiar with date processing are better at making redesign decisions; they are less concerned about the application and thus less likely to make ancillary changes to improve performance or alter style. They also are more likely to enforce standards, use common date routines, identify processes that require business decisions, and employ tools. These people are called *tiger teams*.

A tiger team often provides a significant productivity improvement factor. Working closely together to achieve a common goal, the members are the most likely to continuously improve the process, to assimilate new tools, and to take pride in the speed and accuracy of their work. They generally are more willing to seek advice and expertise from the technical and organization specialists. Tiger teams also are more likely to create mechanisms to deal with conflict and thus handle it most diplomatically.

Forming Tiger Teams

Instead of delegating the correction problem to the organization as a whole, form one or more tiger teams to perform the date changes. Select people who make good use of tools to perform their work. You may start the team with some of the critical talent pool members, but they should be replaced as soon as possible. Those people will be in constant demand to fill knowledge gaps and maintain progress toward deadlines. Tiger team members should be among those who most willingly accept change: They get involved with the newest computer languages, take advantage of technologies such as the Internet, and aggressively seek recognition.

The formation of tiger teams also solves a major problem that most organizations face. Sometimes, being assigned to the problem-repair team may be viewed as a demotion—after all, you are trying to keep your old systems alive, which means fixing old code (in other words, *maintenance*). Maintenance is often considered a task for the inexperienced. Many organizations that have tried to recruit internally for staff to fix old code have met with dismal failure. Nobody wants the job.

Creating tiger teams alters this picture. Everybody in an organization knows who the stars are. Getting these stars on a single team immediately gives the group a certain cachet. Membership on the team is then regarded as a learning experience and an opportunity. Should you lose a member of the team, it becomes easier to recruit replacements. As the members of the tiger teams become proficient with all the tools used in the process, they can be redeployed into the organization to serve as tool advocates and to provide guidance to teams involved in repairing applications that break down due to date problems.

Flying Squad

Face it, things are going to break down. Between 1998 and 2000, anticipate many system failures. Remember, you will not be able to test for everything, and these untested systems will create problems. To cope with them, form a *flying squad.* This squad should consist of three to five of those critical talent pool members who are also skilled in making date changes and using all the tools at the enterprise's disposal. Whenever a breakdown occurs, the flying squad sends in a member to diagnose the problem and provide direction to the application support team to make the repairs. If the support team is inadequately skilled to make the changes in the time required, the flying-squad member can enlist the aid of other team members to make the change and get the application back into production.

Flying-squad teammates can be gleaned from the tiger teams. They should be the most capable and most technically well rounded because they will be faced with multiple platforms, languages, and crisis situations. This squad needs to be empowered to act. In many situations, members will need security clearance to access and make changes to the code or the data. A small group of trusted individuals can be given this level of authority and access.

Large organizations with multiple code-development sites may find it efficient to create a flying squad at the beginning of the update project. This team can take the knowledge of how to define and establish an update process to each of the sites and build a process tailored to that site. A flying squad of this type could consist of no more than three people, each adept at process definition and facilitation, to focus on the topics of applications, quality assurance, and tools usage.

Keeping Project Staff

The number one problem facing most Year 2000 project managers is finding *and keeping* the right skills. The work is tedious, repetitive, not particularly stimulating, and certainly does nothing to enhance a resume after 1999. Worse yet, there is not much of a sense of accomplishment in making a program work exactly as it did before and not fail when the date clicks over the century. Also, as competition for resources heats up, staff will be tempted to go to the company offering the largest monetary rewards.

Money

In the face of these obstacles, how can you attract, motivate, and, most importantly, retain the right staff for the duration of the project? Since the job content won't do it, a more creative approach is called for. Although job satisfaction is traditionally the most effective motivator of technical people, the next best way to their hearts is simply money. A carefully planned monetary incentive program may be the pivotal factor between success and failure, but it must have two characteristics. First, there must be enough incentive in the program to offset the lure of the people pirates calling your staff. Second, the pay out must be deferred so that the reward is for staying the course as well as for meeting the milestones.

The IT shop of one large commercial firm, which does not wish to be identified, has devised such a scheme and it has proved to be very effective. It has set up a deferred payment bonus scheme that rewards getting the job done early. The Year 2000 team is considered to consist of two types of players, and a separate bonus program has been set up for each. Those who work directly on the code conversion and related activities are the Project Team, and those whose work spans the entire project are the Support Team.

The work done by the Project Team is characterized by a series of work elements that can be directly measured as being complete. The repaired code either passes the test or it does not. For example, taking one programming component through the analysis, making the code changes, and performing the development-level testing would be a single work element. This work element typically entails contributions by several Project Team members, such as the manager, one or more analysts, the programming lead, several programmers, testers, configuration management coordinators, and others. Each work element has a standard development time, say, 24 person-hours. Work packages are defined, usually consisting of a major application or family of applications. A typical work package might contain 80 to 150 programs or elements. The package is scheduled according to the standard development time for each element. Based on this planning, a master schedule for the work package is published, showing the expected completion date for each element. Completing a work element on or before the development schedule results in a dollar bonus for the Project Team. The amount of this bonus increases sharply the sooner the work is done, and decreases the later it is done (see Figure 7.1).

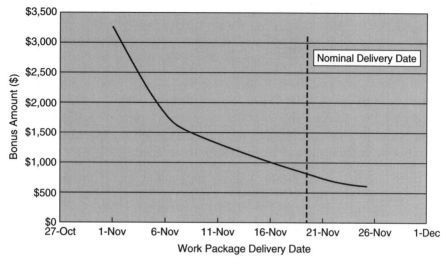

Figure 7.1 Bonus amounts based on work package delivery date.

It should be noted that, although the scheduling is done using a standardized model for the development effort, no one expects that all elements will take the same time to complete. Some will obviously take more, others less. These discrepancies are expected to average out over a reasonably sized work package. Moreover, the bonus is not determined by the number of hours spent, but rather is based on the delivery date of the work package. Thus, if the delivery is made ahead of schedule, an increased bonus is earned. This allows the team to put in extra hours (unpaid for salaried workers) in order to better the schedule, without penalizing the earned bonus. The important thing here is delivery date, not short-cutting the work. As an aside, exempt workers should be required to report their actual hours worked—even though they don't get paid for the overtime—so that the standardized estimating model can be improved in the future.

Once the total bonus amount is determined according to the delivery dates of the packages, it is allocated to the Project Team employees according to a published table. For example, the manager might get 5 percent, the lead programmer 15 percent, tester 10 percent, and so forth. Some portion of the bonus amount is reserved for discretionary awards to participants outside of the project, such as operations, facilities, or others who made significant contributions to meeting or bettering the completion schedule. The Project Team manager decides how to award this portion.

The bonus awards are not paid out until some significant milestone is reached, typically the installation of the complete application work package. This encourages the participants to stay the course, at least until after the important deadlines. Bonuses are only paid to those still on the payroll at the milestone. In other words, they must be present to win. As a further incentive to stay onboard, a matching bonus is banked until the year 2000, or until the employee's defined contribution to the program is finished. This effectively doubles the bonus award for each participant willing to stay with the company until all of the dust has cleared. For key players, the amount of money involved is substantial; but then, it must be, in order to offset the lucrative offers that can be expected over the next 15 (and counting) months. Contractors are not eligible to participate in the bonus incentives. They are covered by contracts for specified periods of time, and besides, their rates already contain incentives.

The Support Team consists of those staff members responsible for planning, training, process development, equipment and software acquisition, program awareness, budget allocation, and myriad other jobs needed to make the project succeed. Their efforts are not easily tracked to a specific code-repair project, but rather form the infrastructure that makes the real work possible. For these players, a different incentive bonus scheme is used. An amount equal to a percentage of each person's total annual compensation is banked each month. The percentage banked goes up each year as year 2000 approaches. For example, the percentage for 1997 might have been 2 percent; for 1998, it might be 3 percent; 1999, 4 percent; and in 2000, 6 percent. A person earning $50,000 per year in 1998 would have $1,500 banked each month, for a total of $18,000 for 1998. A portion of the total banked sum is paid out to the employee at each major Year 2000 project milestone. These milestones are usually the same as the ones at which the Project Team bonuses are paid. There is always enough money in the banked bonuses to make staying with the company and the project attractive, but intermediate rewards for getting the work out ahead of schedule are also provided.

Although money is not the only way to retain and motivate the staff, it is certainly one of the simplest. With contract COBOL programmers likely to command up to $300 *per hour* over the next year, a carefully devised management strategy to prevent total churning within the staff is essential. Of course, some of the staff will remain loyal and stay for other reasons. The bonus program will reward these people as well and keep them competitive within the marketplace and thinking about the work and not the better job down the street.

Another approach used by some firms specializing in these types of complex projects is to use the Year 2000 project as an incentive to bring the IT shops to a *process orientation* (using process development as described earlier) rather than to remain strictly project-based. The staff members that participate in and understand this shift to the process paradigm are the clear winners from a career perspective. Their work is more predictable and controllable, and often more rewarding than it was during normal times.

Other Incentives

Companies that expect to do well by achieving early compliance may also choose to set up a financial award program that includes stock incentives. Other enterprises may offer retirement packages to people who remain through the crisis. A combination of programs may be the best option to keep both younger and more senior staff.

Awarding vacation time is yet another option, especially for newer employees who would not otherwise be eligible. Providing for sabbaticals at the end of the crisis also is a significant enticement for experienced personnel. These sabbaticals can range from an extended time away to paid programs to learn new skills.

Many organizations have let their educational reimbursement programs languish. They have not kept pace with rising tuition rates, nor have they remained flexible so that employees can elect programs not directly involved with their work assignments. Thus, providing credits toward education to be obtained after work hours or after the crisis can be a powerful incentive to many. It will especially appeal to those who would like career changes and increased responsibility. Such programs benefit the enterprise, not only during the crisis but also later, when these people choose to remain with the enterprise as a result of the education benefits.

Empowerment can't be taken to the bank; nevertheless, it is a strong motivator. Building the workflow process creates significant opportunities for empowering the organization to improve itself. Reward systems that support empowerment—such as suggestion plans and acknowledgement awards—provide motivation to stay with the enterprise, with the promise of future advancement and increased responsibility.

Whatever incentive plan you initiate, remember, people are the single most important resource for your Year 2000 project. Make sure your staff is happy and that you are doing everything in your power to reward members for their efforts.

In the next chapter, "A Date with Destiny," the Year 2000 problem is described in more technical detail and the nitty gritty of the work involved for making your systems Year 2000–compliant is discussed.

CHAPTER 8

A Date with Destiny

It's restating the obvious by now to say that the Year 2000 problem is caused by how dates are stored in computers; specifically, there's no standard way to store these dates. This chapter delves deeper into the standardization factor and offers two approaches for confronting the date challenge destined to be disruptive.

To begin, review some of the common ways dates are stored before considering the approaches for dealing with this convoluted situation:

- Dates can be stored as number strings, character strings, or a combination of the two.

- They can be four positions long (month and year), five positions (year and days), six positions (year, month, day in three different sequences), or more (the winner, so far, is sixty-four positions in length).

- They can be stored with a century prefix, with a century flag, or without a century prefix.

- They can be stored with delimiters (for example, /, -, a blank space, or a period).

- They can be stored in strings, as a compressed numeric (where two digits exist in the same space as a character), or as a binary number.

- They can be stored with or without an arithmetic sign: +/−.

Conversely, some programmers don't store the date at all, but instead use a counter that calculates the number of clock cycles elapsed since some base date such as January 1, 1600, or January 4, 1980. Many of these clocks, because of the space allocated to the counter, will roll over to a value of zero during the next century.

The International Standards Organization (ISO) standard allows dates to be stored in all these ways:

DATE	COMPLETE REPRESENTATION		TRUNCATED REPRESENTATION	
	BASIC FORMAT	EXT. FORMAT	BASIC FORMAT	EXT. FORMAT
April 15, 1995	19950415	1995-04-15	950415	95-04-15
April 15 (any yr)	N/A*	N/A	—0415	—04-15
15th of (any mo, yr)	N/A	N/A	—15	N/A
April 1995	1995-04	N/A	-9504	-95-04
1995	1995	N/A	-95	N/A
1995 week 15, Sat.	1995W156	1995-W15-6	95W156	95-W15-6
1995 week 15	1995W15	1995-W15	95W15	95-W15
Any Saturday	N/A	N/A	-6	N/A
1995 day 105	1995105	1995-105	95105	95-105
x5 day 105 (any decade)	N/A	N/A	5-105	N/A
Day 105 of any year	N/A	N/A	-105	N/A

* N/A = Not allowed. Another way of stating this is that the only allowed formats are the ones shown.

Then there's the American National Standards Institute (ANSI), which says dates can

- Be represented as all numeric
- Be presented in year, month, day order
- Contain no delimiters
- Show months in the form 01 to 12
- Show days in Gregorian date views in the form 01 to 28, 29, 30, or 31 (based on month and accounting for leap years)

And to complicate things further, ANSI allows this alternative: The two high-order digits can be omitted if the century referenced is the current century. Of course, ANSI does require that when this representation is used, the phrase "year of the century" be employed in defining the representation. Another option is to use only one digit for the year. In such instances, you must use the term "year of the decade" in the description.

In the United States, programmers are subjected to the following standards, which cover representation of dates in ordinal, or Julian, formats as well as the representation of time. At a Year 2000 forum in 1996, a GTE representative shared the following list of standards the organization must comply with in order to satisfy regulators and customers. The number and variety of standards, as listed in the following table, shows the scope of the problem and leads to additional testing and documentation so that each regulating body can be assured that their standards have been met.

DOMAIN	STANDARD
Department of Defense	FIPS-4-1 (Revised 1996-03-25) procurements
SQL	ANSI X3.135-1992, ISO-IEC 9075:1992, or FIPS 127-2
Exchange of call-billing data	Bellcore SR-STS-00320 (EMI)
Credit, debit, and ATM cards	ISO-IEC 7813, or ISO 4909
Electronic commerce	ASC X12 (EDI draft std.), ISO 9735, or UN/EDIFACT
International concerns for interoperability	ISO 8601

Each of the standards organizations has attempted to create standards that are realistic and relatively easy to comply with. There are some inconsistencies in the formatting of dates allowed in the standards previously listed. They try to regulate the type of date format used in specific instances. But it would be naive, even foolhardy, to assume that everyone—or even anyone—has adhered to these standards in all situations, free as the ISO standards show them to be. Some date-formatting practices defy rational explanation. Here's a sample:

- CYYMMDD—where *C* represents the two digits of the century; 0 is 19, 1 is 20 (there are some instances where 1 is equivalent to 18)
- SCYYMMDD—where *S* stands for a sign and −1 is 18, 0 is 19, and +1 is 20
- AAMMDD—where *AA* is an alphabetic with A0 equal to the year 2000, A1 the year 2001, B0 the year 2010
- SSSYY—where *SSS* represents the season

Some of these formats do not require changes, but implementing a standard fix could create a problem if they are not recognized. Automated Year 2000 conversion packages have to be specially programmed to bypass such dates or to work around them using special instructions. In some instances (e.g., SSSYY), correction may be unnecessary. Some vendors have chosen to adopt them (Hewlett-Packard decided to use the AAMMDD format as a standard).

This can cause significant rework in applications that use data either passed to or received from those applications.

How to Approach Ground Double-Zero

All of this standardization has resulted in two common approaches to solving the Year 2000 date problem, but they require you to first ignore all the unusual date-storage practices and focus on the most frequently used—the Gregorian YYMMDD, MMDDYY, and DDMMYY, or the ordinal/Julian YYDDD. The first approach is called the *logical approach;* the other is the *physical approach.* It would follow, then, that in most applications, it must be a simple matter of choosing the approach that is right for you and your enterprise. But in keeping with the contrariness of the Year 2000 problem, be assured that no matter which approach you prefer, you will find situations where it is best to use the other.

Let's Get Physical

The two approaches differ in both time and cost. The primary difference is in whether you change the data. The logical approach retains the data in the format in which it currently exists. The physical approach requires you to change the data so that it contains four digits, including the two digits of the century.

When people in the industry first began to talk about fixing the Year 2000 problem years ago, they said that the only option was to change the data, thereby making the data accurate and reducing the number of design changes required. Think about it: If you compared two dates that both contained the century, you wouldn't have to worry about having to change most of the logic.

```
IF EXPIRATION-DATE < TODAYS-DATE THEN …
```

When EXPIRATION-DATE equals 20000101 and TODAYS-DATE is 19991201, the process works fine, but if EXPIRATION-DATE equals 000101 and TODAYS-DATE is 991201, the comparison fails, and logic must be inserted to work with the dates.

If you change the data, then the typical processes of computing, sorting, locating, and comparing will continue to work without modification. Because less of the code is changed, there is a chance for less testing. If you reduce testing (typically three to four times the effort of changing code), then you save precious time, and code should function correctly until January 1 of year 10000.

There is a price to pay, though. Changing the data means you have to write conversion programs and temporary bridge programs that create files in the old format to allow unchanged programs to read the data. This adds programming time and requires testing of programs. Writing these programs requires you to study the data and even fix it where the data is bad. Although these programs are not hard to write, and many code-generator programs make them relatively trivial, they still must be written and tested.

The insertion of bridges adds to the processing clock, making certain jobs run longer. Field expansion can add to the data-storage requirements, necessitating more data storage media and even devices. Plus, screens and reports need to be changed, sometimes requiring redesign. There are ways of changing the data definitions so that both changed and unchanged programs can read the same data. The following is a COBOL example.

Where the original data definition is

```
15 INDATE-YYMMDD.
   20 INDATE-YY PIC X(02).
   20 INDATE-MM PIC X(02).
   20 INDATE-DD PIC X(02).
```

the data field could be expanded, and the revised file definition could be changed to read as follows:

```
15 INDATE-CCYYMMDD.
   20 INDATE-CCYY PIC X(04).
   20 FILLER PIC X(04).
15 INDATE-WITHCC REDEFINES INDATE-CCYYMMDD.
   20 FILLER PIC X(02).
   20 INDATE-YYMMDD.
   25 INDATE-YY PIC X(02).
   25 INDATE-MM PIC X(02).
   25 INDATE-DD PIC X(02).
```

It would then be necessary only to recompile the unchanged code to include the new file definition. The revised programs would use INDATE-CCYYMMDD in place of INDATE-YYMMDD, and INDATE-CCYY in place of INDATE-YY. These changes are easy to make with a program editor tool.

It's Logical

If, however, you can retain the data as is, with only two digits for the year, you can save the cost of creating conversion programs, building bridges, and expanding the data-storage space. You can even continue to ignore the bad data that might exist in your files (nobody noticed it before). Further, you won't have to worry about changes to screens and reports, where changes require interaction with the application user and modification of training, documentation, and speed of data entry.

You would start by adding logic to the programs. You could insert vendor-supplied routines (windows) that artificially and temporarily expand the date by supplying some implied century or explicitly add proprietary code to test the range of the years, as in, "If date 1 > 50 and date 2 < 49 then. . . ."

The two-digit, or logical, approach requires more code redesign and thus more testing. Inserting the routines to supply the century information involves some programming and testing time. In situations where processing cycle time is critical, these additional instructions could alter the length of the computer run. These are the obvious penalties.

The less-obvious problems come from several places. First, you are assuming that the processing of dates is correct in the first place and that the data is correct. Second, you believe you know the range of the dates in the files and that they can be handled by a single process. Third, you are adding to the complexity of the code, which means there is more opportunity for problems that will cause breakdowns in the future, thereby increasing maintenance costs. Dilemmas also arise when you consider how to enter and display data with only two digits. Also, data entry tends to be much more difficult because whoever inputs data must start making decisions about it. Today, when a data-entry clerk receives a form that reads "990102" or "010299," he or she can safely assume that the month is January. But what happens with "010102"? Ambiguity. In the first 12 years of the century, without any obvious numerical way to distinguish between years and months, dates will be entered inconsistently, and errors will be much harder to spot and verify.

The same is true of displays. A single report in England displayed the date in the formats MMDDYY, YYMMDD, and the European standard DDMMYY. Needless to say, this caused major confusion. The only way to avoid such confusion is to change the way the data is displayed so that it is always presented in the same format.

There is no right answer, and both strategies entail compromises. Nevertheless, people *do* report an immediate benefit from retaining the two-digit-year format. Reports indicate a 20 to 30 percent reduction in the cost versus what they expected to pay if they made all the dates four digits. (Keep in mind that nobody does it both ways and gathers real statistics.) If you can achieve these savings, then retaining two-digit years is faster; and if time is short, with an impending event horizon, the choice is obvious.

Pick Your Poison

So, what is the best solution? When the pressure is on to meet a date, your only option appears to be the logical approach; but you will be making the sacrifices mentioned. Over the long run, the physical approach costs less because the logical approach introduces more errors and depends on the use of a technique called *windowing,* which is described shortly. But windows do not work forever and eventually have to be closed.

You will have to set your own priorities and then weigh the consequences. Again, you probably will have to make this decision for each application you change. To make the decision that is right for you, you need to evaluate the following factors for *each and every* application:

Time needed to change the code

Cost to change the code

Availability of resources to change the code or the data

Time and cost required to change the data

Time required to process the data

Amount of data to be changed

Cost of maintenance over time

Remember, no matter which option you choose, you cannot escape the cost of testing, which usually demands that you make trade-offs. There is still the problem of what to do with flags, bad date routines, unusual logic, and so on. Another reminder: Neither solution even attempts to deal with the less-common date-formatting standards.

Windows, Bridges, and Wrappers

Here, windows and bridges are described more fully. Another popular technique for dealing with dates is added to the mix: using *wrappers.*

Doing Windows

The windows method for dealing with dates comes in two forms: *fixed* and *sliding.* Both assume a 100-year period. A typical 100-year period is from 1950 to 2049. This might be used as a fixed window of time. A fixed window uses a base year that is dependent on the data. If, for instance, the data does not include a year prior to, say, 1984, you can set the base year at 1984. Then logic can be inserted that enables users to look at any year in the data and assign a century based on the knowledge that, for years between 84 and 99, the century prefix can be assumed to be 19. Subsequent logic in this example then assumes that any year from 00 to 83 can be assigned the century prefix 20.

If you take the current year and subtract 10 and determine the century (e.g., 1997 minus 10 is 1987), you can assume 87 to 99 has a century value of 19. Anything else has a century value of 20—an implied value.

This sliding window works well through 2010, *if* the old data is not kept longer than 10 years and nothing is entered incorrectly with 00 or until the data refers to the year 2087, where the century value is incorrectly implied. You could use a sliding window of 20, which then works well until 2020. Sliding windows are used only with data that is not intended to be retained for a long period of time. If you handle five-year subscriptions, for example, you know that no subscription will be in the file longer than six years; thus, anything in the file will not be older than six years from the current date.

Although sliding windows appear safer because they apparently will adjust themselves, there is a problem with windows in general. Because there are many different dates stored in data, and each may have a different base year or retention period, it is possible that you might be unable to set a base year for all the date data in the program or even to use a sliding window. Chances are, the base date or duration of the sliding window will have to change several times. (There have been as many as seven changes in a single program.) Therefore, you must be very careful in using windows.

Knowledge of the data is important, and the programs must be well documented so that those who change the code later understand the value of the window when a code change is processed. Not knowing the data can result in the placement of time bombs, which occur when the window logic fails. Many times they are difficult to detect and hard to resolve and, consequently, can cause severe damage to data. Some enterprises have already suffered the penalties of making assumptions about their data.

In one such instance, the window was set to automatically attribute 19 to dates with years above 50, and 20 to dates below 51. The system tracked storage of records and files. The system found records created in 2045 and, because that date was greater than the current date, the system rejected them as invalid. They were put on the logical equivalent of a scrap heap. After several months, it was discovered that the files were missing and all backups of the data had been written-over as part of the regular processing by the system. Restoring the records involved weeks of data sorting, recoding, and data reentry.

Building Bridges

Bridge programs read data in either the two-digit- or four-digit-year format and produce a file with the format of the year reversed. The two-digit year is changed to four. The four-digit to two. Another term for a limited bridge used to trap transactions is *filter*. Bridges (or filters) are inserted into processing routines where the data is read sequentially. Typically, a filter or bridge is placed between transaction entry, updates of master files, sorts, and merges. Bridges are also inserted when it is necessary to create a file that is used by another application.

In situations where the application is changed to use four-digit years and the input from another application remains unchanged, a bridge is installed that regularly runs a conversion program that inserts century information in the date fields, creating a temporary file. Windows are often used in construction of such bridges. A single fixed window can be used to handle the determination of century for the bulk of the dates in the data. As long as it is possible to determine the earliest date stored, the window can provide the century. Obviously, this solution will not work if you have date ranges in a field greater than 100 years or dates that extend back or forward more than 99 years from the present year. For these, you may need to write overrides to the century calculations.

In some cases, the use of a bridge may make it unnecessary to change an application—specifically, when the application is scheduled for replacement. A bridge program can feed two-digit information to that program until its event horizon is reached or until 2000. If a bridge is employed between one application and another that performs only *forward looks* at the data (that is, it does not reference historical information), the application may require only minimal changes. Forward-look applications do not perform operations that cannot be solved by inserting a single sliding window, with the current year as the base, in each of the programs.

Bridge programs are relatively easy to construct. Many programs that automatically alter the programs from two digits to four digits automatically produce a template that is used to construct a bridge. You use the two file formats—the old format with two-digit years and the new one with expanded date fields. The simple part involves providing instructions to pass all the non-date data from one file to the other. A window is turned on, and the date fields that fit the window ranges and are in the common format (character strings in the format of MMDDYY or YYMMDD) are moved. Fields that are being converted from one format to another (e.g., MMDDYY to YYYYMMDD, YYMMDD to YYYYDDD, or from strings to packed-decimal or binary) can also be processed using the window. Turning off the window, the other date fields that cannot be processed through the window can be reformatted by special instructions.

Processing of this nature might include inserting century information based on logical relationships, converting end-of-file records, changing date stamps, and altering record key fields. An example of a logical relationship requirement might be found in a situation where an insurance policy is issued to someone whose birth year is 99 and whose parent's birthday is indicated by the year value of 55, in which case the century prefix for both could be assumed to be 19. If, on the other hand, the child was born in 40 and the parent was born in 99, it would probably be correct to assume the parent was born in 1899. You would then insert an 18 into the parent's century position.

Programmers long ago who used dates to indicate that the last record in a series had been reached created a typical set of problems. This happened because a lot of data is processed in sequence by dates. They created a special record in which the date was 999999—month, day, and year all equal to 99. In some instances, a record was actually entered as 991231 to allow the record to survive internal data-validation rules. The programmers would look for a year equal to 99 to identify the last record and then terminate the processing. Recently, improper logic changes have stopped processing before all the data was read because the program thought the end of the data was reached. In some instances, the end of the data record was treated as the year 1999, the end of file was not detected, and processing continued using data that was supposed to be processed by another set of instructions.

Key fields containing numeric years in two digits have been stripped of the date data and replaced with an alphanumeric sequence code. A *key field* is one that is used to determine where to store data. The electronic file is much like a filing cabinet containing file folders. The key field says which folder and where in the folder to store the data. When the key field is altered, the new data can go to the wrong place, or the old data cannot be found because the program looks in the wrong place for it.

The other type of bridge changes the date data from four-digit years to two-digit years. This might require that changes made by one application be reversed. Assume that every program in one application has already been altered to use century information (e.g., YYYYMMDD, YYYYDDD) and may or may not be stored in a different mode (e.g., binary versus character). This data is used elsewhere in the same application or is passed to another application containing programs that are unprepared to use the dates with century expansion. The new format is as follows:

```
05 INDATE.
   10 INDATE-CCYY PIC 9999.
   10 INDATE-MM    PIC 99.
   10 INDATE-DD    PIC 99.
05 INTERM.
   10 INTERM-CODE PIC XX.
   10 INTERM-PERCENT    PIC V99.
```

Compare to the old format:

```
05 INDATE.
   10 INDATE-MM    PIC XX.
   10 INDATE-DD    PIC XX.
```

```
    10 INDATE-YY  PIC XX.
 05 INTERM REDFINES INDATE.
    10 INTERM-CODE PIC XXXX.
    10 INTERM-PERCENT  PIC V99.
```

The unchanged application expects MMDDYY in the old mode, which may
have allowed the date field to contain nondate data stored in the field
(INTERM). One or more conversion routines are needed. The first routine
would look to see if the INTERM data was stored in the incoming expanded
date record, translate the INTERM-CODE from new to old, and move it to the
output record in the old format. A second routine would change the sequence
of date data and store it in the output record. The routine would take the input
date in the mode in which it exists and create the output date in the mode that
is expected, stripping the leading digits from the year field. In other cases, routines may be required to perform compression, decompression, or conversion
from Gregorian to Julian/ordinal or Julian/ordinal to Gregorian.

Under Wrappers

Wrappers are a relatively new solution to date-processing problems. A *wrapper*
usually has many components, which surround a computer process to trap the
inputs and the outputs. There are two types of wrappers. The first is inserted
directly into the program; the second is installed in the job process control and
is sometimes called an *envelope.*

Wrappers are inserted into the code in both old and newly reformatted programs so that they can share the data concurrently. The wrapper corrects old
date data or reverses new date data as it is read. An example of a typical program wrapper presented at seminars by Peritus Software Services follows.

Old program:

```
READ INPUT-MSTR INTO POLICY
     AT END...
       NOT AT END...
END-READ
WRITE OUT-MSTR FROM POLICY
```

New program:

```
CALL "WR-READ-INPOLICY-RECORD"
   IF AT END > 0...
   IF AT END < 0...
END-READ
CALL "WR-WRITE-OUTPOLICY-RECORD"
```

In this example, the new program's read routine would either insert century
information or eliminate century information using a process similar to that

explained in the discussion of bridges. Such routines are often used in transaction processing where screens and reports may not have enough space to handle the display of four-digit years.

Envelopes are used when there is no time to make the changes required to an application, or when the hardware does not handle the Year 2000 dates. An envelope is a time machine that makes the application function as if it were running 28 years ago! The system date in the machine is set back 28 years, thus extending the life of the equipment.

Creating either type of wrapper requires identification of all the date fields to a program or programs being run in a job stream. An input wrapper program is invoked when a job is started. The first type often is inserted by changing the program control language instructions to run the input wrapper component before the first program is run. This program reads the input files and changes the date fields. The job may require an internal wrapper for transaction input that intercepts on-line interaction and changes the dates before they are received by the program. The transaction wrapper component is usually inserted as a call in the processing program.

As noted, the wrapper program is much like a bridge program. The programmer is required to provide the code to change each date field. Often, windows are employed to assign the correct century prefix in the arithmetic activity. The input wrapper used in an envelope finds all the dates in the input files or intercepted on-line entry transactions and subtracts a specific number of years (28) from them. (If the year being looked at is 00, the window tells the program that it is 2000. Subtracting 28 returns a value of 72, which is written over the 00 in the file.) The wrapper, in essence, rolls the clock back 28 years.

The use of the number 28 is not arbitrary. It is required to keep the days of the week aligned with the calendar for the current year. The wrapper contains the logical operations to deal with the years 1901 through 2099 effectively. Since the years 1900 and 2100 are not leap years, the 28-year rule breaks down, and the days of the week no longer line up.

The second part of an envelope collects all the output and reverses the process—adding 28 years to the dates. There might be many components to the output portion of the wrapper: one dealing with files, another with reports, and still another with interactive messages back to on-line users.

Be careful about where and how you apply and test wrappers. Fiddling with dates can become a legal liability if not handled correctly. Do not use wrappers where you are altering customer- investor- or employee-related data. Errors in applying the wrong dates could lead to legal problems. Moving dates backward could make the data subject to laws that were in effect in the past, but have been altered since then. Applying the old rules could change such things as tax liabilities, inheritance rights, and insurance requirements.

The advantage to wrappers is that they can be time-savers. Some organizations are changing all read and write processes to use wrappers. They indicate to the wrapper, by a constant in the data-definition portion of the program, whether the program is millennium-compliant. The wrapper can thus be used permanently, unlike bridges, after all the programs have been converted.

Getting and Using Windows, Bridges, and Wrappers

Windows, bridges, and wrappers can be built or bought. IBM, for example, has included windows as part of its latest release of COBOL. An increasing number of sort routines are being offered with the capability of windowing so that two-digit year designations can be retained without redefining sort parameters. Sort parameters refer to the positions in the physical data transfer where the date field begins and ends.

Many of the rule-based date-conversion programs generate skeleton code for bridges and data-conversion programs. Combined with a proprietary library of subroutines to execute century insertions, the creation of bridges and data-conversion programs can take minutes instead of hours. Further, the latest code-conversion programs are able to install a window or wrapper in the program that is generated. One intriguing solution, but one still under testing, detects dates automatically as part of a background activity that is like the operating system. It would theoretically handle the dates, assigning the right century number without requiring changes to the programs. Sounds great, but then the concern is over data that look like dates but aren't—how can it determine the difference and avoid creating an error?

The pricing of these tools varies widely. Prices change frequently. Service providers change the code for a per-line rate. Current prices are very high—about three times what they should be, according to estimates of the per-line rate and the effort being saved. If the estimate is, for example, $1.50 per line for the total, the cost of the change should be about 8 to 12 percent. This means the cost should be $.12 to $.18. But expect to pay $.50. Prices were expected to drop rapidly as more services came on-line. Demand increases and requirements for detecting date-related design problems at the factory have kept prices high.

Using windows, bridges, and wrappers effectively and efficiently will, of course, be a management challenge. No matter which of these tools you implement, you will have to keep track of what you implement and where. If yours is an environment in which documentation is only a sometime thing, using these tools is risky.

Installing and uninstalling also requires tracking where to put them and when to get rid of them. Many organizations are finding it necessary to build special programs to track where bridges, wrappers, and windows have been installed. Bridges are the easiest to track. If you can determine that all the jobs, applications, and exports that use a bridge have been made century-compliant, you can remove it. This will increase performance but leave possible time bombs in the code. (A window that only works until 2000—1901 is a valid date—must be removed soon to avoid incorrectly processing 2001 data as 1901 data.) For windows, keep track of the type of window, and, for fixed windows, track the date range. Anticipate using wrappers if you are building a tracking tool.

To Test or Not to Test

The importance of testing has been discussed throughout the book, and the enormity of time it will take—from 40 to 80 percent of the entire update project. Not testing is not an option, but as time runs short (as it already has), there are some places where you might be forced to forgo the testing procedure.

Run down your list of applications: Evaluate those that are necessary for your enterprise's survival, those that are required for you to remain competitive, those that make you a market leader, those that provide information, and finally, those that reduce workloads. Only you can determine whether you will allow yourself to be forced not to test. Remember as you evaluate all this, that the testing load is enormous for critical applications. You will want to perform the following:

Complete test script development for all date processes

Baseline testing to ascertain that all dates between now and the year 2000 are handled correctly

Unit testing to assure that design changes and windows work for dates from the year 2000 for each program that is changed

String testing to make sure that data is sorted correctly and passed from program to program within a job, or from platform to platform within an import or export process

Systems testing to determine that daily, weekly, and other time-dependent processes work correctly

Integration testing to determine whether data bridges and other interfaces between applications work as predicted

Acceptance testing to prove to an application's client/user that all changes are working as planned and the program is ready to be returned to production

Parallel testing to give users time to acclimate to changes, and to make sure that critical processing works through period-ending cycles (quarter and year-end processing)

Regression testing to determine whether changes to feeder applications have not altered processing or introduced errors

Forgoing testing is never acceptable, but in the real world, it happens. More than one enterprise has decided not to perform unit and string testing, in the belief that if the application can meet a set of high-level criteria for century compliance as part of a systems test, then it can be returned to production. Further, the thinking goes, if failures subsequently occur in production, they will probably not be so difficult to fix that the application must be out of production for a significant length of time.

In a somewhat similar vein, some enterprises have decided that any applications that do not yet deal with dates beyond year 1999 be reintroduced to production without any testing, with the intention that the application support teams will provide testing during a normal release cycle. And when applications are not involved with extending or maintaining competitive advantage, enterprises must consider putting them back into production without testing. But forewarned is forearmed: If these applications fail, they will increase the workload and force decisions about how to spend enterprise resources.

So what do you test for? The best guidelines shared in public to date in this regard are provided by GTE and are reproduced here.

CATEGORY	SUBCATEGORY	GUIDELINES
General	Current date	Direct set, power-up rollover Reinitialize from cold start Full date ranges
	Calendar accuracy	Days of week in 2000 and 2001 Leap year in 2000 366 days in 2000; 365 in 2001
	Century ambiguity	High-risk values (1999-09-09, 1999-12-31, 1900-01-01, 2000-01-01, 2000-02-29, 2000-03-01) Ambiguous century in user interface Electronic interfaces (e.g., system date)
Technology-specific	Current date	Power-down continuity System date versus current date
	Date representation	Overflow of base-and-offset representation Standards for Gregorian and ordinal date formats interfaces

CATEGORY	SUBCATEGORY	GUIDELINES
Technology-specific	Date manipulation	Date arithmetic Conversion between representations Sorting, searching, indexing Century designation available in storage and interfaces
Domain-specific	Century ambiguity	Accuracy in inferring century for each field in storage, user interface, and other interfaces
	Date representation	Industry standards and contract requirements Human factors requirements Design and coding standards
	Date manipulation	Access to archived data Manipulation of archived data Extended semantics

A complete testing process should evaluate the applications handling of the following years: 1900, 1980, 1996, 1998, 1999, 2000, 2001, 2002, 2004, 2020, 2028, 2032, and 2038. Testing should consider the following period rollovers:

- End-of-day (with special consideration of September 8, 1999)
- End-of-week: last week, this week, next week
- End-of-month: last month, this month, next month
- End of bimonthly period
- End-of-quarter: last quarter, this quarter, next quarter
- End-of-season/semester/and the like
- End-of-year: last year, this year, next year
- Leap year

There should also be testing of date conversions from Gregorian to ordinal/Julian and ordinal/Julian to Gregorian. (For those who wonder about the ordinal/Julian notation, the difference between the two is that the ordinal day starts at midnight, while the Julian day starts at noon.) Also test any conversions from ASCII to EBCDIC and back. Test for the application's ability to handle the following values in date fields: low values, high values, all nines, and all zeros.

It is not recommended to forgo testing applications that interface directly with the public. Nor should you skip unit testing for applications required for you to maintain your competitive position. If you are forced to curtail testing, always make sure that whoever is responsible for the application monitors it.

Clearly, untested changes create vulnerable applications. Several vendors have created tools that allow the same programs to be run several times with the same data. The tool automatically changes the dates in the data to a series of years supplied by the test operator. This improves the number of tests that can be run by diminishing the demand for unique data. The next chapter "Taking a Tool Inventory," talks about software tool requirements for your organization and helps you determine if you have the right in-house tools and resources to manage the fix.

CHAPTER 9

Taking a Tool Inventory

W hen a millennium-update project is started at a new client site, often one of these two scenarios is in progress: Either the client has too few software tools to support code development and maintenance, or the client has too many tools. Where there are too few tools, they may be used and misused for multiple purposes; where there are too many tools, they may be poorly understood or used at cross-purposes. It is difficult to say which situation is worse, but it is safe to say that most organizations have acquired tools without a plan or have integrated them poorly to support their application development and maintenance efforts.

When there are no tools, there are also no *processes* in place to identify requirements, locate vendors, assess tools, train and coach the staff, integrate the tools into the current development or maintenance process, or manage the tools. In too many instances, enterprises do not have a budget for buying software tools, or there is resistance to purchasing tools because there is nothing in place to substantiate productivity claims or prove a return on investment. An enterprise in this state has to find help from the outside to provide the required services and some degree of assurance to management that purchases will be cost-justified.

On the other hand, the enterprise without tools does not have the problem of one that has been aggressive in purchasing tools. Such enterprises often have a toolbox full of *shelfware*—tools that have fallen into disuse, assuming they were ever properly introduced. The problem is that most information technology organizations don't really know what they own. Their tools are not tracked like plant equipment: They usually are not capitalized or depreciated; and they are not associated with a business function (do you know anyone who puts IT in the category of a business?), so the tools expense is treated as overhead.

Also, enterprises may own tools that perform identical functions on the same hardware and operating system platforms. In such situations, loyalty to the tools has become an ease-of-use issue: The group devoted to one tool refuses to use another simply because of the perceived retraining and familiarization costs.

Consequently, to get major corporations ready to analyze, classify, plan, prepare, convert, and reintegrate date-sensitive applications, you must first make them understand that using an effective toolkit is the starting point. If you recognized your organization in one of the preceding descriptions, a suggestion is that you first take a tool inventory. Most organizations fall woefully short when they examine their inventory in relationship to the tasks that need to be supported for the millennium update. (The next chapter, "2000: A Tool Odyssey," discusses the types of tools that you may want to use in addressing the date problem.) That you will need effective tools to process and update your applications is not debatable because, even with maximum tool implementation, industry cost estimates are alarming—but they are even higher without the effective use of tools.

What's in Your Toolbox?

The tool inventory requires capturing two kinds of information. The first category is information about tool ownership; the second has to do with potential use of tools in the process. Taking stock of what you have and where it will be used will identify gaps in your toolbox. Whether you should fill those gaps will require some difficult decision making. A complete tool inventory has four separate deliverables:

Tool inventory list.   Tools owned and their current status

Tool requirements.   Processes to be performed during the update

Gap analysis.   Tools to be purchased (or built) with an estimate of benefit

Tool acquisition and assimilation plan.   Tools to buy, and when and how to implement them

Tool Inventory List

Start your inventory with the operating system environment. Many hardware vendors provide a number of tools with the operating system, such as code library management tools, date routines, and special sort processes to handle the sorting of two-digit years across the century boundary.

Your second source of information about what you own should be the programmers and analysts. In many cases, they use internally built tools, and determining what they are may reveal that some of them could be useful to others. The most common internally built tools include date routines and data-analysis tools.

The third place to look for tools is with your purchasing agent. Some tools may have been purchased and subsequently forgotten. One end-user organization had purchased and installed three tools that were of use in the update project, but the computer professionals were not even aware the tools were on the computers they used every day. (The computer operations and technical support staff who maintained the systems software bought them and never shared the information with the programmers.)

As you locate tools, determine the following:

Version being used.   Is the latest version installed? If it is not, you may find that other actions must be taken before the tool can be employed in the update process. You may discover that the tool has not been maintained because the service contract was not purchased, the number of users is too small, or operating system software has not been brought up to the level required.

Functions performed.   Some tools perform more than one function. The next chapter, "2000: A Tool Odyssey," discusses the functions to look for. For now, just determine whether the tool serves more than one function so you do not buy another tool unnecessarily. In some cases, you will find that the label applied to the function is not consistent with industry definitions. Many vendors strive to create an image of uniqueness, but do not actually achieve it. Investigate to ascertain what the advertised functions really provide.

Platform characteristics required.   Information on the hardware model, operating system, computer languages, and other characteristics of the tool will tell you whether you have duplicate tools or tools that perform duplicate functions on other platforms. If you work off several platforms or in multiple computer languages, you may need to acquire several tools of similar functions.

Date use.   Some tools contain date processes, which may cause some difficulty with a tool if it is not date-compliant. For example, you may not be able to use one in an environment where you are simulating running in year 2000 or later. Watch for data-storage processes that include date stamping. This can make the data unusable from run to run when the system date changes. Test any such tool if the vendor cannot provide you with a clear answer.

Support from vendor. Like application software products, many tools have changed ownership over the last five years. In some cases, this has improved tool support and included integration of the tool into a suite. You may find improved support through hot lines, e-mail, or new and electronic training media. Or you may find that the original support has declined as the number of tool users has decreased, which provides less income for support maintenance. Even when a tool is in frequent use by the technical staff, reassess support. And do not overlook a review of your maintenance agreement. You will want to know the response you are entitled to if the operating system has changed or the tool is sold.

Usage of the tool. Whether a tool was purchased (in use or not) or built, determine its skill requirements, training time, training requirements (manuals, formal classes, coaching, laboratories, etc.), number and location of users, and problems with or limitations to use. Again, this information will be important when you make decisions about implementation. A staff tool-skills matrix may come in handy—you will find that some staff members make maximum use of tools while others do not. The former may be candidates for the tiger teams discussed in the previous chapter, "A Date with Destiny."

Attitudes. When performing tools inventories, it is essential to determine both the technologists' and the management's attitude toward tools; this is part of a context assessment. Some organizations have set up hidden roadblocks to tool purchase and implementation. Examples of these include lack of training facilities, inadequate training or travel budgets, imposition of inflexible due dates, and failure to acknowledge tools use. In some cases, there is hostility on the part of management to tools use, arising from ignorance of what the tool will do to improve performance or from a fear of reprisals if the tool is not implemented correctly. In such business cultures, tool use cannot thrive. A context assessment can prove invaluable in putting together recommendations for purchases and implementation.

Creating an environment. A tool tends to be owned by the department that acquires it. In large, decentralized organizations, this causes pockets of advocates for various tools. It also makes it exceedingly difficult for other staff units to use or share the tools. This may be due to funding issues—maintenance costs come out of one group's budget even though others may use it. The difficulty in sharing tools may also be a result of support issues: It is natural for new users to look to experienced users for help. When the support is departmentally linked, but not enterprisewide, new users can't get the help they need. Review your organization context and define the tools environment. This may lead to recommendations for creating a tools owner who manages all the tools, training, and support.

Automate or Extricate

Experience has taught that automation is only as good as the process. Tools become shelfware when they are bought before the process is defined. Two things must be present before a tool is used: repetitive tasks and frequent use. If a task is not performed the same way *every* time, it cannot be automated. Where exceptions to a process are encountered more than 20 percent of the time, tool users will abandon the tool. Similarly, if users do not invoke the tool frequently enough, they may require a reeducation process, which, if it lasts more than 20 minutes, may discourage use and result in rejection of the tool.

These conditions for tool rejection can be avoided only by having a well-defined process in place. This process should include requirements for use of the tool, steps to intercept and deal with nonstandard situations prior to requiring the tool's use, organization of the work so that those trained to use the tool do so regularly, and measurement and metrics relating to the tool and the task.

If, however, you are well into problem resolution and predefining is not possible, there are some effective ways to determine your tools requirements. Having enumerated your application and tools inventories, you are already aware that you have to deal with a complex environment, including some or all of the following:

Multiple hardware platforms

Different operating systems

Several data management processes and packages

Multiple computer languages

Several versions or extensions to those languages

Code generators, query tools, and report writers

Automated and manual event-driven actions

These factors, which will determine your tools requirements, fall into two categories: *core update processes* and *project processes*. The first category includes those tools used to perform technical work. Update processes include such tasks as code and data analysis, program and data changes, and testing. Project processes include management of code and resources, estimation, measurement, change control, and methodology or process management.

Project administration tools are essential to managing the project. Centralized programs will find tools that enable users to define tasks and track progress so that you can identify the impact of changes in plans and schedules. Although you may normally plan and track projects in your head, don't even consider doing so for this project. Many sophisticated planning tools cannot handle a complete plan for an enterprise that manages 4 million lines of code. Usually, the plan has to be broken up and handled in pieces. Fortunately, project management tools abound, and many enterprises employ two or three PC-based tools.

Another important project tool is a *repository*. But most enterprises do not have a repository, and those that do, find their contents do not reflect the current state of the external application data. A good repository tracks all the components in the environment and their status; it provides information on relationships among components so that plans to implement a change to one component will reveal potential change requirements for other components. Configuration management tools perform some elements of this function, but a true repository captures relationships that include components such as vendor software, hardware, embedded systems, regulations, imports and exports of data, test scripts, and test data. The problem with repositories is that their contents must be loaded without automated input mechanisms, and creation of the contents, called *metadata*, is a major task.

Core tools will be useful but depend on the work to be done. The following is a breakdown of the types of core tools to consider for each stage of the project. A more complete discussion of these tools follows in Chapter 10, "2000: A Tool Odyssey."

PC Assessment

BIOS analyzer.   Tools that test the BIOS to determine if it can handle Year 2000 dates.

Package analyzer.   Tools that scan the information on packages installed on the PC to determine if the package found is Year 2000–capable (user must enter century information if it is not the same as the century in which the processing occurs) or –compliant.

Portfolio Inventory and Estimation

Scanners or parsers.   Tools that look for dates to determine whether code has to be changed and to assess the level of work required.

Estimators.   Tools that forecast the effort required, the cost, and the duration.

Update Planning

Documentation aids.   Tools that recover information on software functions from software code.

Source recovery.   Tools/services that can re-create source code from machine language instructions if the source is lost. Several tools are available for purchase.

Workflow analysis. Tools that describe and diagram workflows and workflow requirements for input and skills.

Update Preparation

Scanners/parsers. Tools that find every reference to dates and date processing so that design problems can be uncovered.

Data analyzers. Tools that look through data to uncover problems such as nondate data stored in date fields, illogical dates, use of date constants, dates stored in fields not defined as dates, and so on.

Code and Data Change

Editors. Tools that allow manual changes to code.

Conversion aids. Tools that upgrade language versions or allow code to be run on another platform.

Intelligent editors. Tools that automatically expand data definitions to four digits and make predefined changes based on rules to date processes.

Syntax checkers and static analyzers. Tools that look for logical inconsistencies in changed code.

Code generators. Tools that assist in the construction of bridges or data-conversion programs.

Data generators. Tools that produce test data based on rules provided by the operator.

Dynamic test analyzers and debuggers. Tools that track the process steps and capture and display the status of fields during testing; some provide test coverage analysis to show which parts of a program were tested and which were not.

On-line simulators. Tools that mimic the entry of test data from terminals.

Date simulators. Tools that cause programs to behave as if they were being run in a different time.

Data migration aids. Tools that transfer data from one file to another and view that process.

Code comparators. Tools that show differences in source code from version to version.

Gap Analysis

A gap analysis is performed to determine the differences between your current state and where you want to be. It is the time to open a discussion regarding any and all tools issues, to recommend actions to promote tools use, or to overcome resistance to tools. If, for example, a tool exists as shelfware and is generally regarded by staff as unusable, the particulars should be enumerated during the gap analysis. If staff skill sets are not up to par, this is the forum in which to reveal that fact and to decide whether you need a tool trainer, a tool manager, or someone to design processes to employ automated tools.

Specifically, for the millennium-update project, the processes to implement and employ the tools must be delineated *before* you can identify the tools you need to build or purchase. Simply put, until your processes are defined, the specific requirements for tools cannot be known. While performing your gap analysis, specific tools should not be itemized; instead, identify a number of tools that fit your general requirements. These can be used to provide a range of costs to do your budget estimations. Specific tool recommendations should be made only in the following three circumstances:

- You wish to resurrect a shelfware product or promote an internally developed tool, in which case you should include specific recommendations about how to reintroduce the tool for general use.

- You decide to build a tool because of proprietary coding requirements.

- You already own tools that are part of a vendor's tool suite and can obtain significant advantage by using another tool in that suite.

A gap analysis should also include the funding requirements for tools, training, process development, tools management, vendor liaison and software maintenance, staff coaching, help-desk support, and supplemental software purchases.

Outside services can perform a gap analysis for you. Several large and small firms have created databases containing information on tools they have used. This is often much faster than a similar procedure can be organized inside an enterprise. Care should be taken that the service is not set up to promote tools from specific vendors—ask if there are any financial relationships between the service organization and the vendor before accepting recommendations. Internally supported studies often do not have the same resources, and options may be much narrower simply because there is little time to do the research. In a large organization in which many tools are owned, there is also severe pressure from advocates of certain tools, which slows down decision making.

A good gap analysis from an outside provider assesses the return on tools purchased. This is most likely estimated based on the difference between doing the update with tools versus doing it without. These are subjective evaluations based on prior experience of the company performing the gap analysis.

Use 'Em or Lose 'Em

The question, "How much should I spend on tools?" often arises. The answer, of course, has to do with your understanding of the role tools play in the project. Simply buying tools will not solve the problem; you must also plan for introduction, testing, training, and integration. Some enterprises with over $500 million have established a fund of $500,000 or more to buy tools and training. This amount can represent from 5 to 10 percent of the estimated cost of the update—this, of course, assumes the maximum use of tools.

The purpose of buying tools is to reduce work and/or cycle time. Certain tasks are virtually impossible to accomplish without tools—scanning for dates, for example. Some activities can obtain up to a 40 percent reduction in effort through the use of a tool—for instance, code changes. Again, any measurable benefit depends on the knowledge and skill of the tool user. The average savings on effort is probably around 37 percent. (A helpful comparison: If your change process is estimated to cost the equivalent of 15 person-years, a savings of this magnitude may amount to more than five person-years. The average fully burdened technologist's rate in the United States is $110,000 per year. You could easily buy a tool suite for a third of that cost.) Cycle-time reduction is significantly affected by management processes, but a well-managed team can achieve an estimated 55 percent improvement in throughput as a result of adopting some tools.

Probably the most difficult question to answer is where in the process to begin spending money on tools. Most enterprises currently spend slightly more than 40 percent of the update-effort budget on testing and 20 percent on management of the process. If you do not have tools to support those two activities, start spending there. If, however, you decide to farm out the work to a code-change service, perhaps you should spend your budget on analysis tools so you can better define your change requirements and test the solution that is provided. If you have to move your code to another version or platform, recover source code from machine language code, or work around a failing vendor product, your purchases are predefined, in the sense that you will need products designed to assist you in reengineering.

Some tools provide some less-tangible benefits. Chief among these are improvements in product quality and application information. A repository, for instance, can lead the way to better control and management of the entire process of systems development and maintenance. Akin to the repository is what is called a *relationship mapper,* a tool that searches for components and establishes immediate relationships.

What is missing in most enterprises today is an up-to-date and complete knowledge of all the relationships that exist between components. It is difficult to research the linkages between programs, system software dependencies, data, shared code members, control language sets, other applications that use the data, and so on. This makes it difficult to estimate the true impact of change on the entire organization. When one component changes, it often causes a ripple effect, requiring changes in other applications; often this is not realized until it's too late. Unfortunately, a tool that constantly queries the environment and maintains the list of dependencies has yet to be developed. Those that are available require the user to keep the data up-to-date.

Code-processing tools are invaluable aids when trying to determine what to test and the path that date information follows within a program or an application. Language parsers can provide dynamic documentation of code so that functionality can be tested and new requirements documented accurately with less effort. Analysis tools can prevent unnecessary decay of code quality, which leads to higher maintenance costs.

The Learning Curve

Which tools you purchase should not be just a dollars-and-cents decision. Don't forget to factor in people issues before introducing tools: Individual capabilities for learning differ, only a limited number of tools can be assimilated at one time, and the duration of the tool's learning cycle can vary.

How successfully tools are introduced depends on how quickly any one individual becomes comfortable and competent with a tool. Nevertheless, certain assumptions can be made for an entire organization. Generally, a relatively simple tool (having a single function with a familiar interface) requires two weeks of training and implementation; a complex tool (one that performs multiple functions) requires four weeks of use to reach the comfort zone. Competency, the point at which the tool starts to recover cost, is usually not achieved until several weeks after comfort is achieved. A second tool should not be introduced until the comfort zone of the first has been reached.

It can take up to six months for people to achieve proficiency with a complex tool. The impact of learning an additional tool is related to the level of success achieved in implementing the first. Simply, if the first is embraced enthusiastically, the second tool probably will be, too. If the tool performs an unrelated activity, the amount of time to achieve competency with either of them is lengthened.

In general, do not expect to implement a large number of tools; and those that you do choose to incorporate should be introduced first to staff members who are already familiar with using tools, as they will be more open to the learning process and thus be able to assimilate the knowledge faster. Choose carefully because some tools require more effort. Configuration management tools, as pointed out earlier, are very difficult to install. Many enterprises have worked unsuccessfully for years to introduce such a tool, so if one isn't already in place, the millennium-update project is not the time to add it. Other tools to avoid, because of the learning investment, include CASE (computer-aided software engineering) tools, new 4GLs (fourth generation languages) or code generators, data dictionaries, and a centralized project management system.

The success of a tool's integration into an organization is greatly amplified when there is someone to champion the tool and encourage others in its use. And, having someone to troubleshoot minimizes frustration during the learning process. Consider retaining someone from the vendor as coach; or you may be able to recruit experienced help from a consulting service.

Buyer Beware

Don't overspend on tools. Specifically, don't be swayed, for instance, by *intelligent editors,* those with the least competition and the most glitz, and regarded by many as the silver bullet. You'll even see them advertised as Year 2000 "solutions." They are not. They simply apply rules to the code and make changes. But beware: If the code doesn't fit the rule exactly, such tools may apply the change incorrectly, thus causing additional problems.

Use intelligent editors just as you would any other editor. This means knowing the rules that are being employed, analyzing the code, making design changes to fit the editing process, then—and only then—letting the editor do its thing. Ultimately, the tool is performing a rather small amount of work, so don't pay a high price. No intelligent editor can promise 100 percent accuracy, so there always must be someone who looks through the code to find out what was missed or incorrectly changed.

Platform Tooling

Not all tools are available for all environments (*environment* here is defined as including the computer model, operating system, database management software, and communications and programming languages). Certain environments simply do not have a large enough base to attract a large number of tool builders. IBM VM, Unisys 2200, and HP 1000 are all processors with limited support from the tool-building community, and few tools support languages such as PL/1 or FORTRAN. In some cases, only the hardware manufacturer provides tools. HP 3000, Honeywell GECOS, and Data General fall into this category for their non-UNIX platforms. In general, more tools are designed for the most common environments.

Not surprisingly, then, the largest number of tools exist for IBM 360/370 architecture, using the MVS operating system with IMS and DB2 for data management, and either IMS/DC or CICS for communications. As for languages, COBOL has the most tools. At the other end of the scale are the low-volume platforms built for niche markets. Tandem, Data General, and Sun Microsystems platforms fit this profile. There are also tools available for multiple environments, an attractive option because all the tools have a similar user interface. Users who become proficient with the tool in one environment can more easily move to another.

Along the same line are tool suites, in development by many vendors. These tools, too, have common interfaces and may work off a shared data-collection file, making it possible to introduce several tools at roughly the same time. Usually it is cheaper to buy the suite than to purchase individual components. The downside is that you may have to uninstall a popular tool in favor of implementing the suite, so be prepared for some resistance if you find yourself in this situation.

An increasing number of tools interface with multiple platforms and run on a PC. This is advantageous for a variety of reasons: Many platforms do not have sufficient capacity to support production, ongoing maintenance support, *and* a concurrent update project. In many cases, the need to alter the system date makes it difficult to schedule testing time. In addition, it may be necessary to add storage to some platforms (an additional cost) and request floor space that is not available. Thus, working off a PC offers several benefits:

Availability and extensibility.   More PCs can be added as required.

Storage.   PC storage capability and capacity is mounting rapidly.

Portability.   It is possible to acquire PCs that run mainframe software so that testing environments can be constructed outside of the production environment.

Tools.   Many tools are being developed that interface with several different platforms. Code and data can be moved to the PC environment, changed, tested, and moved back to the production environment with few or no differences in process.

Ease of use.   PC-based tools tend to be easier to learn and use. The capability to build and employ graphical and intuitive interfaces makes them easier to install. Progress with operating systems is also reducing learning time.

New tools that reduce testing requirements and improve project support on the PC are evolving; watch for them.

One word of caution, though, regarding PC tools: Do not underestimate the impact of introducing PCs if you have not already adopted them in your environment. They require new skill sets and building new communications to provide data transfer; and some routines will have to be recoded to work on the PCs.

Conclusion

An effective suite of tools is essential to application development and maintenance. With the vast amount of code to be analyzed and updated, effective tools are mandatory for the completion of the millennium update. Keep in mind that all the competing technologies, vendors, and environments necessitate an understanding of the tools requirements, a plan for their introduction and use, and a well-trained staff to make them effective.

The next chapter, "2000: A Tool Odyssey," looks at categories of tools by function, examines how each relates to the Year 2000 fix, and provides you with an analysis of potential problems and staffing considerations for each tool class.

CHAPTER 10

2000: A Tool Odyssey

C hapters 1 and 9, "Ground Double-Zero" and "Taking a Tool Inventory," introduced the types of tools most directly associated with updating application code for the year 2000, benefits to be derived from implementing such tools, and selection implications. This chapter examines the tools relevant to the millennium-update project by type. Appendix B contains descriptions of available tools referenced in this section. The tool and service providers will gladly provide references. There are many more tools and services offered than are listed. These vendors have established track records. As Chapter 9 cautioned, you must be wary of any tool offers that make unrealistic promises relating to the Year 2000 conversion effort.

Throughout this period of tool development, expect prices to rise even though competition may be strong. Rising labor costs for development and support will force development and support costs upward. Platform-specific tools will become available for many environments that are tool-poor at present; but their prices will be especially high, reflecting their manufacturer's objective to recover development costs from fewer unit sales. These tools may come with little or no support, but the benefit may be worth the investment and the risk.

Bringing Method to the Madness

The following discusses building a process using methodologies first, since methodologies provide the rationale for the use of all the other tools. Without a repeatable process—a method—work is difficult to automate and a tool may be ill-used or useless. People using tools seldom achieve proficiency.

Primary Function

You start by installing a process. Whenever this is said, most people immediately think of a one-size-fits-all commercial methodology; then they start to laugh because probably the most important and least-used project tool most firms have invested in is a methodology. Computing development methodologies have been around nearly as long as *computer programmer* has been a job title. Few organizations have successfully implemented them. Most methodologies have played their most prominent role as placeholders on bookshelves.

To get the terms straight right from the start, a *methodology* is a collection of methods applied across the system's development life cycle. A *method* is a highly structured process for developing a specific product; it tells the user what to do in a step-by-step manner and, in some instances, offers specific instructions on creating a product defined by the method.

Methodologies differ in their degree of detail, tailorability, amount of automation support, and the linkage to actual processes. At one end of the spectrum, you will find rigid processes that define a step-by-step solution. At the other end, you will find highly flexible collections of modifiable processes designed to be adapted. Most of those used by consulting firms are biased by the kinds of work they were originally developed to support. Because they were designed to be used by consultants who constantly have to obtain approvals, they often do not fit the fast-paced process employed by an internal team. Most are written for software development and provide only minimal direction on maintenance. More than a few suggest that maintenance is similar to development, just requiring fewer steps.

Methodologies *do* provide definitions of products at each step and trace the work as it flows through the process, which can be extremely helpful because of the communication requirements of the Year 2000 activities. Further, methodologies often identify quality assurance steps and practices, suggesting where and when they are performed. They frequently provide forms and product examples and suggest techniques. Some enterprises' standards programs—which define procedures covering communications, project management, quality assurance, and change management—provide standards for some products, such as code or project reports, and effectively constitute a methodology. This is achieved when they strictly define the organization process flow and the format and content of acceptable deliverables.

Year 2000 Relevance

When creating a Year 2000 factory process, one that will enable high-quality and assembly-line conversion of code and implementation, it is helpful to start with a well-defined methodology. Put bluntly, you will not be able to succeed without a factory, and that requires a process!

Although, as just defined, methodologies often are organized as step-by-step processes, they do not have to be employed that way. Rather, a methodology should be viewed as a checklist or set of requirements. You can select the pieces that fit the process you need, tailor the description of the work to accommodate what has to be done, and then describe how to do it *in your organization.*

Idiosyncrasies

Most commercial methodologies prescribe a single right way for developing applications, and thus lack the flexibility required to meet changes in cultural and organizational requirements. A number of them are supported by programmed routines that communicate to planning tools (discussed shortly). The more pragmatic the methodology, the more likely it is to have a project management tool interface. The tool interface makes the methodology more palatable, but structural inflexibility remains a problem.

Nevertheless, new methodologies that specifically address the reengineering of existing applications, and the Year 2000 problem in particular, have found a ready market in enterprises seeking guidance in an information-poor environment. As with all tools, expect methodologies to evolve and mature as they are used. Before acquiring a methodology, do some research to identify one that is built on a strong experience base in fixing the Year 2000 problem. You will find these to be maintenance-oriented and not grounded in software reengineering or development.

Staffing Impact

Handled properly, implementing a methodology has a beneficial impact on staff productivity, as it requires examination of current practices. A methodology provides a starting point for creating process definitions and a common vocabulary for describing the work.

Most methodologies are difficult to implement because they do not fit the actual processes and tools employed by the organization. The numbering patterns they use imply a sequence that cannot be followed due to enterprise practices or organization dynamics. But these deficiencies can be overcome by adapting the methodology to the organization rather than trying to adapt the organization to the methodology. The successful implementation of a methodology generally requires forming a support group to provide coaching and to aid in definition.

Cost Models/Estimators

Primary Function

These tools have two purposes: (1) to establish the budget for the project, and (2) to provide a target for individual work efforts. The typical cost model/estimator provides estimates of the effort (days or hours), cost (based on average workday calculations), and duration required.

Year 2000 Relevance

The coming of the millennium has not significantly altered the makeup of these tools. If you find one that meets your requirements, employ it. Most organizations do not have such tools; instead they rely on intuitive estimates provided by experienced support personnel. Estimates of this nature can be relatively accurate but demand a detailed evaluation of requirements. More often, they are off by as much as 200 percent due to unforseen problems and overconfidence.

Idiosyncrasies

The better cost models/estimators have the ability to enter the incidence of date-related definition and processing lines to be modified and redesigned. The tool accepts input on such important factors as employee knowledge of the application, complexity of the application, documentation requirements, availability of computing resources, schedule and risk constraints, tools usage, data complexity, and management.

One caution—and it's a significant one—with these tools: The tools can be manipulated to produce an *expected* forecast, that is, to produce false information. So, if yours is an organization in which accurate information is welcomed only if it has positive implications, using these tools can result in an underestimation of the costs for the update project, in effect rendering the implementation of these tools useless. Be honest with yourself and your enterprise, and remember, sometimes the truth hurts.

A final note: As you begin to generate estimates, set up a process whereby the actual results are documented against the estimate. Firms that use function points are familiar with benchmarking, which means that regardless of the estimating tool used, such organizations have characteristics that skew the actual performance. Thus, the tool should allow you to apply benchmark results back into the model.

Staffing Impact

Cost modeling and estimating is best left to a few trained staff. One or two people trained in the use of this kind of tool should be sufficient to support a large enterprise.

Relationship Mappers

Primary Function

This tool looks at job-scheduling instructions to determine which programs are run together in a job. It can also tell you where data files are created and used, which programs use them, and which files are passed across system and application boundaries.

Year 2000 Relevance

A relationship mapper establishes knowledge about the passing of data within and between applications. This information is required to plan the building of bridge files and to determine the need for concurrent changes or to set precedence of changes. Such knowledge reduces delays in implementation and can help to prevent constructing unnecessary bridges and performing extra testing.

Idiosyncrasies

A typical commercial relationship mapper does not provide a detailed enough analysis to reveal all components involved in an update project. Its use of job-scheduling instructions automatically eliminates all programs that are performed or executed in real time—driven by transaction events or hardware interrupts. These do not show up in the schedules. They are invoked by the computer when an event is detected by a routine that is constantly running. The problem with this tool, as mentioned in Chapter 1, "Ground Double-Zero," is that it does not take an enterprise view. It is confined to looking at the processes performed on one platform and generates data in the form of charts and diagrams. These are not all that useful until the knowledge they represent is moved into a data store that provides the complete enterprise context—a repository (discussed later). And, be aware that nearly all of the commercial tools of this type are limited to IBM mainframe processors. A few allow databases to be constructed and maintained on PCs. Some of these allow manual entry of information on suppliers, vendors, called subroutines, and embedded systems to obtain a more complete project-scheduling and tracking ability. While these tools are great for Year 2000 work, their true benefit will last well into the future.

Staffing Impact

Running a relationship mapper does not require much technical skill, and it can be learned in a few hours. However, extracting useful information from the run does require an analyst familiar with the application being mapped. Data-entry support usually is provided by staff members who run the tool, since they are familiar with the output. In addition, because information from multiple applications is being captured at one time, it is necessary to provide supervision and coordination to several analysts. Finally, keeping the resulting knowledge base up-to-date requires the implementation of change control. *Change control* keeps track of what components are being worked on and prevents changed versions of them from being used in production without permission.

Repository

Primary Function

In computer parlance, a *repository* is a collection of information about a computing system, including the relationship of the elements of information to one another. The industry has attempted to define exactly what information should be included in a repository and how one should be constructed. Alas, there is still no standard, and, therefore, many different vendors use the term *repository* to refer to their own special files in which they store things that are important only to those using their products.

Year 2000 Relevance

The purpose of the repository in the update project is to track all the knowledge required to manage the work and resources of the organization. Unfortunately, Year 2000 repository requirements are much broader than those served by the best-known repository providers; they must include all the information required to plan and track progress toward fixing the problem. A Year 2000 repository tracks business functions, organizations, applications, subsystems, projects, computer jobs, code components, data components, platforms, hardware components, system software components, embedded systems, forms, reports, screens, test data, and scripts. This information may then become your checklist of what has been changed and what still needs to be changed.

Repository products include a data-collection component, a data-retrieval component, and a report writer. Interfaces enable the capture of status information. Some repositories link to library and configuration management tools and produce project plans and schedules. Others keep track of estimates and record the duration and effort performed. Certain of these tools are sold with optional interfaces; or you may elect to construct additional ones.

Idiosyncrasies

The most important capability of the repository is the building and maintenance of relationship information. All the elements in the repository are related to multiple components. Thus, a repository that limits the number and type of relationships will not provide the information required to manage the update because it is the relationship information in the repository that tells you, for example, the impact of a late vendor delivery on project work schedules, data, other applications, and business functions. Through the chain of relationships, it is possible to show how the failure to replace a PC can cause the interruption of a product line. This knowledge can't be obtained in any other way. Unfortunately, most available repositories are limited in scope to the application code components and do not capture or support any other information.

An ideal product also lists specific lines to be changed or modified, reveals opportunities for setting standards, indicates the location of date routines, identifies efforts required at component level, and shows where bridges need to be constructed.

Staffing Impact

Staffing requirements vary according to the complexity and scope of the repository in use. Implementing a repository may require significant changes to computing management processes; and adaptation of any existent process definitions follow from that change. Support staff is required to manage the data and ensure it is current. Since much of the information required (i.e., information about hardware and systems software, embedded systems, suppliers and vendors, and so on) is not stored on a computer, be prepared to conduct significant research and data entry during the load process. Consequently, there will be ongoing clerical requirements for managing and editing the data.

Project Planning/Tracking

Primary Function

Project planning/tracking tools perform the functions of scheduling tasks, defining precedence and dependencies, and allocating tasks by resource. Some of the oldest and most advanced tools support the functions of project planning and tracking. More than 100 project-planning and tracking tools are available to assist managers with resource load leveling and to identify hidden staffing and hardware resource requirements. Tracking capabilities enumerate completed tasks, problems with estimates and skill requirements, and deviations from the plan.

Year 2000 Relevance

The more complex and time-critical the millennium-update project, the greater the need for project management tools to enable communication of status information and to manage the resources assigned to the project. Studies have shown that projects that are not carefully managed and do not receive management attention are 300 times more likely to fail. Remember, the Year 2000 project is a large and complicated one involving the updating of millions of lines of code and changing of components that do not include code. There is no way to track the progress of the wide range of tasks in a Year 2000 project without the use of a project planning/tracking tool.

Idiosyncrasies

Most planning tools are not sophisticated enough to provide a single complete plan for the date problem. There are just too many tasks. Many enterprises overcome the limitations by dividing the project into smaller ones to plan at different levels of detail. This enables them to use the features of the simpler, but more intuitive, planning and tracking tools that run on PCs. The more complex the functionality of the planning tool, the better it becomes at supporting large project schedules, but the more difficult it is to learn.

Staffing Impact

These products are generally used by centralized project managers, although the technical staff may maintain the plan at lower levels of detail. Build in a three- to five-day training cycle for this type of tool. You may want to delegate task completion and time-tracking data entry to an administrative person. Some enterprises do not use the tool's time-tracking capability, but enter status changes only in the repository. Many tracking tools are interfaced with proprietary time-keeping/reporting and billing products. These are often built by the computing organization and serve the reporting needs of the enterprise.

Workflow Managers

Primary Function

Workflow managers come in several varieties. The lowest-level tool simply provides diagramming techniques for describing workflow processes and interorganization interfaces. Higher-level tools include e-mail connectivity to keep staff informed of activities and move work along.

Year 2000 Relevance

The advantage of having a workflow manager is that it simplifies communications in large, complex projects where numerous people are involved and moving work from one station to another is time-critical. This tool can shave days, even weeks, off the cycle time of important tasks. Managers will find that the tool reduces the need for meetings and gives them greater freedom once they get used to the process.

Idiosyncrasies

The networking requirements to introduce the more advanced tools are significant, but worthwhile. The chief concern in implementing a workflow manager is just getting everyone to use it—if anyone fails to employ the tool properly, it will cause the tool to fail entirely. Usually, getting people to communicate is the cause of a bottleneck, and often, management resists the tool more than does technical staff because they are more comfortable with verbal than with written communications.

Staffing Impact

To launch a workflow manager successfully generally requires two months of training and coaching. But staffing support requirements are minimal once the launch is complete. A local area communications network is required; therefore, an administrative person needs to manage the message files and access security. This is often handled by the network administrator.

Library Managers

Primary Function

Many organizations have used code libraries for a long time. Library managers store code and keep track of different versions. They allow the user to attach code modules and are used by some to track code and test data components. Features of some products help to locate missing components and facilitate identification of obsolete components. Reusable code can be saved as code modules and copied into or included in other programs. Many library managers include a checkout process that allows people to get copies to look at or work on. Conversely, a check-in process allows the system to track changes so that multiple versions of the code can be stored.

Year 2000 Relevance

Year 2000 relevance of library managers stems from the need to provide specific storage locations for all code. Computer people are notorious for keeping code components in private files, team files, and application files, making them difficult to find and manage. Bringing this code under control is part of the inventory process. A library manager provides a minimal amount of control over those components.

Idiosyncrasies

A number of library managers have been implemented on more than one platform, which may prove relevant in a multiplatform environment because common user interfaces cut training time. Many hardware vendors include library management tools with the systems software purchased with the hardware.

However, standards must be created and enforced. Use of the library manager must be universal or the process will break down quickly as new code components are purchased or created. One reason that library management tools fail to be implemented is the absence of naming conventions or control of naming standards. Enterprises that purchase many applications from outside cannot control vendor names, which causes conflicts with internal names and naming conventions. This can cause additional work in trying to keep track of these components. Artificial names are often assigned and tracked outside the tool.

Staffing Impact

If the enterprise has—and enforces—naming conventions, library management tools are relatively easy to implement and require relatively little support and maintenance. On the other hand, an enterprise could find itself faced with months of activity if it must create and implement naming standards. In such situations, the organization may simply not have the time or resources to employ such a tool.

Change/Problem Managers

Primary Function

Change/problem managers track implementation schedules and projects for the operations team. They are used to coordinate changes with the staffs in programming, technical support, database administration, and operations scheduling.

Year 2000 Relevance

The Year 2000 project benefits most from these tools during the migration stage, though they are also helpful for tracking parallel changes. Coordinating the implementation schedule is simplified by the existence of a change/problem management tool.

Idiosyncrasies

The implementation of the change management function is not always easy. Most enterprises already have some form of manual change management process in place. For those enterprises, the greatest difficulty will be to find the tool that supports the process already employed. Changing an existing process to fit the tool will create frustration. Consequently, communication failures resulting from the new process will be viewed as a failure of the tool and lead to its abandonment.

Staffing Impact

Process definition and documentation can require several weeks of effort. Training is very client-specific and includes training in the process and the tool. Analyst and programmer training may require one to two days. The change management process needs to be reflected in the factory process and should be included in project plans as milestones. The tool itself rarely requires support or maintenance.

Configuration Managers

Primary Function

Configuration managers align source code and machine-language versions during the development and maintenance cycles so that the wrong version is not placed in production or lost. They provide excellent information on the relationships of components to other components, job streams, and applications. The tool includes security definitions that limit access to the person who is in the process of changing the code. The configuration manager also keeps track of code-component relationships so that any code checked out for change automatically checks out components. Other staff members can look at the code and even obtain copies, but they cannot release a copy back into the environment except through the individual who has checked out the code. Most configuration managers support one or more interim libraries where the code is retained in various status levels (e.g., work, test, migration, production). Movement of the code from one status to another requires special authorizations. This security measure is necessary so that groups of components can be safely staged for testing or movement to production.

Year 2000 Relevance

Next to methodology, configuration managers are probably the most important tools employed in the Year 2000 project. The payoff comes from validating that all code in a change group is simultaneously moved through the change process and implemented. This payoff includes making sure that code for conversion programs and bridge programs is implemented at the same time.

Idiosyncrasies

Configuration management tools are among the most difficult to implement because they require significant organizational work up front. The reason is that all ongoing work must be transferred to the tool, and no shop has all its applications static at a given point in time. The complexity of the startup is made apparent by the definition of the processes the tool performs. These processes are most often used in concert with change management and library management tools.

Some versions of this type of tool run in several environments—computer platforms and operating systems. Organizations with mixed environments may find multiplatform configuration management tools significantly cut learning and implementation cycle times.

Staffing Impact

Do not implement this tool as part of the Year 2000 correction program if it has not already been started, because preparation can be very resource-demanding. Administration requirements are different among the tools. Some may require only a part-time administrator, while others may require several full-time administrators. If, however, you have a configuration manager in place, it will pay for itself many times over.

Distribution Managers

Primary Function

Distribution management tools are used to schedule and perform the downloading of software from one site to many. Many enterprises have already found it necessary to provide a mechanism for tracking multiple copies of software. Distribution managers were originally developed for use in distributing internally developed mainframe/midsize application software to multiple sites.

Increases in the practice of central distribution of PC software has resulted in the creation of a form of this tool that keeps track of the version of every software program loaded on servers and clients. This often becomes necessary to prevent violating product-licensing agreements. These surrogate managers schedule transfer of software versions to individual computers through network resources. The status of each software program version on every target platform is maintained in a file so that the status of the product's distribution is known.

Year 2000 Relevance

Implementing this tool will help users compile the existing PC software inventory and support the expense of replacing hardware and software. Although the tool is designed to work within a network, some organizations have found its inventory capabilities valuable enough to implement *before* they establish the network. Without this tool, the distribution of PC software can be haphazard. Some remote computers may continue to run old versions of software that can fail, possibly propagating bad data back into the IT environment and thereby damaging enterprisewide services as fast as they can be corrected to support Year 2000 processing.

Idiosyncrasies

Doing the PC and components inventory may take several months, but programs are available to perform this task. User-developed software is often uncovered. These may require additional planning and administration. It is not always possible to tell if the products developed have problems. The existence of the compliant version of a database development product implies that all databases are millennium-compliant. In fact, some may have to be recompiled with later versions of the software. Others may have to be reprogrammed. The availability of macros, small user-developed routines, presents a special problem. These are not inventoried, and even if they were, it is nearly impossible to determine whether there is date processing in them without looking at the code. Enterprises often discover that they cannot substantiate legitimate licenses because copies of some licenses exist on many machines. This is often the result of grabbing the first copy that can be found to reload a PC. Therefore, such enterprises may find it necessary to develop additional management processes. Implementing this tool can be done parallel to the update process.

Staffing Impact

Building an organization to manage distribution is often required. It may take months to achieve but the payback justifies the expense. Distribution management software requires administration support. A small staff of people who support networks and parallel mainframe environments typically runs this product. Training runs from two days to a week.

Version Managers

Primary Function

Version managers make it possible to carry out concurrent change projects and implement multiple changes to the same programs because they provide the capability for simultaneous changes to be merged. Where the tool finds the same lines changed, conflicts are highlighted so that they can be reviewed; the changes can then be combined manually. When version managers are used, then, interim versions can be placed in production, tested individually, or held for a single release.

Year 2000 Relevance

Many organizations cannot freeze application functions long enough to make the changes necessary for Year 2000 compliance. They may be forced by competition, regulatory requirements, environment changes, or Year 2000 failures to introduce several changes while code redesign fixing the Year 2000 problem is under way.

Idiosyncrasies

This tool is important and easy to implement. Many variations provide adequate information to show differences between the original state and the changed state of the code product, potentially making it unnecessary to acquire a separate comparator tool (described later). Unfortunately, version managers are not available for any but the most popular hardware platforms.

Staffing Impact

Version managers do not require much training. Skill requirements for running the tool are minimal. A couple of hours of training is usually sufficient to enable a programmer to use the tool.

Analysis Tools: Scanners and Parsers

Primary Function

Scanners and parsers examine individual computer code modules. Scanners are the simpler versions of the two; they search for matches of character strings in source code, but do not distinguish between data definition (where the attributes of a data element are defined) and process occurrences (each place in the program where the data is accessed), and often do not distinguish between real code and comments. Parsers are a little more intelligent. They recognize the structure of the language and can distinguish not only where a date element is found, but also how it is used. Parsers can be used to trace date movement and find aliases (other names applied to the same location in a record, but which are not obviously date references) that might not be found by a scanner.

Year 2000 Relevance

Scanners and parsers are put to use twice during the Year 2000 correction process: first to estimate the number of lines with date occurrences, and second, in the analysis process, to identify every date occurrence and flag the lines for further study and/or change.

Scanners are usually employed in the estimating process because they are faster, and, when creating estimates, accuracy is not so important. Parsers are used primarily during analysis. These tools are easy to construct, and commercial products are also available that provide the ability to find date fields using many different combinations of date-field name formats. Users will also find it handy to be able to exclude some character strings that would otherwise create false matches (e.g., they don't interpret DD in the word ADD as a date reference).

Idiosyncrasies

Many scanners and parsers have been tailored to support the Year 2000 update process, but they usually support only COBOL. Many specially designed products do not give the purchaser much freedom in defining the search arguments, and the list provided may prove inadequate. This limitation may be a handicap where the application employs naming conventions that are not easily identified as dates (e.g., ADVYRAHEAD, used to specify a table item containing the next year, in which YR is buried in the field name, making it hard to find). It can be a real showstopper when foreign languages have been employed to define data fields.

If you decide to purchase a commercial scanner or parser, look for the ability to exclude terms, because many employ naming conventions using abbreviations such as DA (confusing DATA with DAY) or MO (confusing MOVE with MONTH) to be identified as dates. The exclusion capability allows the user to exclude words or to look for patterns at the beginning of a variable name, possibly followed by a special character such as a dash, and exclude them.

Staffing Impact

These tools are relatively easy to use and do not require much training. Several are available for mainframe use, and they exist for most platforms. The best ones run on PCs, but this usually means that the program code has to download, a time-consuming process for large volumes of code.

Data-Modeling and Design Recovery Aids

Primary Function

These tools have been developed to support product reengineering. While some early data-modeling tools required manual development of diagrams to show the flow, newer products perform the work of decomposing the code into functional blocks or slices. The flow diagrams are generated automatically to show both data and control flow from slice to slice. These diagrams define business rules.

The segmentation of the code is useful for building objects, or discrete functions, which can then be reused. However, the output of these products is not standard. Some will provide new versions of the code that are restructured and cleaned of unused code. Others will produce process flow and data flow diagrams; still others provide quality metrics.

Year 2000 Relevance

Data-modeling and design recovery aids can prove beneficial during the millennium-update project in three ways. Enterprises faced with the possibility of abandoning proprietary code may find these tools essential for analyzing the functions so that they can assess the loss and conduct salvage operations or create specifications for vendor packages. They can supply the documentation needed to redesign programs that are difficult to read and unsupported by experienced staff. They can also assist in defining reusable components such as date routines and conversion programs.

These tools are also useful in populating and automatically maintaining the relationships between code and function in a repository.

Idiosyncrasies

These tools take many forms, but most exist for use on PC-based workstations. They can be beneficial in building models and documenting the process to provide cycle-time reduction improvements during the Year 2000 project. They can aid in assessing product quality, determine the functional paths that need to be included in test script development, and eliminate unused or redundant code that does not require changing. But be aware that these products are computer language–specific, although a number of them can handle more than one language.

Staffing Impact

The operator of these tools is generally not your average programmer; they require experience and technical decision making. Training time is roughly three to five days, and the learning curve is from two to four months.

Documentation Aids

Primary Function

A documentation aid is similar to a reengineering tool, but operates at a slightly higher level. Many provide analysis of job-run instructions, creating job flows that show program and data file usage and highlighting files that are imported from outside the enterprise or the application. Many provide useful cross-reference listings for compiling aggregate information at the application level.

Year 2000 Relevance

Documentation aids are of greater benefit to enterprises that do not have repositories. They can provide much necessary information about relationships of code and data that will help prevent costly mistakes caused when code or data used by other applications is changed without making changes to the other applications. They are not replacements for the repository, which is a more globally useful tool.

Idiosyncrasies

Documentation aids comprise a broad category of tools ranging from the very simple to complex. Most enterprises acquire several documentation aids. Some show the relationships of date fields across programs and data files, and they have been used for data administration and building data warehouses, as well as providing data flow diagrams for reengineering projects. These tools provide input to the repository.

Staffing Impact

Analysts use documentation tools most often. The time required to learn these tools is dependent on the complexity of the tool. If detailed processes and run instructions are defined and constructed by the computer professionals, these tools can be operated by nontechnical staff. Most organizations that purchase these tools create programs to take the data generated and load it into databases or a repository.

Change Tools: Editors

Primary Function

The features included with editors can significantly reduce the workload of the programmer. With many editors, you can perform the following functions: scroll through components based on flow and paragraph execution, view included members on-line, locate field cross references, uncover hidden date components, shorten data entry by providing statement constructs and basic syntax, identify similar modules for creating common routines, and make global changes of words or phrases as in word processors.

Year 2000 Relevance

Program changes are made using an editor. A good programmer with a good editor can process code changes as fast as another can using an intelligent editor (discussed next). Using an editor has the further advantage that it can be used for all work, as it is not restricted only to Year 2000 changes.

Idiosyncrasies

Most computer people already use editors that were provided by the vendor with the hardware platform. The purchase of editors is, therefore, seldom even a topic, although many enterprises have purchased commercial editors in conjunction with programming workstations.

A good editor should have the ability to trace the flow of data through the process from one data element to the next and provide tagging of the lines involved so that when changes are made, they can be captured and fed back to a central store. Many editors provide hot keys, which save the time it takes to type common words and computer commands.

Staffing Impact

Most editors require only a day of training, usually provided by the vendor; but to become proficient may take several weeks. Even though most editors have similar functions, the introduction of a new one often meets with resistance, and thus is best done by a small group of proponents who can encourage the rest of the staff to adopt the new tool.

Rule-Based Change Tools: Intelligent Editors

Primary Function

Intelligent rule-based editors rely on the ability of a human being to provide the definition of what a date is and is not. (For example, when does YR represent *year* and when is it used as a phonetic abbreviation for *wire*? No kidding, it happens!) The rules for making the changes are selected from a set provided by the vendor and constructed in the sequence to fit the situation (e.g., rule 1 might be to reformat dates from MMDDYY to YYMMDD; rule 2 might be to expand years from two digits to four digits when in character strings or to 2 three-digit forms when in packed decimal). The rules have to be validated manually; thus, they require careful definition and, ~~~~~~~~~~~~mization.
The first part of the rule application process is to i⌐⌐⌐⌐⌐⌐⌐e
the code. The second part is to replace the old code

These tools change more than one segment of the ⌐⌐⌐⌐⌐⌐s,
procedure definitions, called subroutines, shared ⌐⌐⌐⌐⌐le
pass. Most intelligent editors annotate the chang⌐⌐⌐⌐⌐ul
hints, and alert the operator to potential problems. ⌐⌐⌐⌐⌐rt
a variety of data management software products ⌐⌐⌐⌐⌐d-
ucts for a single platform. As by-products of the pi⌐⌐⌐⌐⌐or
can provide information on test path requirements and create program templates that can be used to develop test program data, bridge programs, or conversion programs.

Year 2000 Relevance

The label *intelligent editor* is used to describe the myriad tools and services on the market purporting to "solve the Year 2000 problem." The most basic tool of this ilk automatically detects and expands the data definition of Gregorian and ordinal/Julian date fields containing years in two-digit format. This is not as simple as it sounds, however, because the product must handle a variety of date formats and storage techniques.

The most intelligent of these editors perform a variety of date-change functions. They perform process instruction changes for all dates, including fiscal and period dates; they handle mixed dates, where some contain two-digit-year designators and others four; they automatically examine sizes of fields so that screen displays and reports won't exceed parameters; they track movement of dates to new fields (even when field names do not readily identify themselves as date fields) to make sure those fields will accommodate the new size.

Idiosyncrasies

These tools are available on a variety of platforms. While most run on the PC, some are now being sold to run on IBM mainframes. The dominant focus of these tools is COBOL code, since it is the single most commonly used programming language. Tools supporting other languages include Assembler, C, FORTRAN, PL/I, Natural, RPG, and Easytrieve, and other popular languages are increasingly available.

Rules are always developed at some central location by the vendor, and the process can become complicated. As the number of rules increases, the length of time to define a new one also increases. A quick analysis of date validation routines uncovered more than 30 different methods for performing the validation. Some require partial code replacement and others full replacement. Some programs use more than one routine, and the use of different formats may require the alteration of several validations.

Depending on how the rule is constructed and the sequence in which the rules are applied can result in errors being inserted. For example, the first action might be to insert a window. The first test might be to confirm whether the year is 00, then reject it as incomplete data. The test might never be satisfied because the year is now always 2000. You might want to remove the test or replace the initialization routine that loads the data-entry mask with the null values instead of zeros. The year-validity test may require the value YY to be greater than 50 and less than 99, 01 to 97, greater than or equal to the current year, less than the current year, within n years of the current year, and so on, in which case you might want to replace the acceptable range of YY or change the calculation that sets the value of the ranges. If 99 was once used to denote something other than 1999 (e.g., an indefinite date) but is now needed to denote 1999 quite specifically, you might have to change the process that inserts nines in the date and every place it looks for nines. Do not be surprised to hear quotes of up to two weeks to create one or more rules.

The best process for using intelligent editors is to first perform a design review using a parser. Find processes that are not covered by the rules (e.g., replacing calls to retrieve the system date with calls to retrieve a proprietary date), then ask the vendor to add a rule to cover those processes you expect to recur. At the same time, you can make the change manually and proceed with the process so as not to hold up work, thus improving workflow.

Contrary to some marketing claims, intelligent editors are not silver bullets. A typical tool requires the operator to specify date definitions that seed a parser for what to look for to identify dates. The operator may need to make several passes to determine all the seeds and eliminate invalid identifiers. These tools have improved over the months as experience broadened their capabilities. Some have gotten very efficient and achieve extremely high accuracy.

Staffing Impact

Intelligent editors can be bought with or without services. The service providers generally run the code and find the requirements for creating new rules. Where a service is used, plan on human support for it—someone who is intimate with both the rules used by the tool and the application being changed. Maintaining knowledge of the rules may prove difficult if the work is performed in a vendor factory. Multiple clients may be constantly generating rule requirements, rendering it virtually impossible to know the rules in place at any moment.

Installing and sustaining an intelligent editor can be difficult, especially if you take on rule definition, although running the tool is simple enough for a relatively nontechnical worker to perform.

Date (Clock) Simulators

Primary Function

Date simulators intercept program calls to the hardware or system clocks. They are used to force the application to act as if it were running in another time.

Year 2000 Relevance

This type of tool is critical for testing applications that have been changed to be millennium-compliant. It allows the user to tell the program that it is running in the year 2000, on February 29, 2000, or another date such as December 31, 1999. Without this tool, testing on some platforms cannot be completed.

Idiosyncrasies

Date simulators began to appear in 1993 and have evolved significantly since then. Nevertheless, many organizations still encounter problems when using these tools to test in environments where concurrent changes are being made, because the test files get corrupted. Alternatives to using this tool include elimination of calls to the system clock and using a client-controlled clock. Some enterprises have found it more efficient to purchase another processor or to lease time at a service provider that supports Year 2000 testing rather than to change the system clock to the date required.

Staffing Impact

This is another tool that is easy to teach to a programmer, usually taking less than a day. It does, however, require constant administration to schedule its use and manage the date settings so they do not conflict with other tests.

Code (Static) Analyzers

Primary Function

A static analyzer is a programming language–specific tool that audits programs to determine whether they follow the language rules. Violations of syntax rules are highlighted, making this an excellent precompiler diagnostic, hence saving cycle time on the target test computer. Most static analyzers also allow specification of client-specific rules so that infractions can be identified. Nearly every one of these tools performs a quality assessment of the code to reveal introduction of new complexity that makes the program even more difficult to maintain.

Year 2000 Relevance

In a situation where programmers are unfamiliar with the language of the program being changed, this type of tool provides an important teaching function. As resources become more difficult to allocate, the presence of this tool enables less-skilled staff to be introduced to code-change and testing process tasks.

Idiosyncrasies

Very few languages are supported by code analyzers.

Staffing Impact

Using code analyzers is rather straightforward, but building a special rule set may take several weeks and the assistance of a programmer. Goals need to be determined and communicated to the staff, and auditing the use of the tool is required.

Interactive Debuggers

Primary Function

A debugging tool allows the programmer to observe a running program to determine where it is failing and what data or situation is causing the failure. This tool reduces the amount of time required to solve problems.

Year 2000 Relevance

While useful in testing programs that have been redesigned to achieve millennium compliance, the chief benefit of a debugger is in identifying failures in production that occur due to date failures.

Idiosyncrasies

Debuggers are available for a number of computer languages, and many run on PCs or have a much friendlier PC front end. These tools can be impressive when used in testing changes. It is possible to use these tools to temporarily alter the date values at specific points in the program and then watch the value as it is passed through the program. You can actually see the changes that take place and identify the lines of code that are not performing the change as expected. You can even fix the code and restart the process at that point. This may obviate the use of a date simulation tool for some testing.

Staffing Impact

These tools take several days to learn—and weeks for the programmer to become proficient. They require significant programming experience to use, hence it may be prudent to have only the most knowledgeable programmers use them in diagnosing production problems.

Code Comparators

Primary Function

Code comparators perform line-by-line comparisons of two versions of a program or file. When a mismatch is identified, the two lines are reported either on-line, for interactive evaluation, or in a printed report.

These tools are used in two ways. The first and most frequent is to confirm that changes in reports or files have been made as expected. The second is to determine what has been changed in the source code. The latter is usually done when the code is changed by someone who does not work for the enterprise—the purpose being to check for unauthorized alterations.

Year 2000 Relevance

Comparators can reduce testing cycle time and validate not only the tests, but the changing of test data. If code is sent out to a vendor factory, a comparator can rapidly validate the changes made in the factory, and it may be possible to skip some global testing of all routines since it is easy to determine the altered lines that require testing.

Idiosyncrasies

There are few of these tools, but they are easy to build, so most enterprises have constructed their own. They do not have to be language-specific, though some find it useful to build in exclusionary rules for such things as line numbers or changes in comments.

Staffing Impact

Since they are easy to run, comparators can be almost fully automated. The actual review of the output, however, will require an experienced computing professional familiar with the programming language or data.

Code Generators/Fourth-Generation Languages

Primary Function

There are several forms of code generators. Their purpose is to reduce the time it takes to create a program. Code generators make it simple to create the programs that extract data for testing, to make changes to data for testing, to generate data-conversion programs for inserting century values, and to build bridges.

Year 2000 Relevance

This productivity aid will save time in creating conversion programs and bridges, building custom test-data generators, or editing data. If you have to replace missing source code, code generators can save days of coding and testing. Some enterprises build special tools to replace date routines in the source code or to scan for dates.

Idiosyncrasies

Some code generators are not themselves millennium-compliant, which obviously could cause problems in creating some specialized routines or making data changes. Some tools use preexisting data file definitions, while others require that they be reentered each time the file is used.

Staffing Impact

These tools generally take some time to learn and become proficient with, but they can be taught to a noncomputer person. Many of them are similar to the report writers and macrolanguages used to create PC-based programs. An experienced PC person can become an expert with four to six weeks of constant practice. Programmers generally need more time to become proficient because they do not have the opportunity to use the tool constantly.

Test Scripters

Primary Function

Testing is not an ad hoc process. It must be planned so that all the design changes are tested and all variations in the data are accounted for. The test-scripting tool facilitates the planning and documentation so that data can be created and the test run. This is required for several types of tests, including systems and acceptance testing. The playback feature enables the product to run the test. This is important for on-line application tests in which data is normally entered by an individual. The product acts in place of the person entering the data.

Year 2000 Relevance

Test scripters enable the person who is changing the program to communicate with another regarding what changes to test and to what limits. In a factory environment where the testing agent and the person changing the code are different, this will save time and minimize the creation of test data.

Idiosyncrasies

Certain test scripters are more difficult to learn and use than others, and most are written to support only on-line testing, so look for one that produces hard-copy scripts. Most platforms are supported by tools of this type.

Staffing Impact

Scripters are usually used by experienced computer professionals because their many functions can take weeks to assimilate.

Date Routines

Primary Function

Commercial date routines have the advantage of being fully tested. In enterprises that do not have standards, commercial date routines may provide an answer. These are program components that perform such functions as calculate duration, determine the day of the week, and convert from Julian to Gregorian dates and the reverse. A typical package may have 40 or more routines which can be inserted in place of internally developed routines.

Year 2000 Relevance

These routines are tested for millennium compliance. Replacing date processing with tested date routines may save time and reduce testing. When the rules for the date routine are built into a static analyzer, the programming of these routines can be delegated to less-experienced staff.

Idiosyncrasies

If you are using workstations for making update changes, make sure the package supports testing on the workstation. Some are written in Assembler for a specific platform. Choose a set that supports all the ways you store data. This requires some analysis, but it will save time later. Some enterprises store their data in several forms, including variations of size, edit masks, storage form (e.g., character, numeric, packed decimal, and binary), and even two-, three-, or four-digit-year fields.

Staffing Impact

There is a limited set of code modules. Using them does not require specifically trained personnel, but identifying where and which routine to use may not be easy. Clients have employed over 100 routines for everything from date conversions to comparisons and arithmetic.

Migration Tools: Data Analyzers

Primary Function

Many data-analyzer tools have been created to support the development of data warehouses and to help enterprise mergers. They perform an analysis of data files and look for patterns of data. They also find inconsistencies in data where patterns are known, such as nonnumeric date formats or variable date formats.

Year 2000 Relevance

A data analyzer can identify hidden data, such as date data in fields that are not supposed to contain dates, or dates that are supposed to be invalid. In the Year 2000 update process, they can uncover hidden change requirements and be used to test the changes.

Idiosyncrasies

Data analyzers require expertise that may not be available in-house.

Staffing Impact

Data-analyzer tools require specialists. They should be run by a small staff that employs them frequently. Learning curves tend to be moderately high, with proficiency being reached in the third or fourth month of use.

File Definition/File Modification Aids

Primary Function

File definition products are used to create file specifications for new files. They are platform-specific and create files for only a certain number of data management systems. They are, in essence, text editors used to define data files. They support allocating space, browsing existing data, editing data, and transferring data to new files.

Year 2000 Relevance

File modification tools are used primarily to create test files. Where the data requires only the insertion of the century prefix 19, it can be used as a conversion program. Used in conjunction with a test-data generator, it will save time doing global editing of test data to simulate several dates.

Idiosyncrasies

Certain file definition tools provide a full set of functions, but on some platforms, the tools evolved with the functions split; hence, more than one tool may have to be purchased.

Staffing Impact

File definition/file modification aids are used by computer professionals. Since they are powerful data editing tools, they are, in some instances, used instead of building a custom program to change production data, so the output must be tested. They require significant knowledge of the platform and the data management system being employed.

Test-Data Generators

Primary Function

Test-data generators enable the user to define the rules for the data in a file and the limits of that data. The tool then creates a file with the data specified by the rules, which subsequently can be used in each phase of testing.

Year 2000 Relevance

The typical mechanism used for creating test data is to select production data and then edit it by inserting and changing data as required to fit the test requirements. This process is inexact and time-consuming. A test-data generator tool provides a far more accurate and complete set of test data without the additional work of editing.

Idiosyncrasies

Before purchasing a data generator, make sure it is millennium-compliant. It must support dates generated across century boundaries. Some products do not support date definitions that include four-digit years. Although you can work around this deficiency, it is annoying and time-wasting.

Staffing Impact

These tools require one to two days of formal training or workshops. Like other data tools, knowledge of the system software and data management software is essential, which means that experienced computer professionals are required.

Database Conversion Tools

Primary Function

Conversion tools are used by specialists to rebuild databases that have new formats. They are similar to file definition aids, but support data management systems.

Year 2000 Relevance

These tools are used to expand field definitions and file sizes to allow for four-digit years.

Idiosyncrasies

Most organizations already own these tools.

Staffing Impact

These tools are used only by specialists trained in the management of databases built using data management systems. Again, this type of tool is one that requires some formal training, and it can take several months for personnel to achieve proficiency.

And More Tools Everyday

There are now more than 20,000 computer tools on the market. The growing number of tools does not imply Year 2000 opportunists have taken over the tool market. Many vendors are responding to an increasing demand for technology management requirements. Some tools-marketing programs are actually avoiding association with the Year 2000 problem. Vendors may fear that their products will be perceived to have only a limited useful life. Vendors of some tools see a relationship between their products and the Year 2000 problem, but fear that highlighting the problem will decrease the market for other products.

Many tools that are in categories not mentioned here can assist in the Year 2000 work effort. E-mail and rapid-systems development tools are examples of categories of tools not directly related to repair of systems. The first is important for keeping team members current. The second because it may be faster in some instances to rebuild a system than repair it. Reengineering might allow a system owner with a good understanding of an existing application to rebuild a system adding new functionality. This alternative may appeal to those who are looking to extend functionality in the near future, and those who see ongoing maintenance costs for existing applications rising.

The largest percentage of Year 2000 tools is aimed at the mainframe computer platform (IBM MVS operating system is the largest single category). While many of the tools may run on PCs, the target language or connectivity requirement may be aimed at the mainframe application repairs. The disparity in the number of tools aimed at the mainframe versus midrange platforms (client/server, HP, DEC, Unisys, and so on) is enormous. Systemic Solutions, which serves middle-market firms, has been able to build a list of only slightly more than 400 tools that are targeted at the midrange computer user.

An alternative to buying tools is to outsource the code repair and testing. The number of remediation services are increasing, and many have not yet reached capacity. These services often provide some tools-acquisition relief. Some companies have started to provide test facilities that already boast availability of many of the most popular tools. Such sites are particularly attractive if the tool usage skills are available, but the costs of additional licenses for use during the testing phase are a concern. SABRE and Data Dimensions Information Systems are examples of companies offering computer testing time and tools.

The next chapter, "When in Doubt, Outsource," discusses hiring outside consultants to work on your Year 2000 project and how to get the most out of the outsourced service.

CHAPTER 11

When in Doubt, Outsource

E ven when an enterprise is ideally positioned, with the right staff and the management capability to handle the millennium-update project, it still should probably ask: "Can we handle this ourselves?"

The general consensus among service providers is that *if* your enterprise is well staffed and well managed, *if* you've been given the necessary project resources, and *if* you started the Year 2000 correction process prior to 1995—that is, created a plan and a process, tested the process, and began changing code—then your enterprise can probably complete the change without help. Unfortunately, it's no longer 1995, and you *are* reading this book. That probably puts you in the company of about 99.5 percent of the enterprises in the world that are now in some degree of trouble.

Probably no enterprise or organization will be able to solve this problem without some kind of help. Therefore, this chapter discusses why you might consider asking for help, what kinds of assistance you will find, where to look for that help, and what you can do to help the help help you.

Many of the most-experienced Year 2000 consulting companies have reached the point where they are now selective about the clients they are taking. These companies typically are looking for customers where there is a guarantee of post–Year 2000 work. The major accounting firms have stopped providing Year 2000 support for all but their largest existing clients. This does not mean that help is not available.

Many consulting firms have been surprised by the lack of demand for services. Market forecasts for the last three years have not been realized. Some believe that most companies prefer to do the work inside. Others believe that demand will peak in 1999 as the middle-market firms and smaller government agencies realize that their survival is at stake and repair is their only option. These companies have long depended on external resources for systems development and support. The previously mentioned Cap Gemini survey, which found that few companies have spent more than a quarter of their Year 2000 budgets as of April 1998, may indicate that these companies are incapable of performing the work to be done with resources at hand and must now seek external support.

Many consulting and technology labor contracting companies started business or expanded services in the last couple of years hoping to cash in on the Year 2000 problem. Many of these have not yet gained much experience in Year 2000 work, but have lots of background and skills that can be employed. Other companies have been started by individuals around a cadre of Year 2000 experts, as was the firm of one of the authors. There are many that have no experience at all. A May 1998 request for services by an enterprise in Chicago was answered by five companies, only one of which appeared to have any direct experience.

Help is out there. If you want your money's worth, expect to pay for it.

Outsourcing Strategies

Few companies have both the capacity (time, people, facilities, and hardware) and the knowledge (understanding, experience, skill, and perception) required to perform all the work involved in the Year 2000 update project. Sadly, there are those that do not have either. Over the last 10 years, many enterprises have experienced massive downsizing. Further, some have implemented practices to restrict the growth of computer departments specifically. Among the casualties of restrictive measures are technical support staff, training programs, and training facilities.

In addition, techies in some organizations have been replaced with business-minded people, whose eyes are planted firmly on the bottom line and not code lines. Moreover, the educational system produces new graduates who are specialists only in the latest technical fads, while those skilled in computer languages, system software, and existing tools in many organizations have either retired or been forced out. These moves mean that many enterprises are ill-equipped to deal with the massive change demanded by the coming millennium.

Much has been written about outsourcing, and it's recommended that you do a little (actually, as much as you can) investigation before you start working with service firms, especially if you don't have any prior experience. For starters, find a copy of the article, "Strategic Sourcing: To Make or Not to Make," by Ravi Venkatesan, in the *Harvard Business Review* (November–December 1992, vol. 70, no. 6, p. 68). He lists five reasons why you should at least consider outsourcing. They are paraphrased here to more specifically apply to the Year 2000 problem resolution:

1. Improve process
2. Sustain strategic focus
3. Contain costs
4. Improve management control
5. Transfer knowledge

Improve Process

In the first two months of the millennium-update project, many managers will have to perform a number of tasks that are long overdue:

Inventory all computer hardware and software

Find and assess all embedded systems

Prepare an enterprisewide tactical plan

Tool and develop a change process

Build or contract for a testing environment

Implement hardware vendor changes

Identify and contact critical suppliers

In the next four months of the millennium-update project, the technical staff may have to perform all of the following in order to get ready for testing:

Replace or upgrade hardware

Obtain upgrades to vendor-supplied software

Eliminate obsolete code

Update code to latest version of the compiler

Repair or replace application code

Reconstruct missing code

Everyone will have to participate in the following activities in the time remaining:

Test changes to software, hardware, and equipment

Manage enterprisewide risk reduction activities

Prepare contingency plans and business recovery processes

Capacity, which means time, facilities, equipment, and staff, is going to be your first impediment. Time, of course, will always be of the essence, exemplified by enterprisewide planning.

Not planning is not an option. Those organizations that forgo it, thinking it is a waste of time, pay for it later—literally and figuratively. If planning is not conducted *for the duration of the project,* activities can take 30 percent longer and require 50 percent more staffing because things are done in the wrong order, noncritical work absorbs available resources, or mistakes require repair. On the other hand, the planning activity cannot take too long. A plan becomes worthless when applications start failing. By the way, two months is not too long—as long as you build the plan by identifying critical actions first and then executing those actions as you finish planning. This means you can even start changing code while you are planning. Many organizations start their first conversion exercises as soon as they can identify which source code to work on.

Setting up the process in large organizations often still involves technology managers in selling the need to the application users. Only then can they proceed with developing a change process, modifying the infrastructure to support the change process, constructing the process so it makes the greatest use of tools and talent, and figuring out how to get people to adopt the new process so that it is actually employed. Enterprises that never make it to the last step have most likely bypassed one or more of the other steps. If you want your Year 2000 update project to be a success, you cannot bypass any of the steps.

Now that you have the fear of time in your heart, back to where to go for help—outsourcing. There are firms out there that have been through the process of enterprisewide planning for the year 2000, and they can install that process and build a plan in the time required. You will find consulting firms that know what information is required about hardware, software, vendors, data suppliers, and embedded systems. They can provide the infrastructure support systems to support management of these functions.

You will probably have to prepare detailed fallback (contingency) plans for any of the project components not completed on time. Many firms have created disaster-recovery plans for getting their computers back up as fast as possible. The plans required for year 2000 tend to be more expensive. You will find firms that can, within a couple of weeks, provide you with a detailed descriptive analysis of how your business functions relate to your hardware and software systems and show you the ways in which these systems are interconnected. And unless your enterprise maps the dependencies of business functions to applications, you may spend much-needed time on fixing the noncritical and missing the critical systems. Again, outside services, with the right tools, can do this faster and with better accuracy than most internal staff.

You must perform a risk assessment to determine what the penalties will be—lost revenue, violations of laws or regulations, and impact on individuals and business relationships. A consultant can provide awareness training and provide you with an objective risk management planning process for conducting the internal assessment. Some companies can speed the risk management planning by obtaining a facilitator from a consulting firm. Some firms can help companies build a plan as quickly as two days.

Another route that some enterprises take is to reduce the complexity of the environment by reducing the number of languages that have to be changed. Ernst & Young's Cleopatra product converts PL/1 code to COBOL II. A single-language environment makes replacement of date routines easier, facilitates insertion of purchased and tested date routines, and encourages the use of more tools in the date-change process. If you have a lot of Assembler code, you may want to consider Software Migrations Limited's language migration tool, FermaT, that takes IBM Assembler and converts it to C, COBOL, and even other languages. Friedman and Associates provides a service to move code from one platform and/or database system to another. This is only a small sampling of the services you might access. Remember that some tools will come with technical support, but for others you will be required to contract for support.

Sustain Strategic Focus

Many enterprises that try to do it all themselves initially underestimate the complexity of the date problem, but soon discover they are unable to focus their energies to both solve the Year 2000 problem and continue to support business as usual. They find they have too few people with the time, skills, and the interest to perform the change work.

Chances are, you are understaffed. Perhaps the people who built your applications are no longer with the company or are heavily engaged in new key development projects. If the latter is the case, these projects will have to be either put on the shelf or expedited to get them completed prior to the failure of a current application. In many cases, these development projects absorb the time of the most knowledgeable personnel.

Consulting firms can provide the help you need and supply project management talent with date-problem resolution skill and experience. These companies, for the most part, provide training to their new hires in technology and tools, a task that you might not be able to support.

Focusing your enterprise's available resources on fixing the problem may not be possible. Most computer shops say they spend up to 70 percent of their resources on maintenance, but that is probably fudging the truth. Approximately 40 to 55 percent of the maintenance budget is spent in making functional modifications to existing applications. Between 20 and 30 percent of the maintenance effort is spent assimilating changes due to hardware or systems software upgrades. Making adjustments because of vendor software changes absorbs another 10 to 15 percent of the maintenance budget. The bottom line? Only 5 to 10 percent of the budget is currently spent on fixing code errors, which is the nemesis of the computing staff.

As systems start to fail due to date problems, the percentages will start to shift. As they do, less time will be available for the most-experienced staff to spend on design problems or in managing the code-change process. Since the hardware, systems, and vendor application software changes will increase, there will be additional pressure on resources dedicated to code changes. New development will be impacted by the increase in maintenance. Many of these projects will have to be completed on time because they are scheduled to replace applications that are not millennium-compliant.

Needless to say, during all this, competition will not remain idle. No enterprise can afford to lose ground against others in quality or performance. New functionality will be required even against competitors that are not making strides to become compliant. It will hardly serve your enterprise to lose sales as its expenses increase due to the cost of fixing the code.

Contain Costs

If you have a small company, containing costs may be problematic in subtle ways. You may have to find homes for additional staff. There may not be enough telephone lines or terminal ports. Large enterprises, too, will not be exempt from space constraints. One state government agency found itself looking for space to house 40 people for three years. Delays in getting the space increased the agency's staffing requirement to 55.

Outsourcing the work to a company that provides its own facilities will save time and expenses. The tasks of finding the space and setting up furniture, telephones, and the like are all eliminated. And, because the duration of the need is finite, you will also save time and the expense of its ultimate divestiture.

Computer resources may also be obtained from the outside. A number of firms offer computers for disaster recovery and special development projects, and specifically for testing Year 2000 changes. These same firms may be the avenues of retreat if you do not have the storage capacity to handle both the testing and expansion of data fields.

Improve Management Control

A word to the wise: Project teams that were precipitous enough to begin working on the Year 2000 problem early have been stumped by an old foe—poor management control. These early-bird project teams have frequently found the cost of the changes and the duration of the individual correction projects consistently doubling. Why? Because IT organizations literally empty their drawers of every change request that had been put off for years for lack of a financial justification. Since they are now authorized to make changes that have no apparent financial return, Pandora's box has been opened.

Going outside for labor support can be useful in keeping the scope of work in check. Many managers will want to use the opportunity to make other changes. External expenses require hard currency. Having consultants, rather than internal specialists, estimate the costs and added duration to the Year 2000 repair work will take the heat of internal management. Outside help will gladly make the estimates. They will even absorb a certain level of the cost of estimating, but they won't do the changes requested out of the goodness of their hearts; they are likely to project a high cost. In such situations, technology management is given the leverage to curtail incremental project additions. This, then, releases the computer staff from responding to constant estimating requests so they can pursue the day-to-day workload.

Transfer Knowledge

There are many service firms that can provide support in this regard, including but not limited to the following:

- Contract programmers and testers
- Consultants skilled in planning, project management, and testing
- Legal services that perform contract reviews
- Services that determine vendor status and track vendor progress
- Consultants who specialize in tool assessments and implementation
- Business consultants skilled in analyzing business risks
- Process reengineering specialists who can help design replacement applications
- Specialists in source code recovery
- Software factories that can update code in large quantities

Choose a service provider with proven experience in the issues related to the millennium update. The point of hiring help is not just to add a few extra hands and brains, but to expedite the accumulation of knowledge. There is little time for trial and error. It bears repeating: Very few companies are adequately experienced in Year 2000 work. It takes about a year for a company to understand the problems associated with the intricacies of the Year 2000 fix, so be sure to verify references of any firm you are considering.

Taking Out a Contract

The easiest resources to find are contractors, but be sure you know what that means. Contract companies supply people; they do not always supply *skilled professionals.* Don't be surprised to see some programmers and analysts coming out of retirement to cash in on the Year 2000 problem. These people will have all the experience and knowledge, but may require some time to refresh their memories if they have been out of the business for a while. Watch out for people who are inadequately trained and without much technical experience. Care must be taken in the contract negotiations to clearly define the technical knowledge and skills required.

Contract people usually expect to be guided, directed, and managed by enterprise staff. They will require time to assimilate and be assimilated by your enterprise culture. They will require all the care and feeding of a new employee, including orientation and training in practices and procedures. A well-defined process will make this assimilation easier and faster. Contracted help can be introduced to the process piecemeal, with workload expanding, as they become familiar with their requirements.

Before you decide to employ contractors, you may want to review which projects they are going to be working on. Some vendors do not allow contractors to work on their products unless they are licensed. Some systems may require special knowledge about the application. Banks, for instance, find contractors familiar with deposit systems are better when it comes to working on those systems. Some applications may be so sensitive that you will not want an outside person working on them at all.

I'm a Consultant

Hey, who isn't? You may find consulting service providers that claim to have experience in massive conversions, language upgrades, and reengineering projects. They will point to proprietary processes that have been altered to deal with the Year 2000 problem. Trust no one; verify every claim; check every reference. Make sure your agreement is formal, complete, and explicit, not based on hype and poorly defined expectations. Remember, in contract disputes, service providers rarely find it difficult to prove customer complicity.

Planning Consultants

This is not to imply that reliable firms engaged in providing Year 2000 services are not out there; they are, so look for them. Web sites such as those supported by state governments are handy references to local consulting companies. The year2000 and Mitre Web sites list numerous vendors that are still taking work. Look in Appendix B of this book for names of service companies. Such consulting companies can complete a risk management or contingency-planning engagement in about the same time an enterprise can get its staff together and create a project charter. The pricing of these contracts is not always time and materials. Some companies have moved to value-based pricing in which a premium rate is charged for a product that has a high value. The risk management plan is in such a category because companies are under pressure from their bankers and clients to provide evidence of a plan and completion dates. Not all planning proposals are the same, so evaluate the proposal submitted to you from a consultant on the basis of the company's experience and the breadth of the planning effort. Plans must cover technology, supply-chain, customer-chain, operations, and business practices if they are to be complete.

Consulting companies that provide such services as tools assessments and testing are not as easy to find. Many consulting firms have formed alliances with other companies. These alliances include tool vendors, technical contractors, specialized service providers, and integrators (companies that install hardware and packaged software products).

Testing Consultants

There are consulting firms that specialize in testing; they are ideal candidates to test vendor products as well as applications updated by an outside service group. These companies possess special testing tools, which can save your enterprise time and money that might be misspent in searching for tools and implementing the wrong ones. These firms do not need to be experienced in working specifically with the millennium-update project. Most have already sufficiently studied the problem and understand the requirements.

Contract Service Consultants

There are also contract service companies that place an emphasis on supplying project teams. These companies have methods and experienced project management personnel who will be worth their weight in gold during the rush to meet the turning of the century clock. Unfortunately, there are not many quality experts in this regard, so if you do hire such a firm, expect that it will start an experienced person on your project and then replace that individual with someone of lesser credentials. This is not a bad technique. The knowledgeable consultant will establish the process and train your people, then set up the knowledge transfer. The second string maintains and improves the process and manages the work.

Most full-service computer companies divide their offerings into a small number of categories:

Estimating the cost of the portfolio change activity

Helping to plan the code redesign

Providing resources to change the code

For the most part, these firms restrict their services to a single hardware platform and computer language.

Finding the consultant with the breadth of skills required for your enterprise will be a challenge. You may have to or you may choose to engage two or three different full-service firms if you can afford the time and can segment the work to eliminate finger-pointing in the event of problems.

Legal Consultants

Legal consultants do not require any special knowledge of the Year 2000 problem, although the legal community has done some investigation into the problems that may result beginning on January 1, 2000. Legal help thus can be engaged with little coaching and a minimum of preparation time. Use the legal summaries already on the Internet to provide the general direction. Web addresses do get old, but you might try those listed in Appendix C as good legal sites.

Business Consultants

Finding business consultants and business process reengineers with the right kind of experience and focus will prove something of a challenge, because the methods used by most of these firms are designed for quality, not quick change processing. While specific Year 2000 experience is not a requirement for business consultants, these people should at the very least appreciate the urgency of the situation. The firms that will provide the most help are those specializing in rapid deployment of new systems.

Recovery Consultants

If source code recovery is required, you have only a few options. There are a couple of consultants: The Source Recovery Company, LLC, www.source-recovery.com and The Tuskar Company, LLC, www.tuskar.net. These companies offer a narrow band of services. Their service works only with code written for IBM mainframes and is limited in the number of languages it supports, namely, COBOL, Assembler, and PL/1. Plus, their services are very expensive, and the code you get back will not be pretty—nor will it include the Year 2000 changes. Still, having this code is better than no code at all. Expect to employ someone not only to make the Year 2000 fixes, but to maintain them as well.

Consultants via the Internet

Finding Year 2000 assistance has become easier thanks to the Internet. The Year 2000 Web site (www.year2000.com) lists numerous service providers. Subscribers can provide candid opinions of the services provided by these vendors. The Mitre Corporation (www.mitre.org/research/y2k/) provides an independent view of some Year 2000 tools. You can get a vendor's view of its offerings at www.year2000.com. If you are experienced at surfing the Internet, you can find ads from companies specializing in tools, services, and even consumer products such as mugs and T-shirts. (One search returned an advertisement for trenching tools; the advertisement was not computer disaster–related. Surfing the Net can provide you with a source of amusement when things get tough.)

Before You Buy

Before you hire an outside provider, be prepared for internal changes. Two practices employed by most enterprises probably will have to be abandoned when engaging outside help with your Year 2000 repair. The first is the *request for proposal* (RFP), and the second is the warranty on work performed. No, it's not a joke. See the following.

Request for Proposal, Please

The RFP process not only takes a lot of time that you don't have, but requiring a response to RFPs also may eliminate your enterprise from consideration by the firms you send them to. In this period, the demand for resources has created a seller's market. Most RFPs are written without extensive knowledge of the requirements; they demand responses in a specific format and require a consultant's time to create those responses, which are essentially sales instruments. The consultants are much better used in consulting, so companies are reluctant to apply revenue-generating consultants in responding to the RFP. There has to be an overriding reason to allocate scarce resources to this task.

Over the past few years, numerous discussions about the RFP process have been held on the Internet in the Year 2000 mail list. People have questioned what should and shouldn't be included in an RFP and even whether the RFP is useful in a situation where you might be forced to call in outside help and literally cannot afford the time to be choosy.

Here is a random selection of some of the more interesting requirements and queries proposed. These are reasonable requirements and serious questions. It cannot be denied that the answers will enable you to make a better buying decision. As you read them, put yourself in the vendor's shoes and consider what your honest reaction would be to the following.

Impact Analysis

We currently estimate that we have about 100 million lines of code (including comments and command language interfaces) comprising about 130 highly integrated applications. These are primarily COBOL (60 percent); 10 percent is written in an in-house language called INSURE-X, which is based upon an early version of APL; the remaining code spans about 15 additional languages in relatively equal proportions, which include C++, APL, SAS, BAL, Basic, and Easytrieve.

Since our inventory is not yet complete, we estimate these figures to be within 50 percent of the final figures. We have not yet begun a comprehensive analysis of our data.

Given this scenario, we are looking for a service provider to take control of our Year 2000 project. Please provide as much detail as you can to the following questions:

1. Describe the methodology your organization uses to perform the Year 2000 impact analysis. This description must address our unique needs in that we are a multinational company operating in a decentralized control structure.

2. Which programming languages (including version numbers) do you support? What is needed to extend your support to other languages? Can your process support a situation where COBOL has been written by German programmers in German?

3. While our existing documentation is not complete, we see the Year 2000 problem as an opportunity to set strong documentation standards for the future. How will your analysis aid us in that objective?

4. We are already using a metadata repository (PRISMDirectory Manager). Does your solution interface with that product? If not, which products do you support, and do you offer an option to extend support to other products?

5. Is your solution capable of documenting cross-platform interdependencies for both applications and relational databases? Our platforms include PC, client/server environments, and MVS mainframes.

6. We require your analysis tools to operate on PC and client/server platforms due to existing CPU constraints on our mainframe and miniplatforms.

7. In view of the sensitive nature of both our data and applications, we will require that all analysis be performed on-site. We will be happy to supply a fully secure area, since we will also require that we be in control of the security process.

8. Due to past mismanagement, we are missing slightly more than the industry average (3 percent) of source code. How does your analysis methodology handle missing source libraries for COBOL, SAS, and BAL?

Conversion Services

Upon completion of the impact analysis, we will have identified where, when, and to what degree our organization is at risk. The next step is to remove those risks through the process of code conversion. Please respond to the following queries regarding your code conversion services.

1. It is possible we will contract with one company for impact analysis and with another for conversion services. Are you willing to work with us under these conditions? (*Note:* This practice is not unusual with government contracts.)

2. Which languages (include version numbers) do you convert? What is needed to extend your conversion services to other languages? Again, please take into account COBOL programmed in German.

3. Our organization cannot support a big bang conversion strategy. This constraint makes it mandatory that all conversion strategies incorporate automatic creation of bridges and filters to accommodate data transfer from and to applications out of sync in the conversion process. Does your solution provide this service?

4. As in the analysis phase, our CPU constraints make it mandatory that the conversion process take place on the PC platform. Can you support this requirement?

5. Change-control and configuration management strategies of your conversion must be described in detail before your proposal can be given serious consideration.

6. As in the analysis phase, our security requirements will necessitate that all conversions be performed on-site. We will supply a fully secure area, since we will also require that we be in control of the security process.

7. What other resources will you require us to supply during the conversion process? Please detail hardware, software, and people requirements.

Testing

In the past, our testing requirements have been stringent. We have, however, come to realize that a short time frame will force us to accept less than optimal testing using existing strategies. We are looking for a service provider that can overcome these difficulties and guarantee its work via the testing process.

1. As in previous phases, all testing must be performed on-site. We will supply a fully secure area, since we will also require that we be in control of the security process.

2. Describe in detail your testing process, with particular focus on the resources you provide to assist in this process.

3. How are current dates tested on your system? Because of the integrated nature of our systems, we have installed features to keep all system dates synchronized. Will you require separate platforms for testing? Can you provide the hardware resources for these test environments?

4. Which parts of the testing process are you able to automate? How does that process work?

Training and Support

We recognize that in order to automate many of the tasks in the Year 2000 project, we must employ a significant number of new tools. Please describe how your company will assist us in acquiring the necessary skills to gain the required level of proficiency.

1. We estimate that our greatest need for external training and support will arise during the testing and implementation phases. What levels of support can you provide us at that time? Must we commit to these support levels at the beginning of the contract?

2. Assuming we wish to move ahead on training regardless of the assignment of this contract, please provide course outlines, schedules, and costs for all nonproprietary tools.

3. During all phases of the contract, will the resources you supply be provided by your permanent staff, or will they be subcontracted?

4. Assignment of this contract will be contingent upon the successful completion of a preliminary pilot project. Please provide the parameters of a pilot you would consider suitable for the proper demonstration of your solution. Naturally, we are eager to begin this pilot at the earliest possible date.

5. Please specify all resources—yours and ours—required for the initiation of this pilot project.

Guarantees and Fixed-Price Options

The final and most important information we are seeking relates to your company's experience in this area and your ability to service us at optimal levels for the duration of the project.

1. Provide details of your experiences in large-scale system conversions over the past five years. Please indicate your turnover statistics for this same time period so we can estimate how much experience has been retained in your organization.

2. How many customers are currently under contract, and when do these contracts expire? We need this information to ascertain that you will be able to deliver the proper level of support during all phases of our project; it will be too late if we discover in 1999 that you have staffing problems or conflicting service agreements.

3. How many past conversions were completed?

4. How many were delivered on time?

5. Please provide details on the size of these projects. Details should include a description of the change required and the number of lines, programs, applications, and databases changed.

6. Please provide cost estimates for all aspects of your proposal.

7. We are interested in fixed-price arrangements for all the proposed costs. What package deals are you prepared to offer us to secure this contract?

8. We require a guarantee of correctness for the Year 2000 conversion.

9. Please provide analysis of past proposal cost estimates compared to final completion and delivery costs.

10. Please provide references from past projects. These references need not be employed at the original company.

The preceding lists make many sensible and revealing points. Yet how quickly, when rolled up into an RFP, do reasonable questions start to seem like interrogation, with valid requirements becoming unrealistic expectations. Vendors have little inclination to respond to a barrage of questions when their doors are being beaten down by prospective clients wielding purchase orders.

You should fully understand what it is that you are shopping for when you issue your request. Separate discussions of tool purchases from service purchases. If you are seeking services, decide whether you want consulting (planning and management) or contracting. If you want to contract the work, decide whether to do it inside, outside, or a combination. If the work is done inside, tell the vendors what the environment is (platforms, systems software, languages, data types, volume of programs); don't expect them to guess. Anticipate that people costs may escalate.

You, can, however, use a generic RFP, identifying the work to be done, volume of work, and length of time to generate a complete response. The computer service firms will also need to know when the work is to be performed on-site, what facilities and equipment are provided, and that the tools they are expected to use are in place. They will also ask what role your enterprise intends to play, so that they can determine their own. Don't get into discussions of ISO 9000. You are working on your own code, which was not built using ISO standards for documentation. Adding this requirement implies that you expect every bit of documentation to come out of the process. This adds to cost and, when you may be fighting for survival, is meaningless. When it is important to document, pay for it.

Warranties and Pipe Dreams

It is amazing that some enterprises insist a consulting firm give a warranty on its work through the year 2000. On the surface, it may not appear to be an unreasonable demand, but consulting firms will quickly explain that such a warranty is virtually impossible. First, a significant percentage of the changes are made at the discretion of the customer. The consultant can make recommendations, but the client provides the direction. The customer thus shares responsibility. Second, the consulting firm is dependent on the client's definition of *good data* and *bad data* for testing. The consulting firm tests only within the parameters provided by the client. Again, the client is sharing responsibility for the outcome. Third, the consulting company does not retain control over the code. Once the code is turned over to the client, any number of people can alter the code. This automatically voids any warranty.

Fixed-Price Services

Be wary of offers of fixed-price services. Few services can really fix prices, and if they do, rest assured they will add caveats, rendering the fixed prices moot. Don't be taken in by this obvious sales mechanism to attract customers. Too many companies have already found out that such changes are rarely complete. Additional expenses are usually levied for repeat services and services not included in the contract. These expenses will be charged on the basis of time and materials. And fixed-price contracts will require tighter management than time-and-materials contracts.

Finding the Offer You Can't Refuse

There are several valid options for contracting out the code-fix work. Regarding the approach, you can choose manual, semiautomated, or fully automated. For the platform, you can choose to perform the change work on the target platform or move to PC workstations. As to location, you can choose to complete the changes on your computer, send the work to a domestic factory, or use an off-site factory.

Approaching the Runway

Understand the approach terminology before you decide which way to go. For starters, the *manual approach* is not completely manual; it is computer-assisted, using scanners or parsers to locate date references and then using editing tools to make the changes. Testing for completeness employs a debugging tool to trace the logic. This process works for just about every computer language and on any platform.

The *semiautomated approach* employs a similar process. The process starts with the use of scanners and parsers to find the date-field names. These are then fed to the change tool, which performs the process of expanding fields. The tool changes data definitions and logic to the best of its ability and generates programs to assist in century insertion and bridging. Note that the semiautomated approach will not make all your required changes. The change tool will either make incorrect changes or issue warnings that must be dealt with. A common example is expanding screen and report lines, which then exceed the size allowed. These tools cannot replace human judgment and decision making.

The semiautomated approach is best for factories, because they can employ people at a lower cost due to lower skill requirements for some tasks, greater volumes of work uninterrupted by day-to-day problems, higher tools-use proficiency, and more experience in dealing with dates. This approach is currently available for COBOL, PL/1, NATURAL, FOCUS, Easytrieve, and RPG.

As of this writing, the *fully automated approach* is still not totally perfect. The code can be fed into the tool, and changed code comes out the other side. In addition, the client may have the option of having the code provide bridges or insert windows. Many of the tools now find the date fields with as much accuracy as a human. But, even a 1 percent error can close down a company.

Your Place or Mine?

The platform you choose is dependent upon the testing windows available. Some enterprises choose to do the work on computers already set up to support testing. These computers are populated with the tools owned by the enterprise and have such features as security and code management.

A second option is to purchase additional computers. IBM has recently developed a PC that runs mainframe software. These platforms can be populated with the same tools and changes, and testing can be performed behind a physical firewall. A bit of caution: The cost of installing tools on these units might be more expensive than they are worth.

Many enterprises have already moved to PC workstations, which are supported by an increasing array of tools that can be used to perform the changes. If your enterprise has started to move development and support to workstations, you will have the communications support installed and the procedures for doing the work remotely defined. If this is a new technology venture, hire help to get you started.

A third option is to lease time. Several firms offer disaster-recovery and time-sharing services to support Year 2000 fixes. These include security, tools, and management resources.

Regardless of what combination of options you select, be aware that you will need consulting company representatives on-site to organize the work, prepare it for transfer to the people changing the code, handle design questions with enterprise experts, receive the code, and participate in acceptance testing. Doing the work on-site may include setting up a factory environment. Some consulting services are now offering to bring the semiautomated approach on-site; the client is usually required to provide the equipment, communication facilities, and work services to support the factory.

Shipping the code off-site requires the establishment of communications between the host site and the work location. Factories are being set up in various sites around the world, in the United States, Canada, Ireland, and India. Other factories exist in the Dominican Republic, Singapore, the People's Republic of China, and elsewhere. These factories will need to address security issues—some applications cannot be shipped offshore for national security reasons. Another challenge will be time differences, which will impact voice communications and may require remote access during the busiest computer-processing windows.

Obviously, an off-site solution reduces the demand on an enterprise's computer resources and facilities because the changes are made on the consultant firm's computers. Off-site firms may also be capable of limited testing, although the bulk of it will have to be conducted on the enterprise's host computer. Nevertheless, the enterprise is saved the cost of buying equipment, software tools, office furnishings, and support.

Finally, an off-site service provider may offer the advantage of one-stop shopping because of its compatibility with diverse computer languages (such as Pacbase, FORTRAN, and C, in addition to COBOL) and its variety of hardware (including Hewlett-Packard, Digital Equipment, Sun Microsystems, or Unisys).

The Acid Test

If you decide to employ a consulting service, be aware that you will have to develop additional testing processes because your consulting company will no doubt require that all your code be put through a baseline test before it accepts the responsibility of changing it. Plus, your enterprise should establish an acceptance review process before allowing the code to be reinstalled on your computers.

The baseline test confirms that the code operates correctly in processing the current century dates. The baseline test recompiles the code to ensure that all components are available and that the version the code was written in can be compiled with the existing system software. The balance of the test determines whether the date routines handle standard processes correctly—comparisons, computations, searches, and validations, including handling of leap years. Problems found during this test can be repaired either by the client or by the consulting firm—at additional expense, of course; and the consulting firm generally requires that it perform the test or that it be permitted to conduct a detailed review of the test performed by the client. Again, expect to pay for this activity, but do not begrudge the expense; it is not a ploy for getting more money. These tests almost always reveal problems with the existing code and data; thus, they save time in making the changes and may eliminate some testing later.

The primary purpose of the review is to ascertain that all the components have been changed and are in the package and that the integrity of the application has not been compromised. The review also includes running a comparison of the baseline-tested code provided to the consultant and the code that has been changed. The review of the differences will uncover any failings in completeness or integrity. The review should also include a walk-through of any design changes that were required, any questions or issues identified by the people changing the code, and deviations from standard practices. Finally, the better consulting services will alert you to additional requirements for testing the code based on changes that were made.

Before You Sign on the Dotted Line

Before you execute the agreement to obtain services from another firm, be well prepared. Here are a few suggestions for your review; some of this is only common sense, but it never hurts to have a checklist to make sure nothing is overlooked.

1. Prepare a plan.
   - Identify exactly which products or data will be turned over to the service.
   - Enumerate exactly the results you expect when a product or data item is returned. If it is changes to the product or the data, define any constraints. If a new product is to be created, define each content item. Itemize security requirements and copy restrictions. If the service retains a copy, set limits to that retention.
   - Define specifically when the products or data will be turned over. Coordination of rules for handing off requires allowing enough lead time for doing the work as well as putting it back into production. Rules will be required for handling delays at your end as well as the service provider's end.
   - Break down accountability. Make sure each individual understands what he or she is accountable for doing or producing.
   - Define control mechanisms.
   - Document scheduling and commitment procedures.
2. Communicate the plan to your staff. Make sure that everyone understands what is intended before meeting with the service provider. This will prevent misinterpretations about the service provider's role, enabling staff to modify expectations if necessary.
3. Work up procedures with the service provider. Develop communications, performance-tracking, and escalation processes.
4. Reinforce ownership of the work and the process. Review the actual work procedures to make sure that accountability is clearly understood by both your company and the service provider.
5. Assign knowledgeable staff to assist the service provider. There is a tendency in large and small organizations to delegate coordination with service companies to the least-busy members of the staff, who may also be those with the least knowledge or the lowest motivation. Don't pay a lot of money to a company only to have them fail for lack of knowledge.

Once last piece of advice: If you are new to the outsourcing arena and need assistance, don't be afraid to hire a firm to broker the relationship development activities.

What if you can't do it yourself, and you can't find the outside help you need? The next chapter, "Staying Afloat," helps you decide what to do when it is clear you have run out of time, and it is no longer a reasonable expectation that you can perform the fix in time.

CHAPTER 12

Staying Afloat

The Twelfth Hour

At some point in the process, you may come to the realization you are just not going to make the December 31, 1999, deadline. No matter that you have been faithful in bringing your computer hardware into compliance. No matter you have worked hard at making sure proprietary software is fixed and vendor-supplied applications are updated. Despite all well-intentioned efforts, you realize Murphy's Law has caught up with you.

The reasons for missing the deadline are many. There is not enough time to complete testing, or you discover more code that needs to be fixed. Maybe an order for essential equipment hasn't been filled. Maybe your staff is burned out. Maybe you have realized that although your enterprise computer systems have been made compliant, your business will still be negatively affected in other ways. Many embedded systems are not going to work. Many applications considered to be noncritical will fail and take important systems down with them. Some applications that won't be working will create lots of inconvenience for suppliers and customers. They will slow down operations. The suppliers won't be able to supply. Buyers won't be able to buy. Operational processes are going to break down. Investment and cash flow are going to be insufficient, and lawsuits are going to absorb all available time.

The likelihood that hardly anybody will be finished on time is quite high. A Securities and Exchange Commission report to Congress in June of 1997 stated:

> It is not, and will not, be possible for any single entity or collective enterprise to represent that it has achieved complete Year 2000 compliance and thus to guarantee its remediation efforts. The problem is simply too complex for such a claim to have legitimacy. Efforts to solve Year 2000 problems are best described as "risk mitigation." Success in the effort will have been achieved if the number and seriousness of any technical failures is minimized, and they are quickly identified and repaired if they do occur.

What was true in 1997 will remain true right through the end of this century.

A review of the Fortune 250's annual reports by Triaxis Research indicated that 12 percent hadn't even started, and that 48 percent were only just finishing their inventories. A June 1998 survey by Cap Gemini indicated that the number of firms reporting Year 2000–related failures had reached 37 percent in April and 40 percent in June. The survey respondents indicated that 87 percent had experienced processing disruptions, 62 percent financial miscalculation or loss, 44 percent logistics/supply-chain problems, and 38 percent customer-service problems. These problems can only increase as the world nears and passes the year 2000 bewitching hour.

A review of a June 1998 Merrill Lynch report, "Y2K: Implications for Investors," widely referenced as reassurance to investors, raises many questions among Year 2000 experts. Here are some examples—which were picked totally at random:

- The U.S. Air Transport section (pg. 248) indicates that AMR and Delta have budgeted $150 million (this figure for AMR does not include SABRE, which plans to spend $100 million by itself) and $125 million, respectively. UAL Corporation (United Airlines, which is the largest U.S. air carrier) expects to spend only $12 million. How can the largest and oldest airline spend only 10 percent of what its rivals are spending?

- The U.S. Autos report (pg. 290) says General Motors will be compliant, but, as previously noted, its CIO says that all its plants face "catastrophic failures."

- U.S. Natural Gas companies (pg. 354) are only "likely" to be compliant. Not one is listed as "will be compliant." Since many are interconnected, does this mean there is a high probability that many customers will face cold and be unable to cook their food? What does this mean for electricity providers that have installed new gas-fired turbines?

- Japan Software (pg. 213) indicates there is an "accute shortage of computer programmers, the only solution for companies which still have not started working on their Y2K compliance projects is to scrap existing systems and go in for new Y2K-compliant systems." Any computer programmer can tell you that this is a multiyear solution that will take them past the Y2K problem event.

- Japan Retailing (pg. 211) indicates that instead of using packages, the retailers in Japan have used custom-made software, "thus making it easier to modify their programs" while U.S. Broadline Retailers (pg. 384) are clearly spending hundreds of millions changing their custom-made applications.

- European Pharmaceuticals (pg. 165) indicates that while the companies find the Y2K problem a bigger issue than the Euro (monetary conversion), dependency on third parties risks business disruption.

- European Paper, Packaging and Printing (pg. 163) is not guaranteeing its supply chain, and it is expected to be compliant because the "majority of the hardware acquired in the last two years is compliant." The same report reveals that equipment is depreciated over 10 to 15 years. Are readers to believe it has recently replaced most of its equipment?

The only salvation to the situation may be that everyone is suffering equally. A more realistic view may be that it is not millennium compliance that companies should be worried about, but what Systemic Solutions (Seattle, Washington) calls *millennium viability*. *Viability*, by definition, is the ability to stay alive—meaning to stay in business—after all the dust clears. It is possible to fail at millennium compliance and still be millennium viable, given a carefully devised set of workarounds and contingency plans for the processes that cannot be made to work.

Even today, many companies still believe the problem can be solved by throwing money at it. One major manufacturer claimed that it had spent $5 million through 1997 and was preparing to spend $450 million in the remaining time. The corporate officers have failed to realize what it takes to ramp up a project of that size and complexity. No amount of money can solve the Year 2000 problem when time runs short. Read *The Mythical Man-Month* by Frederick P. Brooks, Jr. (Addison-Wesley, 1995) and *Software Runaways* by Robert L. Glass (Prentice Hall, 1998) if you doubt this assertion.

So now what? There are two management approaches that, if implemented now, can assure millennium viability—risk management and disaster recovery.

Risk Management

The risk management process has two parts. The first is *risk assessment* and the second is *contingency planning*. Explaining each of these is probably best left to other experts, and many books have been written on both topics. For the reader with time and the information technology project responsibility, the book *Assessment and Control of Software Risks* (Capers Jones, Yourdon Press, 1994) makes excellent reading—as do the books by Brooks and Glass previously mentioned.

Ten Steps to Safety

Year 2000 risk management involves ten steps. The first five are associated with risk assessment, and the next five arrive at a contingency plan.

1. **Identify risks.**   Most risk identification can be done through straightforward analysis, brainstorming sessions, research of problems at other firms, and just common sense. For a start, ask yourself: "What could possibly go wrong?"

2. **Determine potential impact.**   If the risk actually comes to pass, what will be the result to the business? For example, if a given computer system should fail because of an undiscovered or uncorrected Year 2000 problem, what business decisions could be based on faulty information? What customers will be affected? What business processes will go awry?

3. **Identify times of potential failures.**   Not all failures will occur at the stroke of midnight on December 31, 1999. Some may have already occurred. Some may not become evident until days or weeks after the witching hour. Some may occur as a result of government actions, litigation, customer reactions, or general market economy changes. Try to estimate when you will know for sure that the shoe has dropped.

4. **Describe how the risk will manifest itself.**   How will you know that something has gone wrong? In the case of a computer problem, only a few errors will result in an abend or error message. Most of the Year 2000 software hits will result in bad data, files sorted out of order, invalid invoices, data deletions, or other *quiet* time bombs. You may not even know that the problem has occurred until the phone starts to ring. Of course, some of the risks will be more obvious than others, such as when the process server shows up with a subpoena.

5. **Identify current processes that could mitigate the impact.**   If you have listened to anything in this book, or in any of the relevant literature for that matter, you probably have a set of activities underway to sniff out and correct as many Year 2000 problems as possible. Fixing the in-house-developed computer software is where most of the emphasis on the problem has been focused, and many firms have put projects in place to deal with this. Take a good look at the risks you have identified and see what the likelihood of serious business injury will be, and what safe-

guards may already be in place. Start with a review of your insurance coverage. Bring aspirin.

6. **Establish root causes of the risks.**   None of the Year 2000 grief will have mystic roots. Discovery of the cause is not rocket science. Your computers may start cranking out invalid information because they can't figure out what century it is. Your suppliers may have trouble getting your needed goods and services to you on time. Your customers may be diverted from their usual buying habits by their own Year 2000 activities. Your business processes may be dependent upon computer reports that suddenly are a mess. Your process control systems may decide that maintenance is 99 years past due.

7. **Identify possible chain reactions.**   Businesses and working processes are so interconnected these days, mostly through electronic communications, that there are relatively few isolated breaks. "For want of a nail, the shoe was lost"—except in this case, it may be: "For want of a JIT part, the assembly was late" and "For want of a delivery, the contract was lost." These dependencies are complex and difficult to trace, but some trigger effects will be fairly obvious. List your dependencies, and concentrate on shoring up the weakest links first.

8. **Establish nature and amount of costs.**   If ever the old saw "An ounce of prevention . . ." held up, it would be in this situation. Or maybe its modern-day advertising equivalent from the Fram oil filter people would be more appropriate, "Pay me now or pay me later." It is probably safe to say that no one, including you, will be able to foresee and prevent every possible risk. Pick the biggest, most devastating, and reasonably likely and get some expertise working on it. The costs may be consulting fees, temporary staff to do things manually that the computer used to do when it was working, legal fees, extra inventory, a backup power generator, or just extra incentive money to keep the staff from going into new lines of work.

9. **Define steps to stop or minimize the risk.**   There are many ways that a Year 2000 problem may affect your business. But the more insidious risks are those that you don't anticipate—the blindside blows. For these, the more expert help you can get, the fewer surprises you should encounter. Start with a consultant who can give you a 360-degree assessment of your readiness. Armed with this, you can determine where effective actions could ward off downstream problems. Talk to your attorney, or better yet, with a law firm specializing in Year 2000 litigation. You can bet your competitors are. Reassess your insurance coverage. Make sure that your policies still cover things like the sprinkler system going off because of some bizarre linkage through the building safety monitoring system computer having a Year 2000 seizure. Some insurance companies are tak-

ing a stand that, if it can be traced in any way to a Year 2000 failure, then it is not covered because you knew it could happen and didn't take the right steps to prevent it.

10. **Create policies to stop or control costs.** Once risk mitigation teams are put in place, they can develop a life of their own. Make sure Year 2000 activities are reviewed regularly, that the expenditures of time and money are showing adequate results, and that a clear set of ending objectives are identified—so the team (and you) will know when they are done.

Finding the Roots of Risk

Systemic Solutions has developed a practice based on making enterprises millennium viable. Systemic's philosophies provide a useful reference for addressing risk management. These philosophies look at the risk at two levels. The first level concerns itself with the *sources* of the risk to the enterprise. The second level is the analysis of the risks to understand where the *break points* exist by looking deeper into the situation.

At the first level, *risk sources,* the problem can be seen in five parts:

1. **Supply and vendor support.** Initiate an analysis to determine the likelihood and effects of the key suppliers not being able to get critical goods and services to you because of Year 2000 computer problems, reduced ability to function, business failures, breaks in the transportation and distribution chains, and other related issues.

2. **Sales and customer relations.** Determine how the Year 2000 issues might degrade your customers' ability or willingness to buy your products. They might be strapped for cash, go out of business, be unable to order your products, or have a reduced demand because of general economic downturns. They may want to increase orders late in 1999 and then cut demand in the beginning of 2000 to avoid transportation problems.

3. **Business Administration and Finance.** Will your bank still be willing to advance credit if it believes you are not stepping up to the Year 2000 risks? The banks themselves may have cash problems or be mired in Year 2000 computer problems. The federal regulatory agencies are directing particular scrutiny to banks to make sure that no money is lost through computer malfunctions. Many banks are more concerned about being closed down by these agencies than about possible runs on the bank by misinformed citizens who want their cash in hand. Insurance companies are eliminating coverage for Year 2000 problems—unless enterprises can demonstrate diligence in trying to avoid business interruptions and losses. Company-

sponsored employee retirement and investment programs may be at risk if the providers are not diligent. Health insurers may not be adequately prepared for year 2000. The enterprise shares responsibility for employee issues in many countries for providing these programs.

4. **Operations and regulatory compliance.** To the extent that computers play a part in your business, the Year 2000 problem could degrade or even disrupt operations internally. Failures in systems could upset such things as hazardous waste disposal and accidental escape of toxic wastes. Even if a company has taken all of the steps to become compliant, the various government agencies may not be. As a result, you may see a blizzard of stopgap regulations requiring special reporting, additional inspections, or tax changes.

5. **Computer and embedded systems functionality.** And, of course, there is the Year 2000 problem in the computer center and anywhere else that a computer chip may hide. Little black boxes keeping track of the mainte-nance schedules on your equipment, the expiration dates on chemicals or consumables, the operation of the building systems, and the security sys-tems could stumble on the Year 2000 error and do unexpected, and usu-ally bad, things to the business functionality.

Notice that only the last item has to do with what is typically perceived as the source of the Year 2000 problem. The focus here is on enterprise survival, not simply millennium compliance. While many service companies offer support in some of these domains (for example, legal audit, supplier surveys, vendor status reporting, and so on), the Systemic approach differs in that it looks at each problem or concern from three perspectives:

- What is the current and anticipated environment going to look like?
- How does technology contribute to the problem?
- Where do shortcomings in current policies and practices increase the risk?

An example or two may serve to explain how its approach actually uncovers more risks than other methods might discover. Following are two examples of the risk management approach used by Systemic Systems: a food import com-pany and an agribusiness.

These two examples show the value of going deeper to determine where break points may exist that are not apparent even to the business owner. Defining the risk is important so that a contingency plan can be formulated. In the two pre-ceding situations, the contingency plans were as follows:

1. The food importer asked the freight handler to determine if the con-tainer's refrigeration units are millennium-compliant containing no

Example: A Food Importer

The food importer might see supply as a significant business risk. Its business is entirely dependent upon being able to purchase foodstuffs at one point and getting them delivered to another without spoilage. It sees its problem as one of identifying who will supply the foodstuffs and how they will get from the foreign producer to the shelves. To the importer, it is a matter of making sure that it has a supplier that can deliver food to the dock and a shipping company that will have a ship to carry food to the destination. It puts pressure on the supplier to guarantee delivery and the freight handler to make sure a ship is going to be there to load it. The first analysis shows that there is no problem, that a Year 2000 effect won't interrupt the chain.

Systemic Solutions views the supplier issue as not so cut and dried. It notes that the food being shipped is frozen fish. Since the port of shipment is cold during the winter, the dependency upon refrigeration is not immediate, but the voyage may be several days and may take the shipment across the equator. The container refrigeration must be operating throughout the voyage. It is then determined that current practices are to prepare the paperwork for customs and duty the day before the shipment is to dock. Should there be a break in the communications, the paperwork may be delayed, and the ship may not be able to unload its cargo. The containers can only maintain freezing temperature for a few days. If the paperwork does not arrive, the fish may rot in the hold of the ship.

Example: An Agribusiness

An agribusiness may see its exposure to Year 2000 problems as minimal. After all, it is the winter months and, surely, everything will be running as usual when the planting season arrives. An examination of current practices indicates that during the first part of January there is a field spraying to prevent diseases from appearing during the sowing season and to kill off insects that lie dormant during the winter. The chemicals cannot be mixed until just before the spraying and must be shipped separately. The grower is dependent upon air delivery because the chemical effectiveness diminishes rapidly and air traffic might be curtailed by problems with air traffic control and delays in freight handling. Delaying the spraying could force the seeding to be pushed back later because the spray interferes with the germination process. This, in turn, might push the seeding into a traditionally rainy period, which would drown the seeds.

embedded microsystems which will shut off the refrigeration. It also required the freight handler to guarantee to provide all the paperwork to the ship's captain at the time the fish are loaded.

2. The grower determined to complete spraying in mid-December.

John Munyan and Lisa J. Downey of Systemic Solutions, Inc. provided Appendix A as a case study of how one enterprise mitigated risks through management action. The company in the appendix has to deal with very specific potential interruptions. Larger businesses and smaller ones will be faced with their own set of problems, but you can use the appendix as a model for your own risk management assessment and to develop a plan for mitigating the risks.

Monsters under the Bed

Defining the sources of risk for a specific firm cannot be fully accomplished in a book designed for a broad audience, but it is possible to expose them at some level. The following section may get your brain working and help you convince those in authority to launch a detailed investigation. Appendix A shows how a company with only a modest amount of technical dependency deals with the problems it has seen for its company. During the discovery period, it is also useful to evaluate the reality of each risk. In other words, what is the likelihood that the problem you have identified will actually occur?

Supply and Vendor Support

Enterprises long ago stopped being totally self-sufficient. Few firms own the raw materials, transportation, intermediate processing, final assembly, or distribution of products. Even the smallest enterprise relies on stationers, delivery services, postal services, telephones, electricity, sewers, and cash registers and/or calculators. The larger firms rely on hundreds, or even thousands, of firms to supply parts, materials, or ingredients used to produce something as uncomplicated as the paper in this book.

Manufacturing facilities throughout the world are dependent upon embedded systems that will fail. A survey performed by General Motors in all its assembly plants found that every single plant was potentially at risk. It has collaborated with the other automobile manufacturers to raise awareness in their immediate supply chains. It is clear, however, that secondary suppliers have not yet recognized the risk. For many, it is the small- and medium-sized businesses in Asia, Europe, North America, and South America that may stop production for a time, waiting for parts or computers that must come from far away.

Many of these sources of supply are local, but the products they provide to the business usually come from outside the immediate vicinity and many from outside the country. It is unlikely that any enterprise is not dependent to some extent upon international trade. The small business may have a cash register manufactured in Japan or Germany that may require parts, microprocessor chips, or reprogramming that originates in that country. How will the parts arrive if shipping channels are interrupted? Air, rail, ship, and even truck transport may be assailed by a lack of fuel, incomplete shipping manifests, or tracking-system shutdowns.

Parts must be ordered using telephones, fax, or mail, all of which are dependent upon computers. If any one of them fails, the order may be lost or delayed in transit, as may the receipt of the item required. Mail systems outside of the local area may be tied up for weeks or even months. Witness what happened in the United States when United Parcel Service went on strike in 1997. Imagine the same thing with the added complication of the U.S. Mail and all the other delivery services going out at the same time. The result may be more than inconvenient.

Ask yourself a number of possible questions:

- What products and services are key to enterprise survival?
- How much is normally on hand?
- How long will that supply last?
- Is there any expiration concern?
- Is there a local source of resupply?
- What is the enterprise experience in tapping resupply?
- Is there sufficient space to store additional supplies?
- Are there alternative sources of supply?
- What is the cost of buying more or buying from another source?
- If the needed component is manufactured, what is the normal lead time?
- What is the likelihood of the supplier not being able to produce the needed service or products?

This is not meant to be an exhaustive list, so don't limit your thinking to these questions. Think about the supplier, its suppliers, the transportation requirements, the paperwork and regulatory requirements, and the costs associated with the risks. Don't limit the thinking on cost to just money. Costs may come from turning to a new supplier, changing processes, and having to take on new debt.

Consider the following table to be a starting list (there are lots of others) for determining which suppliers may pose the greatest risk:

SUPPLIERS	SERVICES	AGENCIES	UTILITIES	TRANSPORTATION
Appliances	Accounting	Bonding	Cellular phone	Air
Chemicals	Advertising	Customs	Clearinghouses	Automobile
Computers	Banking	Fire	Electricity	Barge
Data	Brokerage	Inspection	Gas	Bridge
Fasteners	Building services	Judicial	Radio	Ferry
Fuel	Catering	License	Sewer	Rail
Furniture	Consulting	Mail	Stock exchange	Roads
Gasoline/fuel	Contracting	Patent	Telephone	Ship
Goods	Help desks	Permit	Television	Subway
Ingredients	Hotels	Police	Video cable	Truck
Lubricants	Insurance	Tax	Waste disposal	
Machines	Internet	Title	Water	
Materials	Janitorial	Trademark		
Networks	Laundry	Weather		
Office supplies	Legal			
Packaging	Maintenance			
Paints/finishes	Messenger			
Parts	News			
Pharmaceuticals	Overnight mail			
Software	Payroll			
Subassemblies	Rental			
Tools	Repair			
Vehicles	Warehousing			

Courtesy of Systemic Solutions, Inc.

As you consider the dependencies listed in the table, realize that it is only a starting point of a long list of primary and secondary suppliers and support organizations. Your enterprise should concern itself not only with how Year 2000 problems might directly affect operations, but also your suppliers. In addition, consider your employees' ability to come to work and function.

Sales and Customer Relations

Along with suppliers and vendors, there should be an equal concern about customers. New Year's Day is a big day for many businesses throughout the world. Some of the largest celebrations ever planned are now scheduled for that New Year. How are the celebrants going to fare miles from home? Is the business going to be at added risk if employees cannot return to work? If cash registers don't work or telephones are out of service or jammed, how will retailers process cash and credit card transactions?

Risks to cash flow are not insignificant if the normal supply functions are interrupted. Technologists concerned about possible breakdowns in the distribution system are advising consumers to stockpile food and other necessities before the new millennium. In case of stockpiling, the enterprise needs to be concerned about the possibility that sales may fall off after the Year 2000 whether problems manifest themselves or not. Businesses also need to be ready for a sharp rise in the purchase of some products prior to the millennium New Year and recognize it as a sales blip rather than a trend.

For a start, the enterprise should consider the following:

Who are our most critical customers?

What is their Year 2000 vulnerability?

Will they be able to buy our products as usual? And pay for them? On time?

What will their preparations be?

How could our customers be affected if we cannot provide the service or products we normally supply?

How can we deliver our products if transport systems fail?

What will a temporary or protracted loss of sales do to our cash flow?

Elective medical services, janitorial services, and restaurateurs may find themselves susceptible to a significant drop in revenues should the Year 2000 be the disaster some predict. Nonessential services may be the first casualties in a poor economic climate. For them, the issue may be to increase revenues prior to the New Year event.

Business Administration and Finance

The Year 2000 problem can create special administration problems. Keep the following in mind:

A legal audit should be performed which looks at contracts (supplier and customer), insurance, warranties, and liability issues. A risk assessment may review investments, loans, and financial obligations.

An accounting review may be required to avoid stockholder lawsuits and determine what records must be kept manually in case of system interruptions.

Sustaining insurability in the absence of some systems and services may become a problem.

A determination of the risks from degradations in record-keeping functions should be performed by your business or obtained from others. If ever system backups are needed, now is the time.

An assessment of risks over employment issues—provisions for layoff, losses in employee investment and retirement programs, interruption of health insurance programs—should be made.

A discussion of your situation with the bank, covering such topics as relief from loan defaults, need for additional credit for inventory, temporary help, alternate suppliers, and legal defenses would be prudent. It would also be a good time to make sure the bank itself is going to be viable through the ordeal.

A review of the enterprise's investment policies for 401(k) and retirement funds is in order. Given the predictions that a significant number of companies will cease to exist as a result of Year 2000, it is important to make sure that the enterprise's investment portfolios are purged of the likely nonsurvivors.

Operations and Regulatory Compliance

Regulatory compliance may prove to be a problem that peaks at the year 2000. During the months to come, many agencies are expected to impose data- and record-keeping regulations that will be difficult to meet and implement in time. Not only are domestic regulations changing, but so are those of other nations.

Businesses run on processes, most of which are supported by devices. The role of computing systems in supporting the processes is obvious, but there are thousands of other devices and systems that play hidden roles. For each piece of equipment, and for any process that uses computer or microprocessor interfaces, the enterprise should ask the following questions:

- How important is the system to the key business of the enterprise?
- How will failures of a system manifest themselves?
- How can the system be tested for potential Year 2000 problems?
- How will failure of the system impact production? Sales? Cash flow?
- How long can the system be down?
- How long do repairs normally take? If failures are widespread, how long might it take to get parts and service?
- How long does it take to return to normal operations?

While the focus of the questions may appear to be a factory floor issue, it is not. A butcher is severely affected by the loss of service from a scale; a grocery store may find itself encumbered by the inability to take stock inventories, scan UPC labels, or put labels on packages. The issue here is not the equipment, but the processes the equipment affects.

Computer and Embedded Systems Functionality

Not all of the operational risks will come from boxes that look like computers. Many will come from other devices that have computer chips and date-dependent logic built into them. These are collectively called embedded systems. The typical enterprise is at the mercy of both its computer systems and embedded systems.

The embedded systems risk issues are discussed in Chapter 3, "The Monster in the Closet." Risk assessment for these pieces of equipment should consider the following:

- Is this equipment critical to the functioning of the business?
- Does it impact a significant line of business?
- Does faulty operation of this equipment risk injury to an individual?
- Does the data output of this equipment affect decisions made by customers or management?
- Is there a backup process for this equipment?
- How long would it take to replace this equipment?
- What is the cost/benefit return on this equipment?

For computer systems, the risk assessment process is best handled through the triage process (see Chapter 4, "Avoiding Future Shock," and the section entitled, *Triage: Business Style*). The risk assessment questions should include such things as the following:

- How will a system failure be detected?
- How will operations be monitored?
- When is the system most likely to fail?
- How many people depend on the system?
- Is this system critical to support primary product lines?
- What are the current and expected workloads of the system?
- Are record-keeping functions damaged by an interruption of the systems?

- How does this system affect customer service?
- How does this system affect management decision making?
- Are regulatory requirements met by this system?
- What other systems are dependent upon the data provided by this system?

Ashes to Phoenix?

The alternative to successful risk management is disaster recovery. Depending on the degree of risk management success, the game may not be lost. Through a carefully considered triage process, many firms may get through the initial period with their critical business systems intact. If they have performed risk management, they may even have minimized the impact on revenue and kept legal action at bay. These firms are ideally positioned to acquire competitors.

For many, disaster recovery will not be possible. When a company's losses exceed its ability to remain viable, the company will have to fold. The Y2K is the proverbial monster under the bed. It may be totally unforgiving. A public company may see its last hopes die in legal actions from investors. Insurance for business interruptions is disappearing if the cause is Y2K.

If the enterprise has not weathered the millennium-compliance storm well, but still has some life in it, there is still some hope it can remain viable—if managers or owners can make some minimal preparations. But, given the scope and magnitude of the problem, some simply will not make it. Some Year 2000 experts believe that as many as 30 percent of the enterprises in the world will succumb. Hopefully, they are wrong. The Great Depression saw the failure of about 13 percent of the businesses in the United States over the course of three years. The loss of businesses due to failures could reach that level in the first six months of 2000. Not a comfortable thought. There is hope that businesses today are much more resilient than they were in 1929. A power outage in Auckland, New Zealand, in early 1998 put several thousand downtown businesses in jeopardy. It is believed that while the outage lasted six weeks, not a single business failed because of the outage. (It will never be known how many weak enterprises collapsed because this was one burden too many.) The difference between the New Zealand situation and the Y2K situation is that people could escape the problem by leaving the city in New Zealand. When Y2K problems hit, they are likely to hit everyone and there won't be anyplace to escape.

Hopefully, everyone will start to take the Year 2000 problem seriously before it is too late. Contingency planning can do much to soften the business-disruption possibilities. One of the authors tells his audiences to be prepared for two to eight weeks of serious business interference. For small business owners, an eight-week interruption of income could prove disastrous if they are not prepared. Could this set off a recession? Coupled with deteriorating economies in Asia and less than optimal Y2K attention in Europe and Latin America, the stage might be set for a severe economic problem. Visit Ed Yardeni's (Mr. Yardeni is the economic strategist for Deutche Morgan Grenfell) Web site (see Appendix C) for insight into the possible economic impact of the Y2K problem. The impact of Y2K-related failures could easily impact the world economy for 10 to 20 years.

Those businesses that are noncompliant but still running may take several actions short of selling themselves off to the highest bidder. Taking some actions can enable disaster recovery. The following is a list of actions that might help a firm return to being viable, even though their systems have failed:

1. During the week of December 26, 1999, make backups of all data files and programs being run on all of the enterprise computers.

2. Schedule at least half your employees to be on call for possible work on Saturday, January 1, and Sunday, January 2.

3. Capture the status of all accounts with banks, investment firms, insurance agencies, suppliers, and vendors.

4. Retain a hard copy of all transactions enacted during the week. Place these records in a fireproof vault or safe.

5. Make a duplicate copy of all computer electronic files and store them off-site.

6. Cancel any electronic transactions for which there is no audit trail.

7. Keep paper copies of all audit trails dated and signed by a responsible manager.

8. File all government-regulatory paperwork with the agency even if it is early.

9. Process payroll checks by no later than Thursday, December 30, and tell all employees to bank them not later than Friday.

10. Turn off all nonessential equipment on Friday before midnight. (This includes computers and networks.) Shutdown manufacturing facilities.

11. Cancel all overnight transaction processing (especially financial transactions) for the evening of December 31–January 1.

12. Have someone on the premises to observe and guard against unlawful intruders.

13. On January 1, begin an organized restart of systems. Start with equipment first. Reset any system dates you can to the correct time and date.

14. Test the systems using fake transactions that are easily recognized. Review the output. If the enterprise systems have failed, the contingency plans can be implemented.

15. Contact key suppliers and customers as early as possible during the week to determine their status.

16. Notify key suppliers and customers of current requirements and review the status of transactions known to be in process.

17. Begin replacing failed systems with purchased packages. (*Note:* Do not modify the systems, change the organization to fit the product. Install key functionality first. Modifications and rework to fit custom needs or practices can come later. This is a time to return to basics. Many businesses can survive with little more than a spreadsheet program and a word processor. Until 1965, almost every business subsisted using 10-key adding machines and 12-column ledger sheets.)

18. Evaluate the work environment of all employees and their ability to perform their jobs.

19. Locate suppliers or customers, interested in supporting the enterprise, whose systems have not suffered from system failures, and see what it might take to lease time on their computers.

20. For all systems that fail, create a startup record for all ongoing business and current employees using January 1, 2000, as the start date. (You can clean up any of the mess this makes manually and enter historical data later.)

21. Pare business activities as necessary to only essential services. Redeploy people to support those processes.

22. Inventory all supplies and determine how long they will last to support the essential services.

23. Meet with key customers, bankers, and investment representatives to coordinate survival responses. Renegotiate contracts as necessary.

24. Meet with suppliers to determine how to manage the supply requirements and payments. Again, renegotiate contracts as necessary.

25. Notify any regulatory agencies of any inability to comply with rules and determine what can be done in the interim and how long any deviations are allowed.

26. Notify shareholders of actions taken, status of the business, and issue any warnings of possible revenue or legal implications.

Combined with a *serious* risk management program, these 26 steps should give the enterprise from 6 to 12 months to reestablish itself and return to full productivity. The company that is seriously financially damaged may have to seek broad support from clients, investors, and suppliers to recover business. For many, disaster recovery may be government grants to overcome the losses.

The next chapter, "The Price of Failure," explores some of the legal risks and costs associated with the failure to meet the Year 2000 compliance deadline.

CHAPTER 13

The Price of Failure

Legal costs of the Year 2000 crisis are impossible to predict with any accuracy. It is likely that the actual investment in fixing the problem will be dwarfed by the legal costs. Some lawyers estimate the bill will be $1 trillion. Much of this will be spent not on preparing and preventing Year 2000 problems, but on resolving disputes involving the unprepared: companies who never attempted to address the Year 2000 problem, those who tried but failed to fix it in time, and service providers who waited too long to bail out the companies who hired them. The companies who lose will suffer because of inadequate knowledge of the Year 2000 problem and inability to predict the consequences of system failures.

Most laws that will address the Year 2000 problem haven't been written yet. The Ontario Bar Association has developed a list of 128 specific topics that are involved in the Year 2000 problem, and it is likely that more will be added to the list as cases come to trial. No legal precedent exists for many of the issues introduced by the Year 2000 problem. The Y2K cases that go before the courts, as lawsuits or criminal action, will be breaking new legal ground.

Obligatory Legal Disclaimer

This chapter deals with issues in the legal domain. It is a layperson's view, and it is important to note that what is presented here is in no way meant to substitute for qualified legal advice. Readers are subject to the laws of many nations, as well as local laws, traditions, and customs that also take on the aspect of law. To say a legal audit of an enterprise's position is worthwhile is an understatement.

The legal implications should be of concern to everyone and it is important to take risk mitigation actions now. Since it is recognized that the United States is a litigious society, it is a reasonable place to start in describing potential local as well as international legal risks. The topic is exceedingly complex, and growing more so each day.

Consult your legal counsel and possibly a law firm specializing in Year 2000 issues—they are growing in number.

Enterprise Headaches

Perhaps the best way to look at the topic is in the context of a typical enterprise. There are several points of view that are informative: that of a provider of services or products to the enterprise, that of a consumer of services and products of the enterprise, and that of the manager of the enterprise.

Managers could be faced with a number of legal problems—breach of warranty, breach of contract, product liability, failure to meet accounting disclosure regulations, and their own fiduciary obligations to shareholders head the list. At the very least, any of one of these could give even a superhero a headache.

Preparing for and avoiding legal claims based on any of the preceding is essential for an enterprise, because litigation will create havoc. Not only do lawsuits run up significant legal expenses, they absorb time and impose substantial stress on key managers and executives. Time taken away from the business to participate in the defense and prosecution of cases may put a severe strain on an enterprise already struggling to survive the Year 2000 fallout.

Warranties

Warranty issues may be the most common legal issues facing the enterprise. The number of class action cases against computer-based hardware and software providers continues to grow. Rumors are that by May 1998, over 200 cases involving warranty claims had already been settled out of court. The common theme of the filed cases appears to be the provider's willingness to correct the problem without forcing the client to incur additional expense if the product was sold after January 1, 1996, when the Year 2000 problem was already being widely publicized. Statutes of limitations on express warranty claims are generally four years from the sale of the software. Implied warranty limits, however, vary widely and, where physical injury or death is involved, are subject to even broader interpretation by the courts.

Some software vendors are being warned by their legal counsels to remove any language from packaging and manuals that in any way implies that software will run without problems into the next century. Some courts may entertain as a warranty claim the words in a brochure, "Handling all your future needs." Even when the product has been tested to meet millennium compliance policies of the builder, a customer may perform an operation, unexpected and untested, that leads to a breach of warranty claim.

In many cases, the software and hardware industries have been able to reduce the warranty periods by writing terms in the purchase agreement that say the purchaser has 90 days to accept the product. Further, they have established a practice under which they can, under contract terms, release a new version and automatically obsolete older versions. Under these conditions, the operator of an obsolete version is compelled to update to the new version or lose software support and warranty coverage.

Parties may limit warranties by contract. Where there is no express limitation or disclaimer, generally, certain warranties are implied. What obligation a party has to fix defects, and so forth, depends on what was bargained for.

Some legal analysts predict that courts will take the stand that manufacturers of products that are (or contain) computer-based be required to provide a product that works if there is a reasonable possibility that the product *could* have been designed to work and yet wasn't. This gets back to the general knowledge rule, which claims that knowledge of how to get around the Year 2000 problem existed, was available to the designers, and yet was not incorporated into the design. Here, rules of merchantability and fitness might be invoked as a defense when it can be shown that software, thus designed, would not function within the prospective customer's computing environment or with the data rules currently being employed.

Basically, a firm may be held to an obligation to fix the problem—that is, to supply parts and service as represented—and to do so without additional cost, if it can be shown that the design was defective. On the other hand, if the customer knew about the Year 2000 problem (through public disclosure) and did not notify the provider that it would be held accountable for problems with its product, the provider may be able to successfully defend warranty claims.

If the product was designed and built according to the requirements and specifications provided by and/or approved by a client, the client is most likely accountable for any Year 2000 omissions in the design. However, the client may argue that he or she was relying upon the builder's expertise to design viable software or systems. It is also possible to make the case that the products were designed according to prevailing government and industry standards, so that manufacturer/developer was not realistically capable of building a design to work correctly into the next century.

Instead of focusing entirely on what manufacturers do to get out of the warranty coverage, the software purchaser should start now to establish warranty-coverage obligations on new purchases and in renewals of software maintenance licenses. Manufacturers should review past contracts and enter into new contracts, which more thoroughly define warranty limitations. All parties should be aware of the potential implications of the customer being forced to fix the code internally or to use an unauthorized third party.

Voiding the warranty responsibility may be a strategy for some software-manufacturing companies. This allows the customer to make necessary changes and releases the manufacturer from responsibility to make the change without losing ownership. The cost of making a Year 2000 fix can break a software company if there is insufficient income through maintenance licensing to pay for it. Many have announced that some older products are no longer supported. Other firms attempt to recover the millennium-fix cost by providing additional features along with the fix and selling them as a new version. (*Note:* This is most often the strategy that, if not exercised prudently, leads to lawsuits.)

Breach of Contract

The first of the potential problems facing any enterprise is failure to meet contract commitments—breach of contract. The enterprise may be unable to meet contract commitments to its customers because of failures of its production systems, inability to receive necessary supplies or services, or interruptions in its distribution channels, which prevent delivery to the customers. Many enterprises have substituted just-in-time supply techniques for conventional inventories. A brief break in a supply chain can result in factory closures. For example, hospitals and other health care providers might not receive critical medications from the prescription fulfillment services that have replaced on-site pharmacies.

Many contracts provide that contractual obligations are suspended under certain *unforeseen* circumstances. These provisions, often referred to as *force majeure clauses,* are not much help in dealing with Year 2000–based failures. These clauses are typically strictly enforced, with only totally unforeseeable events falling within their orbit. Most courts would likely find that companies have received adequate notice of the possible Year 2000–related interruptions and have had ample time to prepare. Since the Year 2000 problem has been widely publicized, it can hardly be considered an act of God.

It is best, then, to specifically address the Year 2000 problem in your contracts, to provide, for example, for reasonable delays in performance in the event of interruptions due to the Year 2000 problem not directly within the enterprise's control. If a contract addresses interruptions without special reference to Year 2000 issues, the scope of enforcement of such provisions is uncertain.

Liability Claims

Courts may find that economic losses, with no associated damages or injury, fail to justify a liability claim. Even when damages or injury occur, there will be a question about who will be held accountable—the computer manufacturer or the software provider. Apparently, courts, up to this time, have treated software as part of the hardware.

You may find, because of this, that claims for damages to computers by software may not be recoverable no matter what the cost. Damaged computer components and circuit boards thus may not be covered by liability claims. Damages to peripherals (interface cards, power supplies, and external devices) that can be shown to be directly caused by a Year 2000 problem may be covered—if the claimant can demonstrate that a Year 2000 computing failure was the cause.

Damage to data by the computer is a different problem. Contracts for software products typically limit damages to the value of the contract. Where the software was created under contract for a computer or circuit board (hardware) manufacturer, the damage claim against the software provider may be limited by the contract negotiated by the manufacturer. A hardware manufacturer's liability for damage to data may be limited by failure of the customer to perform prudent actions—such as performing data backups or monitoring a device which has been identified as potentially capable of experiencing Year 2000 problems. Here, warranty limitations may come back into issue. If the product is under warranty and the vendor notified the customer of even the potential for a problem, the customer may find it contributed to the problem by not being watchful. If the product is no longer under warranty, the client may be found to be responsible for not testing or watching the computer product for problems.

Can software and hardware cause bodily injury or death? Computers are used in process control equipment, robots, and decision-support systems. A sudden shift in schedule from what is scheduled for Saturday (January 1, 2000) to what is scheduled to happen Thursday (January 1, 1900) or a complete shutdown in the midst of a critical operation could easily result in injury or death. An aluminum smelter in New Zealand narrowly escaped such claims when a computer failed to recognize leap day, February 29, 1996, and suffered only huge losses in equipment destruction.

Embedded computer chips contained in process control modules or devices present a particular hazard to both manufacturers and users. Manufacturers often do not know who is the ultimate purchaser. While the manufacturer may issue a warning to the immediate buyer, it may be impossible for that enterprise to know where the component was eventually used. For the manufacturer, a broad public statement as to the risk involved may serve as protection against a liability claim. It may be possible that the broad coverage of the Year 2000 problem could be inferred to provide sufficient independent knowledge of potential hazards.

If an injury or death event happens, the courts will be most concerned by evidence of malfeasance, misfeasance, or culpability of the product builder and/or its distributor. If it can be proven that the builder was, or should have been, aware that a problem could exist, the builder and/or distributor could be held liable. Manufacturers that build equipment known to be hazardous to operate or equipment whose failure to operate correctly presents a hazard to others may find the courts will rule that their liability exceeds any warranty limitations. The courts may also rule that any product manufacturers may be found liable because they had, or should have had, knowledge of their products' potential for material loss or injury. Manufacturers of Year 2000–related products should perform detailed testing not only of current products, but also those manufactured years ago that are still in use in order to protect themselves from liability claims.

Firms providing computer-based products or services may find themselves at risk even though they did not build the computer-based component or software. If it can be shown that a product is not safe in its design, that it could have been designed to be safe, and that the design fault contributed to a physical injury or death, the manufacturer, distributor, or even the company using the hardware or software may be sued. Manufacturers and companies who use computer systems to make decisions in life and death situations should review all systems hardware and software in depth.

It is not clear where liability limitations exist. The builder of a manufacturing process control system may be found equally as guilty as the manufacturer of a black box that was purchased to schedule maintenance that shut the system down. By the same token, the company that does not halt operations over the Year 2000 New Year event may be found to be negligent when the system fails even though it was diligent about testing the operation. Many plant managers are opting for shutdowns for maintenance to avoid litigation risks.

Software and information liabilities are currently being defined for the first time in the United States. The proposed amendments to the Uniform Commercial Code, known as UCC2B, redefine damage definitions and liability limits for information providers, including software developers. It is not known at this time when these new laws will be adopted, but Year 2000 legal actions may accelerate their adoption and implementation. The full impact of the adoption of the proposed changes can only be guessed at, since they are still in review, but customers may find their positions weakened by their passage.

Follow the Rules, or Else

Perhaps the most difficult legal impacts to predict are within the domain of government and industry compliance. Many regulatory agencies are still defining requirements and redefining old ones.

Many industries (such as banks and pharmaceutical manufacturers) are required by regulation to maintain records for a certain number of years. These records are frequently maintained in electronic form. As the format and technology used to archive the data change, the ability of the enterprise to retrieve and process the data diminishes. This is especially true where the data is not actively used. If the records cannot be processed by existing systems, or the processing returns invalid results, the enterprise could be found to be in violation of the record-keeping requirement.

Records kept electronically are often encrypted. The encryption codes frequently involve date processing. As these records are kept past the next century, the date processing may not function properly, making these records inaccessible. When these records are kept on behalf of other enterprises or the public, the enterprise with the maintenance responsibility may be accused of violating good business practices.

The federal government has posted requirements that systems it purchases for many types of uses must be Year 2000–compliant. For the most part, it has adopted the Department of Defense's definition for *compliance.* Should a firm sell a system or a component of a system that is not compliant, it will certainly run the risk of government actions. Even more important, if the firm that sells products and services to the government is not fully compliant, the government will hold the firm responsible for all costs incurred in remediating any problems caused by the use of the product or service.

Agencies governing the banking industry have issued Year 2000 compliance guidelines and policies to financial companies. Some financial institutions have already received strong warnings that if they do not comply more rapidly, they will be shut down. One regulatory reviewer has indicated that as many as 30 percent of the banks may be forced to close in 1999. Some analysts believe that recent bank mergers have been motivated in part by the Year 2000 regulations, and that all such mergers are being scrutinized to see if they facilitate or impede Year 2000 compliance directives.

The securities industries in most countries require disclosure of financial events or risks. Many enterprises who face large expenses due to Year 2000 repairs avoid reporting the expenses if they determine that the cost "represents no substantial material effect on the business" of the firm. If it comes to pass that there *is* a serious impact, such enterprises could find themselves in violation of Securities and Exchange Commission (SEC) disclosure rules for not reporting the expenses, or not reporting them in a timely manner.

Accounting practices require identification of financial risks. These risks may be associated with expenses, loss of revenue, or interruption of business. Many enterprises still do not recognize that the risk to business is not necessarily from their own computers, but from the inability of others to supply or of customers to buy. Such enterprises, and their auditors, could be accused of violating accounting-practice rules if reporting is not handled correctly.

It may not be necessary to disclose the actual expenses related to the Year 2000 repair. In fact, enterprises that mitigate the problem by buying both hardware and software so that they can be capitalized often do not report the cost as Year 2000–related, but simply as an investment. An example of an astute disclosure is one that achieves the following points:

- Recognizes that internal systems are not, or may not be, millennium-compliant.
- Hardware and software purchased by the firm may not be compliant.
- Failure of either internal or purchased components could result in unanticipated expenses that may have a material effect on the enterprise.
- Expenditures by customers to mitigate their own Year 2000 problems could reduce sales and have a material effect on the enterprise.

Breach of Fiduciary Duties

Managers should be particularly concerned about the personal consequences of a failure to properly address Year 2000 impacts on their businesses. In the case of corporations, each director or officer owes a fiduciary duty to the shareholders to protect the shareholders' interests. Managers who negligently ignore the Year 2000 problem and fail to prepare their businesses are open to being sued by those shareholders.

Shareholders who have lost 30 percent or more of their investments due to Year 2000 negligence may argue that management had been adequately warned of the Year 2000 threat. Laws were written to protect the absentee owners of businesses from managers who were hired for their qualifications and their ability to minimize risks. Management is not supposed to be caught unaware by problems it had adequate notice to address. The Year 2000 problem has been widely publicized far in advance of the critical window for action.

The question management will be called upon to answer is whether it acted in a timely manner. Shareholders may hold that if the enterprise did not act when the problem became known, then management may be held accountable. Some believe that management was sufficiently warned or had the knowledge to understand the potential impact of the Year 2000 problem as early as 1992. Evidence exists that management was restricted from acting by equipment and software constraints, industry standards, and competitive conditions. Also, managers may argue that the cost of repair was too high to undertake in the early 1990s, when hardware and system software that could handle Year 2000 testing were not available. Media hype and tool vendors claiming to be working on solutions to the problem made it financially unwise to invest in a solution that proved too expensive. Even so, those that feel injured may hold that management could have started redeploying resources to head off large financial impacts in the late 1990s. It is probably safe to say that any publicly traded enterprise's management team that waited until 1998 to take action is going to be severely mauled by its shareholders.

The management team may try to defend against any claims by demonstrating diligent attempts to minimize problems before they occurred. Fortunately for management, courts and the law do generally provide managers with wide latitude in making business decisions on behalf of their companies, and any decision that would not have been patently unreasonable at the time will likely be respected. However, this latitude will not be extended to managers who failed to take any action or make any effort to assess Y2K risks.

Don't Feed the Bears

Dealing with hardware and software vendors can become like a visit to the zoo gone badly. Get too close to some animals, and you could get your arm ripped off. This is especially true if your firm proceeds without due caution. Keep in mind as you read the following that the hardware and software providers are reading it also. Wear strong gloves with lots of padding.

According to lawyer friends, it is unclear whether the UCC (Uniform Commercial Code), which applies to transactions in goods, covers contracts and licenses for computer software. Apparently, it is not easy to determine whether the delivery of software constitutes a sale of goods, a license of goods, or the performance of services. The courts have so far relied on the particular factual circumstances of the original sale to determine if contract liability exists. This includes expressed warranties such as promises, product descriptions, or any sample or model used to induce the sale. Consumers may claim implied warranties when the seller suggests it fully understands the needs of the customer in the product's advertising or product claims. Before claiming a breach of implied warranty, it may be best to have a lawyer examine the purchase contract. In many cases, courts find that purchase contracts void any implied warranties made prior to sale.

Who's Responsible?

A big problem for developers and customers alike is to determine whether the Year 2000 problem is a design flaw that must be corrected. For customers who provided the specifications for the code that was created or purchased, this might be a special problem, as the specifications may have unintentionally required the creation of design flaws leading to the Year 2000 problem. Consumers of mass-market products may find that contract terms on the package say that they accept the product "as is" and that the time allowed to discover any flaws is limited.

Where specific contract terms do not exist, design changes (enhancements that improve the functionality) of software are usually made at the discretion and scheduling of the vendor. Software repairs (the correction of flaws) are required by most warranty clauses to be performed within a reasonable period of time. The exact date of repair is open since the changes required are not predictable. The repair of the code to achieve millennium compliance may take too long to be useful, may not be started in time, or may not be performed in a manner consistent with the customer's definition of millennium compliance.

How do you define millennium compliance? Customers may have their own definitions that differ or compete with the software vendor's. Which party has the right and/or obligation to make the definition? Who is contractually obligated to establish the definition of compliance, and how do the parties reconcile their differences? Vendors may argue that they made a reasonable attempt at fixing the problem, but the customer interfered by changing requirements.

Source code for many custom high-end software products is often held in escrow for licensees or purchasers. These escrow accounts may be opened under certain circumstances. If the vendor is unable to repair the code in the time frame required by the customer, the licensee/purchaser may attempt to withdraw the source code from escrow. This may or may not be possible under the terms of the escrow agreement. Mediation or arbitration of disagreements about access may delay any action until it is too late. Any legal claims as to the lack of action may find either or both parties at fault, depending on how each case is handled.

Lease and License Obligations

Enterprises with established computing departments should thoroughly review the status of all their hardware and software contracts and licenses prior to taking any actions to pursue claims against vendors or to exercise lease and license terms. There are many instances in which Year 2000 corrective actions may be frustrated by past decisions or operational errors. Following are a few examples.

An enterprise seeks to terminate the hardware lease of computer equipment that is not millennium-compliant. The lessor asserts that this is a violation of agreement. The lease contract had no provisions for failure of hardware and software. The lessor handled only the financing of the equipment, not its selection. The enterprise got rid of the hardware, but paid penalties.

A software vendor claimed that it was under no obligation to the licensee because it violated the terms of a lease. The licensee failed to maintain a contract by payment of maintenance fees. In another instance, the licensee lost the argument because it had failed to notify the licensor of the transfer during an acquisition. Even though the new firm continued to pay on the maintenance contract, the product had been moved to a new computer and the contract called for the specific registration of the hardware serial number of the computer on which the product was being run. In another case, the licensed software was installed on the wrong computers, violating the terms of the license.

In another case, the licensee was surprised when the vendor found that a product licensed to run on only one computer showed up on more than one. The licensee had to buy several new licenses and pay back maintenance for several past months. It turned out that operators did not know the license terms and loaded the software on the other computers to simplify application testing. The firm found out the cost of the licenses was not justified by the convenience, but they had already violated the contract and were obligated to buy the additional licenses.

In another instance, the software lease contract invited the customer to create its own code and insert it in the package as long as it fit specified rules. The intent was for the customer to create custom business routines. The vendor later found that customer-developed routines often contained special date processing that interfered with the correction of the vendor-supplied code. The vendor simply could not expand dates or install a solution without violating a clause in the contract, which stated that it would maintain the protocol, which allowed customers to insert code.

Some software license holders find that their licenses prohibit them from allowing a noncustomer employee or a noncertified party to see or modify the product code. In one instance, the license holder found that it did not have staff that was authorized and it could not find a certified party to make the changes. The problem was compounded when it was discovered that the vendor was no longer providing training. So, even if the license holder decided to train a person, it couldn't.

In another instance, the company discovered that though it had sent a number of products to an offshore code remediation factory, federal laws governing technology transfer inhibited shipping certain of its software. Though the software was very old and not even considered a proprietary product, the time and effort it would have taken to get permission exceeded the window in which the code had to be fixed.

A software product was sold by its manufacturer to another vendor. The end customer was told of the sale but did nothing about contacting the new vendor with its concerns about Year 2000 problems in the product. The original manufacturer had started a project to fix the code, but the new owner could not retain the staff and failed to notify the customer about the status of the project or any delays. The customer did not discover the problem until the application failed. Neither the customer nor the new owner was in a position to fix the code. Contract terms failed to protect the customer since it did not work with the new owner.

Consultants

About consultants—don't expect to recover costs from them if they make a mistake. It could be extremely difficult to prove malpractice. Consider that any damages are most likely to be caused by the Year 2000 problem and not introduced by the consultant. As long as the consultant can demonstrate reasonable and prudent adherence to industry standard practices, the client (your company) usually retains responsibility unless there are specific terms in the agreement that cover performance. The client would probably have to demonstrate either intentional or negligent misrepresentation of the resulting changes or negligence in following standard practices. Damage reimbursement is most likely to be limited to the actual cost incurred in getting the code to work—hardly worthwhile if the business is collapsing.

It is unlikely that any consulting company would encourage the client to implement the code "as is" after the Year 2000 remediation work. It is rare for consultants to accept liability. They normally require the client reassume responsibility for the code when it is delivered from the remediation consultant. The logic that prevails is that the consultants were hired to perform specific changes, limiting what they can do to the code. They assume no responsibility for any code design problems to do with dates or any other data processing. Further, they do not control the environment in which the code is executed. The code must be recompiled and, at that point, any clear responsibility is lost. There is also the problem of maintaining control so those date problems cannot be reintroduced after the changed code is delivered. The customer would have to lock up the code. The client can rarely demonstrate that the code was not touched in any way after the consultant changed the code.

It is not uncommon, even under normal circumstances, to find that the operations staff continues to run an old version of the software instead of an updated version. There have already been instances where a company complained to its consultants that the Year 2000 fix was not made only to find, on investigation, one of its operators had loaded an old version accidentally.

As the Year 2000 deadline approaches, expect consulting customers to find that firms will only be able to make best-effort commitments to their clients. The demand for staff is expected to affect both the consulting companies and their customers in keeping commitments. Consulting companies may seek stiffer requirements for customer performance.

Inventory Risks

Lawyers will tell you that it is best to find out what your risks are and deal with them before they are realized. In talking with several firms and searching through material available on the Internet, the following advice seems to appear consistently.

- Inventory existing contracts with vendors, suppliers, and customers.
- Assess your liability and theirs based on the compliance claims made by them and by yourself.
- Evaluate your insurance coverage and requirements. Don't assume any Year 2000 problems are covered.
- Perform due diligence for future contracts and transactions.
- Create a high-level corporate strategy around Year 2000.
- Document all the preceding actions in detail.

Legal matters pertaining to year 2000 are starting to appear. Get very familiar with your attorneys and their knowledge of the Year 2000 legal issues. They may soon have to become part of your corporate family. What has been indicated here are the principal conditions that may be involved in legal actions. Many more may come up. "May the force be with you!"

Many law firms are beginning to pay close attention to evolving actions relating to the Year 2000 problem. Some interesting material can be found on the Internet at the following sites:

www.year2000.com/archive/audit.html—Michael Scott; Howsie Wes Sacks & Brelsford

www.2k-times.com—Thelen, Marrin, Johnson & Bridges, LLP

www.year2000.com/archive/NFbeyond.html—Warren S. Reid

www.tamu.edu/cis/teams/yr2k/links_legal.html—Links to legal aspects of the Year 2000 problem

www.state.tx.us/year2000/legal-issues.htm—More links to legal issues

Insurance

The most relied upon bulwark against litigation claims is insurance. All insurance policies are expected to be impacted in some way by the Year 2000 risk including directors and officers, business interruption/property, errors and omissions, general and employers' liability, product liability, boiler and machinery, environmental liability, and professional liability. The insurance industry is rapidly side-stepping the Year 2000 risk.

Business-interruption insurers are seeking status information from their clients. Clients may be put in the position of supplying information that the insurer could interpret as not sufficient to support a claim, or that later might be termed as a misrepresentation and used to deny a claim. Some of these insurers initially started to create exclusions, but competitive pressure forced them to back down when other insurers did not participate. Businesses should review their policies to make sure coverage is granted if suppliers fail to perform and a waiver of material damage proviso is present.

Machinery insurers appear to be introducing Y2K exclusions in all policies fearing the presence of embedded microprocessors. The embedded systems problem is also a concern for product and environmental liability insurers. They are looking for full disclosure information. If companies do not provide such disclosures they may find themselves without insurance coverage. By the same token, those same manufacturers must be careful to make such reports accurately. They must be concerned about changes in models and versions of chips used in their products. Companies may want to review their insurance limits.

Professional liability insurers are already introducing Year 2000 exclusions in some cases. Nobody knows yet when the Year 2000 problems will manifest themselves and how anyone can determine specific responsibility for actions taken in the past. The injured party may be totally unable to substantiate a fault, and the insured may find it equally difficult to process a claim where fault cannot be proven. There may also be a problem of determining when a wrongful act occurred, which could trigger a rejection of a claim if suspicion exists under prior acts exclusions.

Fiduciaries are expected to come under increasing pressure from insurers as governments enact laws requiring fiduciaries to investigate recommended investment opportunities for Year 2000 vulnerabilities. Some insurers of directors and officers are including Year 2000 exclusions in policies, but clients are finding them ready to withdraw them if a substantial history exists. Directors and officers are particularly vulnerable because investor fears of possible Year 2000 problems could trigger a problem prompting many companies to minimize their reporting. At the same time, failure to adequately disclose the depth of possible problems could create problems. In the first, disclosure could trigger a market sell-off and a shareholder class action suit. The second could be grounds for class action suits because investors were not warned. Companies may find it prudent to raise their limits in either event.

Year 2000 insurance does exist. Several firms (J&H Marsh & McLennan, American International Group, Axa Global Risks, and AON are a few) offer insurance addressing business interruption, director and officer, and professional Year 2000 liability coverage. These policies require an intensive third-party audit. The risk profiles these audits set determine the rates and the deductibles for the policy. These policies tend to be looked on as disaster insurance for firms that have already invested in Year 2000 risk reduction programs. It is fairly safe to say that if there is not a comprehensive Year 2000 project underway that is fairly certain of success, the premiums would be so large as to make the cost of the insurance as high as the value of the insurance policy.

The best insurance is an enterprisewide Year 2000 project that looks into all the aspects of the business to determine risks and then mitigates those risks. Documentation of plans and actions taken will provide the best legal and insurance coverage. Not taking any action at all is almost guaranteeing some kind of legal or insurance problem.

TruAuto: A Year 2000 Case Study

Introduction

The case study in this appendix represents a snapshot of a hypothetical business in the process of evaluating Year 2000 risks. For our purposes, we will call the model company TruAuto. Systemic Solutions, a real company that does Year 2000 consulting, completed this review of TruAuto in January of 1998. It begins with a *company overview,* where the general results of the study including Year 2000 vulnerability are presented. The following sections are a series of *area reviews,* where each of the principal business areas of TruAuto is discussed. The assessment of each area is further subdivided into

- A section called *Area Overview,* which describes the status of the area being discussed
- A section called *Vulnerability Assessment,* which describes the vulnerability identified by TruAuto as a result of the Year 2000 assessment it has completed or has underway

Company Overview

TruAuto began its work on Year 2000 preparations in November of 1997. The TruAuto management team, led by the vice president of finance, grasped very early the complexity of the Year 2000 problem and the inevitability of the work that must be completed to remain viable past December 31, 1999. The TruAuto management team also saw the possibility of using an early state of Year 2000 readiness to gain competitive advantage and increase its market share.

The vice president of finance was the first to launch an assessment of Year 2000 impact. The first assessment was made in finance and in the front office area. He also requested the other areas to begin their own investigations of their Year 2000 vulnerabilities.

TruAuto determined the magnitude of its vulnerability using an *iterative estimating process.* The iterative process allowed the estimates to increase in accuracy as experience demonstrated how much time and effort was actually required to address the problems found. Initial estimates were made quickly by management on the basis of experience and manager speculation about what could go wrong. These estimates were sufficiently high to generate concern and to free resources to conduct more analytical estimates. The Year 2000 team prepared estimates of both what could go wrong and costs to correct problems in each area of vulnerability. One challenge it faced at this stage was difficulty in gathering sufficient credible data to gauge the Year 2000 condition of external entities, such as customers.

TruAuto chose to focus its primary Year 2000 attention on mitigating Year 2000 vulnerabilities in operations, facilities, sales, and computers and technology because of the substantial consequences it identified in those areas. Only limited vulnerability was identified in finance and so little effort was focused there. TruAuto is also conserving resources to be able to respond to government agencies, which are expected to present problems to TruAuto beginning in mid- to late 1999 because of their lack of Year 2000 preparation.

TruAuto has made a great deal of progress in mitigating its Year 2000 vulnerability because of the active stance it has taken. Early planning conducted by TruAuto management assures the likelihood resources will be available to handle government requests. Vulnerability in areas of operations, facilities, sales, and computers and technology is now reduced because of risk mitigation efforts.

Business Overview

TruAuto has been in business for 15 years and currently enjoys annual sales of approximately $29 million. TruAuto's principal business is the manufacture and sale of gasoline cans and zinc-coated buckets, funnels, and related items for automotive use. TruAuto occupies a central niche within a web of raw material suppliers, services, and marketing and distribution channels that serve the Northwest, California, and Southwest automotive retail markets.

TruAuto employs a total of 125 employees. There are 95 employees at the man-ufacturing site in Kent, Washington. Eighteen staff and a small number of con-tractors are employed at the administrative offices in Renton, Washington. Sales offices with five staff each are maintained in Los Angeles and Dallas.

TruAuto is a family-owned privately held company with a board of directors of close friends and family members. TruAuto is organized as depicted in Fig-ure A.1.

Overall Vulnerability Assessment

TruAuto management believes Year 2000 issues are under control.

All TruAuto employees have been made aware of the impending Year 2000 event and of the work underway to mitigate its effects. Most employees have actively supported the compliance work.

Year 2000 resource deployment has been accomplished primarily through out-source expertise and subcontractor assistance. One primary consultant has

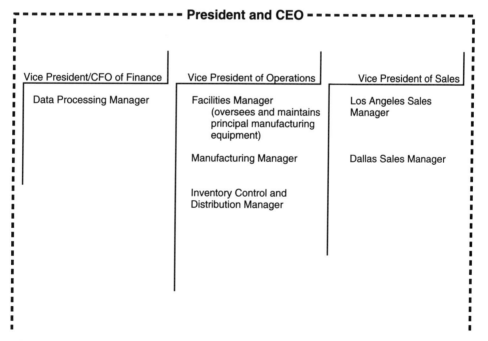

Figure A.1   TruAuto executives and corporate organization.

been employed for guidance and business consideration. Several independent contractors have been employed from RHO Process Engineering for facilities and systems remediation. Additional programming and testing resources have been contracted from Division Labs, based in Tukwila, Washington, for assistance with programming and testing changes of the data processing and operations departments.

TruAuto's anticipated completion date for Year 2000 readiness is August 1999. Year 2000 compliance began as a formal project within the company in November 1997. Year 2000 work is currently underway with formal plans and regular progress reports delivered by each primary area of TruAuto.

The vice president of finance (who originally brought Year 2000 compliance issues outside of computing technology to light) is TruAuto's primary sponsor of the Year 2000 project. The data processing, operations, and facilities managers have committed themselves to visibly cosponsor the Year 2000 efforts. Each manager has taken a key role in mitigating the potential impact and risk the Year 2000 issues might have to TruAuto's ongoing operations.

Legal counsel has been contacted for assurance of activities with regard to potential litigation (either initiated or defended by TruAuto). This in turn has accomplished the following:

- Triggered regular reviews of contractual obligations with existing and new potential business partners
- Furnished a structure for the questions asked of suppliers and business partners

Year 2000 Efforts

The vice president of finance leads the Year 2000 efforts as TruAuto's primary sponsor. He also distributes formal reports of the remaining Year 2000 tasks, progress, and schedule. He distributes a companywide newsletter with announcements and acknowledgments of key milestones reached.

The president and the key managers of the company meet every other week to review Year 2000 progress and assist in removing any obstacles delaying efforts.

A substantial annual budget allocation has been set up for Year 2000 work throughout 1997, 1998, and 1999. An additional sum will be set aside for cleanup activities during 2000. Budget allocation has been funded primarily by funds previously planned for company expansion. These funds were to be used for acquisition of a like company/facility in Dallas, Texas, in 1999; however, the acquisition has been delayed. Another facility may be purchased at a more attractive price in 2001 due to the possibility of Year 2000 business failures in the area.

Area Reviews

The specific area reviews of TruAuto include the following:

Finance and front office operations

Sales

Use of computers and technology

Operations (purchasing, order processing, manufacturing, inventory control and distribution)

Facilities

Government agencies

Finance and Front Office Operations

TruAuto is only mildly vulnerable in finance and front office operations. Year 2000–readiness preparations already in progress under the leadership of the vice president of finance have mitigated all internal vulnerability. Outside entities that pose a risk include outsourced company payrolls, temporary workers required to handle peak loads, and company investments. The company has an outside funds manager who handles the employees' 401(k) plan, and it is believed it has not given due consideration to possible Year 2000 problems. Plans have been written to mitigate concerns with outsourced services, and the company is making good progress with these objectives.

Area Overview

The following reflects the situation in financial and front office operations at the start of the Year 2000 evaluation process.

Payroll

Payroll depends on a paper timekeeping system within TruAuto and computer processing by Data Wonders in Auburn, Washington. Data Wonders is a local source of payroll processing using a homegrown payroll system that also supports 79 other area companies. Paper records (time cards) are delivered to Data Wonders on odd Fridays. Payroll checks, payroll registers, check reconciliations, and so on are returned to TruAuto on even Fridays.

Finance

Financial reporting, budgeting reports, and the like are completed internally by data processing using the Dunn & Bradstreet accounting system (see the upcoming section, *Computers and Technology*). The company maintains funds and an investment account at Central National Bank, a local bank in Kent, Washington. The 401(k) plan is managed by a team of fund managers at Washington Investment Corporation of Seattle, Washington, and includes several fund placements.

Contract Employees

On a regular basis (usually on payroll Fridays and at month end), the company acquires contract employees for temporary day work in finance from Andover Temps and Wonder Workers both of which are local temping agencies with offices in Kent, Washington.

Office Supplies and Equipment

Office supplies are acquired from Costco, Office Depot, and Office MAX on an as needed basis, with vendors chosen depending on prevailing prices. The front office uses several fax machines and a U.S. postage meter for correspondence.

Vulnerability Assessment

TruAuto will address the vulnerabilities in finance and front office operations in the following ways.

Payroll

The vice president of finance has contacted Data Wonders to inquire about the status of the payroll system and payroll processing with regard to the year 2000 and has received a letter of explanation. Four staff from Data Wonders have been assigned to bring their payroll system into compliance. A windowing technique will be used.

The actual modification (conversion) of the payroll system is well underway and the core system is already converted and in test. Implementation of the system is planned for Q3, 1998. Assurances have been given, although not contractually, that the system will be functional and without deficiency in time for the millennium rollover.

Finance

The vice president of finance feels confident Central National Bank is well along in its Year 2000 conversion effort and the investment accounts TruAuto has placed there are secure. Central National Bank has described its Year 2000–compliance work in some detail and has shared its experience and its progress with the TruAuto conversion team.

Questions raised with Washington Investment Corporation by TruAuto about the management of the 401(k) funds have received friendly but uninformative response. The letters sent by TruAuto have received relatively vague responses referencing work being done to bring Washington Investments Corporation's internal systems into compliance. No information has been supplied about the steps being taken by the investment managers to assure the compliance of those companies whose stock they are acquiring for the 401(k).

Contract Employees

Temporary resource requirements have increased recently in the front office to support the inquiries and letter-processing requirements imposed by other areas of the company for Year 2000 information from suppliers, customers, and distribution channels. Temporary staff have recently been harder to obtain.

Andover Temps has been unable to provide skilled staff on a regular basis and untrained staff have been furnished (and returned) on more than half a dozen occasions. Wonder Workers, who continues to provide sufficiently skilled temporary resources, has informed TruAuto that it is experiencing increased demand but has been unable to increase staff accordingly. This has led to an increased workload in the front office, and some Year 2000 information gathering has slowed as a result.

Office Supplies and Equipment

Acquisition of office supplies has been categorized as a lower priority than other issues because they are readily available from a variety of sources. The front office manager, who is also the president's administrative assistant, has asked the facilities manager to include the fax machines and postage meter in his department's remediation plans.

Sales

Year 2000 preparations are underway under the leadership of the vice president of sales. TruAuto depends upon a relatively small number of customers with whom it deals directly and three primary distribution partners. The vulnerability uncovered thus far is with several customers who were late in starting Year 2000 preparations. Steps have been taken to mitigate that vulnerability.

Looking forward, a worst-case scenario based on the latest information would leave TruAuto only slightly vulnerable to Year 2000.

Area Overview

TruAuto sells many of its products through three distributors who deliver 80 percent of TruAuto's annual revenue. Distributors sell and distribute Tru-Auto's products to approximately 180 end customers. Some end customers are chains with 75 or more sales outlets. TruAuto also sells direct to 86 customers, and 25 of these provide the primary customer base.

Vulnerability Assessment

TruAuto has mounted a strong campaign to assure and support the preparation of its customers and supply chain through the year 2000. The vice president of finance and the vice president of sales have examined the customer base, made five-year revenue projections, and developed a prioritized list of key customers. An orchestrated set of letter inquiries to gather information about the Year 2000 readiness and ongoing viability of direct customers and distributors was begun in November 1997. A general meeting was conducted in mid-December 1997 to review the Year 2000 situation and its associated risks with the 25 key customers and to gather information regarding their respective Year 2000 readiness. TruAuto is continuing to develop information about the situation at each of its key customers. As of January 1998, the survey was scheduled to be complete in March 1998.

The 3 distributors and only 15 of the 86 customers have furnished formal responses containing guarantees of ongoing business viability past December 31, 1999. The distributors have reported they have major project efforts underway and have uncovered deficiencies. The scan guns and box supplies for the distribution channel are at risk (see *Operations* section). Four key customers have admitted being at significant risk for year 2000 and beyond because of a late start and a misunderstanding about the scope of the Year 2000 problem.

TruAuto is also working with its three distributors to extend the Year 2000–readiness inquiries to the distributors' end customers, particularly the customers with the larger sales volumes.

Computers and Technology

TruAuto identified high vulnerability in its computer systems and technology. The risk lies in application use and the resulting user files (e.g., spreadsheets), the user applications, and the inventory management and shipping (IMS) system. The IMS system was originally designed and built six years ago by the individual who is now the data processing manager. Additional resources will need to be deployed for the conversion and test activities for this system.

With the early proactive steps begun by the data processing manager, most hardware system changes are nearly completed. The data processing manager has completed a thorough inventory and assessment of the computers and technology used throughout TruAuto. A great deal of the computer and technology remediation and testing under TruAuto's control has been completed. The data processing manager used an industry standard for compliance to certify the hardware, network, and software changes being made. This has been useful for his team to better understand how to approach validation of the changes made and has given the data processing manager the assurance needed to consider the system components Year 2000–compliant.

Area Overview

TruAuto has a primary computer complex consisting of the following.

Hardware

- A central server.
- 14 workstations used by managers, administrative support, and supervisors (largely used for an internal e-mail system).
- 4 workstations in manufacturing used for job statusing. The workstations on the factory floor act as dumb terminals for the processing systems. These workstations are linked to the Matsushita, Chicago Pneumatic, and Paano manufacturing equipment, and the chemical containment systems which exist within facilities. Each of these systems portrays and executes specific commands per each processing system.
- 2 workstations on the shop floor used for facilities management.
- 4 workstations in traffic and distribution used to receive orders and control in-process inventory and shipping.
- 12 workstations throughout each of the office staff; finance, sales, and operations teams used to manage order processing; accounts payable and accounts receivable; and sales bookings.

Nearly all of the workstations are 386 or 486 processors employing older BIOS chips, which put these devices at risk with regard to Year 2000 compatibility.

In addition, some office staff have stand-alone workstations used for special purposes such as handling special correspondence for the president or security reasons to access the Internet and certain bulletin boards germane to the company's business.

Operating System and Software

Most of the computers are networked together employing Microsoft's NT server product; the operating system of the workstations is Windows 95.

General software includes the following:

- Microsoft's Office 95 (the main application in general use)
- Microsoft Exchange (the manager's e-mail system)
- Microsoft's Internet Explorer 3.01 (for Internet access on stand-alone workstations)

Business Applications

TruAuto's computers operate three principal business applications. The shop floor has four workstations for its equipment commands and processing which include the following.

Order-processing software. Acquired from ALPHA four years ago. The Order Processing System contains approximately 230 programs and utilizes Crystal Reports as its report writer. Order Processing is

- An integrated user interface, reports, and data query system based on a Sybase database
- The front end to the IMS system
- Utilized primarily by the front office staff for order entry and processing

Inventory management and shipping (IMS). This system utilizes Symbol Logics scan guns. The data processing manager developed and implemented IMS at TruAuto a little over six years ago while still a consulting programmer. IMS contains three major applications:

- Parts and supplies inventory
- Product inventory tracking
- Replenishment shipping and freight management

IMS is made up of approximately 300 programs and includes a module deployed as remote functionality to the chemical crib within operations for tracking receipt and expiration dates of the chemicals.

Financial reporting. This software was acquired from Dunn & Bradstreet five years ago. The application includes the following financial systems:

- Accounts payable and receivable (AP/AR)
- General ledger
- Invoice processing

- Tax preparation and audit reports
- Company revenue forecasts and 10K reports
- Investment profiles and processing
- Benefits reporting
- Annual budgeting and quarterly reports

Other Business Application Concerns

TruAuto has been asked by Sears to accept orders and other related information using electronic data interchange (EDI) via the Internet by January 1, 1999. The data processing manager is now exploring that possibility.

Operations tracks certain of its data using an Access database to provide details of operational components for the operations manager. This database also supplies the preliminary time sheet information delivered to Data Wonders every other Friday.

Vulnerability Assessment

All software employed within the computer complex has been inventoried, vendors have been contacted, and/or their software products have been tested for compliance of century date functionality. All desktop hardware and network components have been inventoried and assessed for noncompliance. Only a few Year 2000 issues remain within the major business systems infrastructure including the following:

Microsoft Office. Microsoft Office components requiring minor work include several Excel files and the operations Access database. The database is currently being investigated for date impact, with completion expected by end of March.

IMS. The inventory management and shipping (IMS) application. IMS needs updating and corrections for century compliance. The screens of the IMS application must be resized and adjusted to accommodate the newer hardware recently installed in the manufacturing and distribution areas.

Financial programs. Many of TruAuto's financial programs are already in compliance and the remaining few will be made compliant before year-end. These systems, originally purchased from Dunn & Bradstreet, are under remediation by the new OEM, GEAC out of Vancouver, British Columbia. GEAC has contractually committed to completion of these changes no later than December 31, 1998.

Order-processing software. The order-processing system is under conversion by ALPHA, the original design and implementation house. ALPHA has furnished descriptions of plans to bring the financial applications into compliance. ALPHA says it is implementing fully compliant date structures in data files and this, in turn, simplifies the programming task at TruAuto to modify homegrown programs using these files.

Year 2000 software. The data processing manager is using Microsoft's Year 2000 Issues and Solutions document for identifying potential failure and correction data. The Microsoft document is incomplete in regards to specific uses employed by TruAuto. Little information has been obtained from Microsoft. Testing has begun in several areas albeit more complex than anticipated.

Operations

Operations includes purchasing, order processing, manufacturing, inventory control and distribution. TruAuto is conducting its operations preparation quickly and efficiently. The operations manager and the operations team have been proactive in reviewing readiness and acting where deficiencies have been identified. Their research outside the company has been thorough and their risk mitigation efforts appropriate. This includes the activities defined by the manufacturing and inventory control and distribution managers. The facilities changes are outlined in detail in the following sections.

Contingency plans for the suppliers and supply chain as well as the distribution channel are largely defined and alternative suppliers are already identified in most cases. Still, some key vulnerabilities remain to be mitigated. These include clearing up with greater certainty any weaknesses in the supply chain, assuring a continuing supply of corrugate, and determining how inventory will be counted.

Area Overview

Vendors. The vendor list contains the names of 47 companies. Seventy percent are located in this country, 20 percent (10 companies) in Latin America, and 10 percent (5 companies) in the Pacific Rim. TruAuto receives its principal raw materials from three suppliers:

- Apex Metals located across the street from TruAuto
- Janus Minerals and Chemicals of Edmonds, Washington, with chemical plants in Honduras, Saigon, and Pittsburgh, Pennsylvania
- Minerales Perfectos, S.A. with a sales office in Tacoma, Washington and a chemical-processing facility in Monterrey, Mexico

Sensitive inventory. Chemicals with limited shelf life are stored in a chemical crib supervised by the material manager and withdrawn on an earliest date FIFO (first in, first out) basis. A networked workstation is maintained in the crib for inventory management and control.

Ordering.   TruAuto receives orders by telephone, fax, and mail from distributors located across the United States and directly from large retail organizations such as K-Mart, Sears, Target, and Coast to Coast.

Orders are entered into the ALPHA order-processing system, a vendor-supplied software package running on TruAuto's central server. The ALPHA system is linked with the inventory management and shipping (IMS) system.

Scan guns.   Symbol Logics scan guns are used to secure inventory counts and furnish data for input to preparation of bills of lading and shipping notices. From the research conducted by the operations manager, these guns are in use by 85 Symbol Logics customers, including TruAuto.

Shipping.   The inventory management and shipping application tracks finished goods inventory and shipping activity. Finished goods are stored on-site at the Kent facility. All shipping is done using Indian Express Trucks, Nationwide Shipping, and Forrester. Special shipping (ones and twos) is done using Airborne Express. Finished goods are shipped in partial as well as full truckloads depending on arrangements made with receivers. On occasion, special arrangements are made to ship ones and twos for favored customers.

Vulnerability Assessment

A plan has been developed by the operations manager outlining the changes required for assuring readiness of the manufacturing equipment. This plan was presented to and approved by the president of TruAuto in the fall of 1997.

Vendors

The operations manager has met and corresponded with the primary equipment manufacturers to identify potential malfunctions. The results of this correspondence have been turned over to the facilities manager who has Year 2000 accountability for all non-data-processing equipment.

The operations manager has also spoken with representatives of the primary chemical suppliers (and, in two cases, met with their representatives). Apex Metals, Janus Minerals and Chemicals, and Minerales Perfectos S.A. have provided assurance of their Year 2000 readiness via correspondence including the following:

- Several levels of documentation

- Formal enterprise project bulletins

- Written guarantees of compliance for uninterrupted supply of goods

Customs

The manufacturing manager has investigated import/customs issues that may be potential failure points for the raw materials received from offshore suppliers. The current customs regulations and the importers already processed and operating will remain in effect. No potential changes to regulations are anticipated at this time per the broker and customs agents (refer to the upcoming section, *Government Agencies*).

The manufacturing manager is working with the customs broker to further assess and inquire about the preparedness of the warehousing agents he currently utilizes. He has delivered a list of questions to the customs broker to determine those steps being taken to assess Year 2000 readiness at the warehouses. Answers to the questions are to be returned to the manufacturing manager by the end of Q2, 1998. Contingency plans are currently being discussed within operations should the results show substantial risk.

Supply Chain

TruAuto has begun to act on a comprehensive plan to assure the viability of its supply chain. All major suppliers, including the freight carriers, have been polled for readiness via a letter and phone campaign conducted by purchasing. Thirty-one of the 47 suppliers have responded formally with letters describing progress. Six have responded more informally by telephone with verbal reassurance. Ten suppliers have furnished no response. Company representatives are following up with the last 16 to obtain formal assurances. TruAuto has found 6 of its suppliers have not yet begun Year 2000 compliance efforts.

Distribution

The distribution channel has been polled for readiness. A deficiency within Sandforth, the major distribution house in the Northwest, has been identified. This deficiency has to do with lack of date compliance in the scan guns used by Sandforth and TruAuto to inventory all their goods. These scan guns are known to have problems with date management of the century field for receipt and outbound processing of goods.

Corrugate may become more difficult to acquire in a timely manner. TruAuto has learned of a potential deficiency in the packaging of goods including to and through the distribution channel. The box supplier and manufacturer (Seattle Container) who generally supplies both TruAuto and Sandforth with corrugate for shipment, anticipates a supply-chain failure with its chemicals supplier. Chemicals needed for the corrugate production may be in short supply in the latter part of 1999 because of lack of readiness by the upstream chemicals supplier.

Facilities

TruAuto's vulnerability within facilities is moderate to high. A plan for achieving facilities Year 2000 compliance including remediation of the manufacturing equipment has been approved and is underway, although the final completion date is not yet known. Changes to the facilities devices such as HVAC, building access systems, lighting and landscape systems, and so on are planned to start in 1998 with completion expected by the end of the first quarter of 1999.

The facilities manager has a list of the equipment where Year 2000 remediation is needed. It was developed following a walk-through of all TruAuto facilities with an outside expert in Year 2000 device and process compliance. This list encompasses the equipment and processing systems throughout the facility and identifies specifically each device with an embedded chip suspected of noncompliance.

The remediation plan developed by the facilities manager includes the steps required for the remediation effort for each item, as well as the steps necessary for testing and validation after corrections are made.

Area Overview

Facilities. TruAuto conducts operations out of rented facilities built approximately 35 years ago.

Equipment. Manufacturing equipment has been obtained from a variety of sources including Matsushita, Chicago Pneumatic, and Paano. This equipment is serviced and maintained by the facilities manager. Some of this equipment is computer driven and/or contains computer chips for functionality and processing.

Utilities. Propane (used in large quantity in the manufacturing process) is acquired from U.S. Propane in Auburn, Washington. Natural gas and electric power are purchased from Puget Power. Sewage services and chemical disposal are furnished by the City of Kent. Garbage disposal is furnished by Lathrop Disposal of Renton, Washington.

Phones. Telephone services are provided by US West and AT&T. A ROLM telephone system with 65 phones, voice mail and forwarding, 15 pagers, and a Sprint connection with Dallas and Los Angeles was purchased in 1991 and is used companywide.

Misc. Food Services of America provides sandwich, snack, coffee, and soda vending machines. Building access is monitored and provided by Honeywell Systems in Seattle. The front office manager has asked the facilities manager to include the fax machines and postage meter in his department's remediation plans.

Vulnerability Assessment

The facilities manager has conducted a walk-through with an outside Year 2000 consultant of all the manufacturing facilities and administrative offices to identify Year 2000 vulnerabilities.

A number of embedded chips with potential date compliance problems have been identified for further exploration. These include the following:

- Automatic lighting and landscape systems
- Backup uninterrupted power supply (UPS) and generator systems
- Fax machines and U.S. postage meter
- Fire suppression systems
- Heavy equipment and freight hydraulics
- HVAC and clean air systems
- Hydraulic doors
- Load lifts and forklifts
- Pressing molds and assembly processing and manufacturing equipment
- Security and surveillance systems
- Sewage and chemical disposal systems
- Telephone systems
- Workstations for manufacturing, inventory, and distribution personnel

Out of the survey list, the following components were tested by an engineering firm specializing in chip testing and were found to be at risk for Year 2000:

Automatic lighting and landscape systems.   These operate on a month and hour basis and, because of leap year processing, are believed to be noncompliant.

Backup UPS and generator systems.   These are standby systems for the current energy and computing facilities. They were installed by RHO Engineering and have been assessed by RHO for Year 2000 readiness. The backup UPS and generator systems do have deficiencies and will need corrections to assure viability.

Fax machines and U.S. Postage meter.   This equipment processes functions using date fields and will need to be replaced or updated.

HVAC and clean air systems. These systems are a little over a year old and RHO Engineering provided support for the original installation.

Pressing molds and assembly processing and manufacturing equipment. Matsushita, Chicago Pneumatic, and Paano are the primary processing and equipment manufacturers.

Security and surveillance systems. These systems were delivered and installed by Honeywell and are over five years old. The facilities' entryways, shop floors, and grounds are scanned and taped daily with archives cataloged by date. The camera and scanning equipment is initialized and operates on hourly and date triggers and is monitored by Honeywell Systems. The facilities manager has learned from Honeywell Systems that equipment modifications are required to achieve Year 2000 compliance.

Telephone systems. The facilities manager has tried several times to obtain information from US West and AT&T for determining Year 2000 compliance of the equipment and systems purchased in 1991 and later (e.g., the pagers). All attempts for obtaining formal information from either vendor have been inconclusive.

The pagers. These were acquired subsequent to the phone system installation, and PageNet, the vendor, claims compliance. The facilities manager has deemed this equipment compliant because PageNet has provided test results and a formal guarantee of Year 2000 readiness.

Workstations used by manufacturing personnel. The workstations are 386 PC-compatibles and have deficient BIOS chips.

Several other devices, because of their age and general condition, were found to be beyond repair and will have to be replaced.

Government Agencies

TruAuto's projected vulnerability to outside governmental agencies is estimated as negligible for two reasons. First, TruAuto does not depend on services from government agencies for operation or continuance of its business except for U.S. Customs. (U.S. Customs has oversight of the importation of foreign materials TruAuto uses in its manufacturing processes.) Second, TruAuto has positioned its resources with respect to Year 2000 so as to be able to respond promptly to any requests that may be forthcoming from the government.

It is widely reported that government agencies (city, county, state, and federal) have done little to prepare their information systems to deal with the year 2000. Industry sources expect that sometime in mid- to late 1999, this lack of preparation will result in a number of demands by government agencies for changes in the way data is to be exchanged with others. If the government agencies do experience problems with attaining readiness as predicted, TruAuto will be affected. Depending on the requirements imposed, the needs of government agencies may use up a considerable number of TruAuto's resources.

TruAuto has anticipated possible future requirements from government agencies and has planned its own Year 2000 compliance to be largely complete by August 1999. This plan, if successfully implemented (much is already complete), will assure TruAuto's readiness well before the earliest date when government demands are expected to arrive. Not only will resources be available, but TruAuto's systems will already be Year 2000–compliant and thus not open to the difficulties posed by concurrent development, that is, being repaired to serve the two different purposes of meeting Year 2000 requirements and satisfying the requirements of government agencies.

Area Overview

TruAuto is in regular communication with local, county, state, and federal government agencies in Washington, California, and Texas. Communications with U.S. Customs are handled by TruAuto's customs broker. Interaction with government agencies occurs via fax and modem to report business and operations taxes, payroll tax, compliance with regulations governing manufacturing, land use and zoning, usage and disposal of hazardous substances, and importation of raw materials for manufacturing.

TruAuto does not depend directly on government agencies for service (with the exception of U.S. Customs) although it does exchange data with many government agencies in Washington, California, and Texas.

Vulnerability Assessment

The vice president of finance has taken the lead in gathering information about government agencies and has corresponded with each agency with whom TruAuto has a history of exchanging data.

Responses have been received from most government agencies. The State of Washington responded with a great deal of candor describing its investigative efforts, budgets allocated, and anticipated completion dates. Its plan, although it shows late completion (beyond January 1, 2000) for some items, does not indicate any effects that might be felt by TruAuto. No major problems are being raised by government agencies at this time. However, responses from most government agencies have been vague about the scope of the issues being addressed, the budget allocated, the quantity of resources being deployed, and anticipated completion dates. All Year 2000 effects from government agencies are expected to manifest themselves as change requests to modify data transactions in TruAuto business systems.

The vice president of finance and the vice president of operations have met with the chief of the U.S. Customs branch overseeing customs operations in the Port of Seattle and the Port of Tacoma to assure continuous flow of materials to TruAuto's manufacturing operation. These are the ports of entry for goods destined from overseas to TruAuto. The branch chief offered verbal assurances that no obstacles were foreseen in the processing of goods through customs.

Business may be affected by the fact that customs officers are dispatched directly to bonding warehouses on the basis of requests received by telephone and fax from the customs brokers. Work is underway to add Internet dispatching by the end of the second quarter of 2001.

Current assessment by the vice president of finance confirms that little is known about the Year 2000 preparations being made by government at any level. Little more can be predicted regarding possible impact to TruAuto's business systems from government agencies. Beyond letter writing, not much can be done to spur government agencies or gather more definitive information.

Year 2000 Vendors

The following list of vendors contains only established firms with proven product and service offerings. Their appearance on the list is in response to an invitation by the authors. The authors make no expressed or implied warranties for these companies or their products.

Company: 2000 Assembler Conversions

Address: 11300 N. Central Expressway, Suite 404
Dallas, TX 75214

Phone: 214-363-7600

E-mail: info@systemssourceinc.com

Languages: MVS, VSE, Assembler

Description: 2000 Assembler Conversions provides the Assembler Conversion Engine, ACE, a PC-based tool for accurate, predictable, and fast Year 2000 remediation of Assembler language code. ACE is offered as a comprehensive code conversion factory service or tool. ACE is automated and it analyzes, finds, and remediates date-related fields in an application. The unique level of automation achieved begins at the customer site, where the Assembler Collection Tool, ACT, is used to automate the collection and inventory process ensuring all copybooks and macros required to assemble and run the programs are obtained and accounted for. ACE and ACT as a solution are unmatched in the industry.

Company:	21st Century COBOL Conversions, Inc.
Address:	2035 Winding Oaks Drive Palm Harbor, FL 34683
Phone:	813-781-0035
Web site:	www.custom-software.com
E-mail:	sales@custom-software.com
Description:	21st Century COBOL Conversions specializes in COBOL legacy systems conversion projects, offering a spectrum of services from impact and methods analysis to source code and data conversions, and testing and implementation. All contracted work from mainframes to mini networks is done in its continental U.S. factory. It also offers YEAR2000.EXE, an automated COBOL conversion tool. It operates on a Win 95/NT platform to convert COBOL source code including mainframe, HP3000, and DIGITAL under MVS, UNIX, and VMS. This company's current Year 2000 clients span major companies (Sigma-Aldrich and Dyno-Nobel Corporation), government agencies (State of Illinois and Los Angeles County), and utility companies (Louisville Water Company).

Company:	Alydaar Software Corporation
Address:	2101 Rexford Road Suite 250 W. Charlotte, NC 28211
Exchange:	NASDAQ: ALYD
Phone:	704-365-2324
Web site:	www.alydaar.com
Platforms:	MVS, UNISYS, DEC VAX, Wang, HP, and others
Languages:	MVS COBOL and other dialects of COBOL, PL/1, RPG, Natural, FOCUS, TELON, EZTRIEVE, FORTRAN, and Assembler
Description:	Alydaar offers computer language translation and migration services, including Year 2000 analysis, remediation, and audit (verification/validation of fixed code). It specializes in reducing your risk, time, and cost.

Company:	Analysts International Corporation
Address:	7615 Metro Boulevard Minneapolis, MN 55439

Phone:	800-800-8699
Exchange:	NASDAQ: ANLY
Web site:	www.analysts.com/y2k
E-mail:	year2000@analysts.com
Description:	Analysts International Corporation (AiC) is a premier information technology consulting firm with more than 4,500 consultants and over 40 branch and field offices in the United States, Canada, and United Kingdom. AiC Year 2000 consulting competencies include analysis, project management, conversion, and testing. Due to the broad range of client needs, its approach focuses on helping clients make informed decisions concerning their Year 2000 strategy and tools. AiC customizes its methodology to conform to the client's business environment.
Company:	AnswerThink Consulting Group
Address:	One Van de Graaff Drive, Suite 203 Burlington, MA 01803
Phone:	781-229-0850 ext. 4000
Exchange:	NASDAQ: ANSR
Web site:	www.answerthink.com
E-mail:	kcopins@answerthink.com
Description:	The types of service AnswerThink provides include the following:

- Program office.
- Assessment and planning.
- Infrastructure preparation.
- Conversion.
- Testing and compliance verification.
- C.era, an industrywide collaboration of vendor companies aimed at solving the Year 2000 and other enterprise challenges.
- Desktop management.
- Application warehouse.
- DART (discovery, analysis, reporting, and transformation). Based on a clearly defined measurement process, AnswerThink's DART program was designed to provide clients

rapid, accurate assessments to help ensure their Year 2000 projects are completed in time and on target.

- Testing strategy.
- Program management office.
- Enterprise warehouse.
- Embedded systems.

AnswerThink Consulting Group is a knowledge-based consulting and technology implementation company focused on improving business results through technology-enabled transformation solutions. AnswerThink addresses its clients' strategic business needs by providing a wide range of integrated services or solutions, including benchmarking, process transformation, software package implementation, electronic commerce, decision support technology, technology architecture and integration, and Year 2000 solutions.

Company: Apex Information Systems, Inc.

Address: 2200 E. Birchwood Avenue
Milwaukee, WI 53110

Phone: 888-400-YR2K (9725)

Web site: www.apex-isg.com

E-mail: info@apex-sig.com

Description: Apex Information Systems provides businesses with information technology solutions. The talented staff of experts works with you and your organization to provide a wide range of consulting services (training, awareness presentations, project management, audits, testing, compliance certification, and more) pertaining to year 2000. In addition, the company offers consulting services for small business specializing in PC, network, and midrange environments (OS/400, UNIX, SSP, Windows 3.X/95/NT, Novell) and Access, Assembler, Autocad, Basic, C, C++, Clist, COBOL, Dialog MGR DTU DYL250, FORTRAN ISPF, Pascal, RPG, SAS, SQL, and Visual Age for Java languages.

Company: Ascent Logic Corporation

Address: 180 Rose Orchard Way, Suite 200
San Jose, CA 95134

Phone: 408-943-0705

Web site: www.alc.com

E-mail:	Marketing@alc.com
Platforms:	Windows 95, Windows NT
Description:	Ascent Logic Corporation provides Y2K risk assessment/management software and consulting services. Ascent Logic Corporation is the world leader in systems engineering, an automated approach to risk management. Today, Ascent Logic offers a risk management solution specifically for Year 2000 conversion planning. Integral to the process is Ascent Logicis Year 2000Plus software suite. Year 2000Plus serves as a powerful tool for forging a management plan for reducing risk. This same technology is used to perform risk audits for qualification for 2000Secure insurance from J & H Marsh McLennan.

Company:	BindView Development Corporation
Address:	3355 West Alabama, Suite 1200 Houston, TX 77098
Phone:	800-749-8439 or 713-881-9100
Web site:	www.bindview.com
E-mail:	info@bindview.com
Description:	NETinventory significantly reduces the time it takes organizations to assess their Year 2000 exposures on the PC LAN. NETinventory goes beyond other PC testing tools by performing 16 automated tests on the BIOS and CMOS/RTC to check for Year 2000 bugs. NETinventory runs from the network, performs hardware and software inventory and Year 2000 assessment and tracking. It includes a database with software manufacturers' statements on compliance of their packages and provides a mail merge utility for faster generation of compliance letters. NETinventory recently received the Best of LAN TIMES award for its Year 2000 capabilities.

Company:	BlackHawk Information Services, Inc.
Address:	2420 Camino Ramon, Suite 212 San Ramon, CA 94583
Phone:	925-244-6701
Web site:	www.blackhawkis.com
E-mail:	info@blackhawkis.com
Description:	BlackHawk Information Services offers full-service IT consulting services ranging from Y2K to placement. It specializes in addressing Year 2000 issues for companies of all sizes. Its struc-

tured methodology, BlackHawk 2000, applies automated tools to solve the problem for both business and technology issues. Rapid Development Methodology, based on BlackHawk 2000 and the company's substantial experience across a broad range of companies and technical platforms (Tandem, IBM mainframe, client/server, and PC/network environments), can help companies expedite Y2K compliancy. BlackHawk is a Tandem Alliance Partner.

Company:	Blair and Associates, Inc.
Address:	7257 Parkway Drive, Suite 211 Hanover, MD 21076
Phone:	410-712-7205
Web site:	www.year2000-tools.com
E-mail:	bai@baiengineering.com
Description:	Blair and Associates offers two categories of service:

1. It licenses the use of the BAI Slicer for the remediation of C source code on Windows NT and UNIX systems.

2. It offers solutions for Year 2000 problems in the areas of assessment, remediation, and testing on various platforms with many different languages.

BAI's talents include assessment, in-house code renovation, consulting, and tool development. The BAI Slicer, for C source code analysis, modification, and testing, is probably the best tool for the money. It is superior for Y2K remediation work, and it attests to the capabilities of BAI's staff.

Company:	Branco International, Inc.
Address:	91 Main Street Kings Park, NY 11754
Phone:	800-528-7445
Web site:	www.millennium.nl
E-mail:	branco2000@hotmail.com
Description:	Branco is the exclusive distributor of the Official CountDown Watch and Wall Clock. There's no better way to keep Y2K top of mind than with Branco's countdown timepieces, the only products on the market that show regular time while simultaneously displaying a digital read-out of the hours, minutes, and seconds left to the year 2000. They can also be used to count down to any other important date like a product launch,

new software release, sales competition deadline, or any target date that has special meaning to your company.

CountDown timepieces can be easily and inexpensively customized to keep your company name, slogan, or timeless message in the forefront. They'll capture the constant attention of people who use them and not be stashed away collecting dust on some file cabinet. The international award-winning design and attractive packaging make Branco's timepieces ideal for special-event marketing, recognition awards, and motivational incentives.

Company:	Bridgeway Systems, LLC
Address:	4040 Civic Center Drive, Suite 200 San Rafael, CA 94903
Phone:	415-492-1484
Web site:	www.bridgeway2k.com
E-mail:	info@bridgeway2k.com
Languages:	Independent Language Support: Assembler, C, CMS2, COBOL, FORTRAN, Natural, PL/1, ADA, Jovial, RPG
Description:	Bridgeway Systems is a leading provider of second-generation automated Y2K solutions. Bridgeway provides comprehensive knowledge-based program transformation technologies, products, and services that automate the Y2K impact analysis and remediation process as well as independent Y2K verification and validation. Bridgeway's Program Factory approach assures a rapid, accurate, and cost-effective solution to the Y2K problem. Automated impact analysis and remediation services can be provided off-site at one of Bridgeway's program factories or on-site at the location of the customer.

Company:	CACI International Inc.
Address:	1100 North Glebe Road Arlington, VA 22201
Phone:	703-841-3720
Exchange:	NASDAQ: CACI
Web site:	www.caci.com
E-mail:	npeters@caci.com
Platform:	Independent, OS-independent
Language:	Independent

Description: CACI's ITAA-certified Restore 2000 methodology, based on its award-winning reengineering approach, is the centerpiece of a solutions set that includes testing and independent verification and validation; risk management and contingency planning; templates and lessons learned databases; program management, training, and personnel support; value-added preparation for future reengineering; and partnerships with leading tools and services vendors. Celebrating its 35th year in business, CACI specializes in developing systems, software, and simulation products and services for government and commercial clients worldwide.

Company: CADAS Software

Address: 12707 High Bluff Drive
San Diego, CA 92130
United States of America
52 London Road,
Twickenham Middlesex,
TW1 3RP United Kingdom

Phone: 619-350-4358 (United States)
or +44-(0181)-831-6800 (United Kingdom)

Web site: www.cadas.com

E-mail: general@cadas.com

Platforms: Mainframe, AS/400, Wintel MVS, VSE, OS/400, Microsoft Windows (3.X, 9X, NT); CADAS provides a number of Year 2000–based tools and services, including CADAS Data Ager.

Description: In an easy to use package, CADAS provides the most complete range of business and calendar rules for future date testing combined with database independence. Its desktop services use Check2000, from GMT, as the basis of a full Year 2000 desktop solution. CADAS provides a full service package to resolve the issue in larger organizations. Its remediation services include, in partnership with ConSyGen, fully automated remediation of COBOL and PL/1, on any platform at a fraction of the price charged by other vendors.

Company: Cap Gemini America LLC

Address: 1114 Avenue of the Americas, 29th Floor
New York, NY 10036

Phone: 800-Y2K-TODAY

Web site: www.usa.capgemini.com/y2k

E-mail:	sbroderi@usa.capgemini.com
Platforms:	Cap Gemini America's TransMillennium TM Services' ARC-driveSM toolset supports a mainframe platform.
Languages:	In addition to being able to scan almost any language, Cap Gemini America's ARCdrive is an automated toolset that is able to renovate COBOL, PL/1, TELON, IDMS, Easytrieve, FOCUS, and Natural. The toolset supports languages running on an IBM MVS operating system.
Services:	Cap Gemini America's formal methodology and smart technology help it to be flexible to its clients' needs. It offers a wide range of services including assess/strategy, renovate/validate/implement, renovate only, 20XX testing services, QUICKcheckTM (smart data aging for 20XX testing and smart code walk-through), end-user license, and PMO.
Description:	TransMillennium Services, Cap Gemini America's Year 2000 group, uses a highly automated and factory-based approach to the date change issue. Cap Gemini America's artificial intelligence–based ARCdrive has already helped more than 300 businesses worldwide address Year 2000 issues on over three billion lines of code.
Company:	Century Services Inc.
Address:	20251 Century Boulevard Germantown, MD 20874
Phone:	301-353-9500
Exchange:	NASDAQ: ZMAX
Web site:	www.zmax.com
E-mail:	busdevelop@csi.zmax.com
Platforms:	All mainframes and midrange (IBM390, AS400, Unysis, HP, etc); all operating systems except client/server
Languages:	All versions of COBOL, PL/1, RPG, IDEAL, and so forth.
Description:	Century Services provides Y2K remediation, testing, and consulting services at its factory or on-site. It uses a proprietary toolset and will license the tool. Century Services is a software reengineering company focusing on all aspects of Y2K compliance. Its extensive consulting division is also available.
Company:	Century Technology Services, Inc.
Address:	1313 Dolley Madison Boulevard, Suite 203 McLean, VA 22101

Phone:	703-749-7840
Web site:	www.ctsi2000.com
E-mail:	ctis2000@aol.com
Description:	CTSI provides full Year 2000 analysis and conversion services. Target2K is a sophisticated data analyzer that scans samples of data records to identify mathematical patterns that match known date formats. Target2K can increase the effectiveness and accuracy of any code-scanning tool. T-Scan2K is a robust, text-based scanner that runs on mainframes, midrange systems, and PCs to identify dates in any text-based language. Low Impact Expansion is a proprietary process that remediates code with a permanently expanded 8-digit date in a minimally invasive, nondisruptive way. CTSI also provides solutions for embedded systems problems through its Century Processor Remediation (CPR) system.

Company:	Cipher Systems Ltd.
Address:	Suite 110, 259 Midpark Way S.E. Calgary, Alberta, Canada T2X 1M2
Phone:	403-256-8877
Web site:	www.ciphersys.com
E-mail:	info@ciphersys.com
Platforms:	Mainframes, midframes, client/server, PCs
Languages:	COBOL, Assembler, C, C++, Natural, PL/1, and other legacy codes
Services:	Complete Year 2000 services, including project management, inventory assessments, conversions, audits, testing and implementation, and embedded systems.
Description:	Cipher's RENAISSANCE2000 SOLUTIONS has been providing exceptional Year 2000 expertise to clients for over four years. Cipher's resources are available to assist with any or all aspects of your Year 2000 project.

Company:	Class Solutions LTD
Address:	Frerichs House, 14 Frerichs Close Wickford Essex SS12 9QD United Kingdom
Phone:	+44 (0) 1702 480675
Web Site:	www.class-solutions.com
Email:	info@class-solutions.com

Languages: Microsoft Visual Basic 3.0, 4.0, and 5.0 Microsoft VBA in MS Excel and Access, Windows 3.1, 3.11, 95, NT, Visual Basic source code

Services: Impact analysis, remediation, and coverage testing.

Description: Adopting Class Solutions' pseudoautomated methodology accelerates the conversion process and eliminates the risk of human error.

Company: Cognizant Technology Solutions Corporation

Address: 1700 Broadway
New York, NY 10019

Phone: 888-937-3277

Exchange: NASDAQ: CTSH

Web site: www.cts-corp.com

E-mail: Bschule@cognizantcorp.com

Platforms: Mainframe, client/server, operating systems: All

Languages: Languages supported: All

Description: CTS provides end-to-end Year 2000 services using a proven on-site/offshore methodology, with high-quality, cost-effective results. CTS provides software development, maintenance, and reengineering services for the Fortune 500, including Year 2000 and Euro compliance. CTS's expertise extends across a range of technologies encompassing client/server, Internet solutions, data warehousing, object-oriented development, and legacy applications.

Company: COMMTEC Systems 2025, Inc.

Address: P.O. Box 3712
Scottsdale, AZ 85271-3712

Phone: 602-994-1875

Web site: www.doitnow.com/~commtec;

E-mail: commtec@doitnow.com

Platforms: QIPP supports all platforms and O/S

Languages: QIPP supports all languages

Description: QIPP is the next generation of Y2K toolsets. It is a fully integrated system for analyzing and remediating any system for Y2K compliance. QIPP can keep applications running that have no source code, and it doesn't have the 99-year limitation of older windowing tools. It can generally be installed in 15 percent of the time with less then 10 percent of the labor required to do a 4-digit conversion. It will run on any mix of platforms, application languages, and operating systems simultaneously. It also handles multiple sites with mixed platforms. QIPP is so unique that it was just granted a patent, with 16 claims, by the U.S. Patent Office.

Company: Compuhope

Address: 3528 Torrance Boulevard, Suite 209
Torrance, CA 90503

Phone: 800-437-8321

Web site: www.compuhope.com

E-mail: team2000@compuhope.com

Description: Team 2000 is Compuhope's team of qualified trained professionals which include project managers, analysts, programmers, engineers, developers, and testers. Compuhope has the resources to recruit professionals who will meet the demands of the Y2K issues specific to your company's platform, languages, and applications. Compuhope has a proven track record in providing Y2K services and solutions.

Company: Computer Associates International, Inc.

Address: One Computer Associates Plaza
Islandia, NY 11788

Exchange: NYSE: CA

Phone: 888-4-2000YR

Web site: www.cai.com

E-mail: challenge@cai.com or info@cai.com

Platforms: Mainframe, desktop workstations

Languages: COBOL, CA-ADS, CA-Easytrieve, CA-Ideal

Descriptions: Computer Associates Discovery 2000 solution helps clients address the unique technical and business challenges created by the Year 2000 problem. It is a complete, end-to-end solution including powerful tools and services for addressing Year 2000 inventory, project management, assessment, remediation, testing, and implementation issues.

Company: Computer Horizons Corporation

Address: 49 Old Bloomfield Avenue
Mountain Lakes, NJ 07945

Phone:	973-299-4000
Exchange:	NASDAQ: CHRZ
Web site:	www.computerhorizons.com
E-mail:	information@computerhorizons.com
Description:	Computer Horizons provides its global customers with systems integration, network services, staff augmentation, education, software products, and its industry-leading Year 2000 and European Monetary Union solutions for mainframe, midrange, and desktops, including assessment, remediation, and testing. Computer Horizons, founded in 1969, is a diversified information technology services company with 4,000 employees and 50 offices throughout the United States, Canada, and United Kingdom.
Company:	Computer Reserves, Inc.
Address:	150 River Road, Suite H-4 Montville, NJ 07045
Phone:	800-882-0988 or 973-263-9800
Web site:	www.cridon.com
E-mail:	y2k@cridon.com
Platforms:	Mainframe, AS/400, client server
Languages:	COBOL, PL/1, Assembler, RPG, MVS, DOS/VSE, OS400, UNIX, Windows
Services:	Year 2000 assessments, conversions, testing, and critical partner compliance audits. Computer Reserves has provided IT solutions since 1968.
Description:	Its consulting services include Year 2000 compliance and testing, Year 2000 critical partner compliance audits, mainframe software audits, mainframe outsourcing, and application development and maintenance.
Company:	Computer Software Corporation
Address:	24864 Detroit Road Cleveland, OH 44145
Phone:	800-908-2000
Web site:	www.dateserver.com
E-mail:	CSC@dateserver.com
Description:	Computer Software Corporation's DateServerTM 2000 software is currently called millions of times each day. It has been

solving the Year 2000 date-processing problems for COBOL and Assembler application systems since January 1994. It is the most efficient and comprehensive set of mainframe date sub-routines available, processing most date formats with either two-digit or four-digit years and providing the date compari-son and the date calculation routines needed by legacy appli-cation programs to make them Year 2000–compliant using either a procedural or a date expansion approach. MVS/VSE versions are available.

Company:	Countdown Clocks International Inc.
Address:	734 Franklin Avenue, Suite 343 Garden City, NY 11530
Phone:	516-739-7800
Web site:	www.countdownclock.com
E-mail:	budd2.ix.net.com
Description:	The Millennium/Y2K Countdown Clock is an LCD clock with continuous display of days, hours, minutes, and seconds to the big day. It has a unique design for desktop and includes won-derful graphics. A wonderful tool for motivation and aware-ness.

Company:	Data Dimensions, Inc.
Address:	411 108th Avenue NE, Suite 2100 Bellevue, WA 98004
Phone:	425-688-1000
Exchange:	NASDAQ: DDIM
Web site:	www.data-dimensions.com
E-mail:	marketing-mail@data-dimensions.com
Description:	Data Dimensions works on all vendor-supported hardware platforms and operating systems and addresses all software languages. Data Dimensions specializes in developing solu-tions and services to help organizations manage enter-prisewide systems changes. Since 1991, it has helped over 200 companies plan and implement programs for resolving Year 2000 problems. It has been in the Year 2000 industry longer than any other company and has more than 20 licensees and resellers operating in more than 50 countries around the world. Hundreds of companies, including 50 of the Fortune 500 com-panies, have chosen Data Dimensions as their Year 2000 solu-

tion provider. Besides information technology and business-consulting services, it offers Y2K products and other services: Ardes 2k, Provisia, Interactive Vendor ReviewSM, Training Solutions 2000+, and Year 2000 testing facilities.

Company:	DATE/2000
Address:	P.O. BOX 600084 San Diego, CA 92160-0084
Phone:	619-282-6792 or 877-RPG-3636 (toll-free from the United States, Canada, Caribbean)
Web site:	http://members.aol.com/date2000/web
E-mail:	date2000@aol.com
Platforms:	IBM midrange AS/400, System/36, RS/6000, RPG, SSP environment
Description:	DATE/2000 is a Y2K tool for RPG legacy software. The SCANNER identifies date occurrences in RPG programs, OCL, sorts, and Data. It provides include and exclude capabilities. The ESTIMATOR provides statistics including total statements scanned and total statements with date occurrences. The PROJECT/CHANGE management tool interface creates flat files.

Company:	DCI
Address:	204 Andover Street Andover, MA 01810
Phone:	978-470-3880
Web site:	www.dci.com/2000ad/
Platforms:	Conferences, seminars, and expositions
Description:	DCI offers the most focused educational events to help your organization prepare for the Year 2000 date change. Acquire the knowledge and solutions you can implement immediately from experienced consultants, industry experts, keynote presenters, and solution providers.

Company:	DSQ Software Corporation
Address:	4300 Stevens Creek Boulevard, Suite 222 San Jose, CA 95129
Phone:	408-249-1497 or 732-767-0007
Web site:	www.dsqsoftware.com
E-mail:	dsq-skb@worldnet.att.net

Platforms: Mainframe, AS/400, HP, DEC, SUN, IBM RS/6000, Unisys, PCs

Languages: COBOL, PL/1, C, C++, Assembler, FORTRAN, Synon, Obsydian, RPG, COBOL, DB2, CL, C, Query, SQL, SSET, CATIA, Sybase, Oracle, Ingres, SAP, BAAN MFGPRO, MAPICS, PRISM, PROTEON, ORACLE APPS, CATIA, PRO/E, CADDS5 AUTOCAD, CABLECAD, IMAP OS: MVS, OS/400, UNIX, WinNT, Win95, Novell Netware, OS/2 offshore software development, remote maintenance, on-site contract services, Year 2000 date correction, software development/maintenance/migration/conversion/reengineering, CAD/CAM/CAE modeling and design, CAD/GIS conversion, telecom and networking solutions, Internet-based solutions

Description: DSQ Software is a software solutions company with an international presence. With an employee strength of over 1,300 engineers, 5,500 cumulative years of software development experience, and CMM level 4 certification from KPMG Quality Registrar, DSQ strives to exceed client expectations.

Company: Effective Management Systems

Address: 12000 West Park Place
Milwaukee, WI 53224

Phone: 414-359-9800

Exchange: NASDAQ: EMSI

Web site: www.ems.com

E-mail: marketing@ems.com

Description: ERP and MES EMS is an application software implementation specialist that helps discrete manufacturing improve the speed and predictability of product delivery while reducing costs.

Company: Execom (US) Pty Ltd

Address: 104 Riverbend Boulevard
Longwood, FL 32779

Web site: www.execom.com.au

E-mail: davidp@execom.com.au

Phone: 407-774-3211

Languages: IBM MVS (and compatibles), Cobol 74/Cobol 85/Cobol II, CICS/IMS DC, DB2/DL1, ICL VME Cobol, Micro Focus Cobol, Natural, MVS, VM, VSE, VME

Description: Execom's FixIT 2000 remediation centers provide automated Year 2000 code correction services for COBOL and Natural languages. Execom is a leading international information technology conversion and reengineering solutions provider, involved extensively in providing Year 2000 automated remediation services.

Company: Fidelity Technology Solutions

Address: 82 Devonshire Street A9A
Boston, MA 02109

Web site: http://tracer2000.fidelity.com/

E-mail: tracer2000@fmr.com

Platforms: Supports all platforms, all operating systems

Languages: Supports all languages

Descriptions: TRACER 2000 is a source code analysis and remediation support tool that can be used on all software from mainframe to client/server to desktop. TRACER 2000 was developed as an internal tool for Fidelity's Year 2000 conversion team and has proven itself on hundreds of conversion projects.

Company: Forecross Corporation

Address: 90 New Montgomery Street
San Francisco, CA 94105

Exchange: VSE: FRX.U

Web site: www.forecross.com

Phone: 415-543-1515

Languages: COBOL (AS/400, DEC/VAX, HP, MVS, Tandem Unisys, VM VSE, and Wang), C, C++, CA-ADSO, APS, CLIST, CSP, CA-Easytrieve, CA-IDEAL, IMSADF II, MetaCOBOL, PL/1, Powerbuilder, REXX, and CA-Telon

Descriptions: As a leading authority on migration software, Forecross Corporation has more than 15 years experience in developing software solutions and technologies for companies worldwide. Based on proven, time-tested methodologies and technology, Forecross provides one of the most comprehensive solutions for legacy migrations and Year 2000 compliance on the market today. Its legacy migration and Year 2000 fully automated factories allow it to automate up to 100 percent of an application reducing the cost, time, and risk required compared to other solutions.

Company: Formal Systems America Inc.

Address: P.O. Box 1235
Cherry Hill, NJ 08034

Web site: www.fsamerica.com

E-mail: inquiry@fsamerica.com

Phone: 877-482-0400

Languages: Natural 2.x structured and report-mode

Services: Y2K automated impact analysis and remediation.

Descriptions: Over the past two years, NXL2000 has been used to complete automated Y2K processing on over 170 million of lines of Natural structured and report-mode source code. NXL2000 delivers outstanding value to Natural users by providing date field identification (all dates and problem dates), portfolio-wide analysis including local and global control and data flow, automated remediation of Y2K date defects in 2.x structured and report-mode Natural source code. NXL2000 services can be purchased separately or combined into a package to meet customer needs.

Company: Global Software, Inc.

Address: P.O. Box 2813
Duxbury, MA 02331-2813

Web site: www.Global-Software.com

E-mail: GILES@Global-Software.com

Phone: 781-934-0949

Platforms: Mainframe

Languages: JCL, CICS, Natural, COBOL, PL/1, Assembler, Mantis, IMS, DB2, ADABAS

Services: Easytrieve, Model 204, CSP, IE, Focus, SAS; Operating systems: OS/390 (MVS) Tools for Y2K detection, inventory, remediation, and impact analysis, quality assurance, and euro conversion.

Descriptions: Established in 1979, Global Software of Duxbury, Massachusetts, began working on OS/390 (MVS) Year 2000 solutions back in 1994, making it one of the more mature players in the field. Global draws upon the insight and experience gained from developing parsing technology over almost two decades, including the population of dictionary/repository tools such as IBM's DB/DC Dictionary.

Company: Greenwich Mean Time

Address: 4301 N. Fairfax Drive, Suite 400
Arlington, VA 22203

Web site:	www.gmt-2000.com
E-mail:	ussales@gmt-2000.com
Phone:	703-908-6600
Deployment Platforms:	Novell NetWare 3.11, 3.2, 4.11, 5, Microsoft Windows NT Server 3.51 and 4, Microsoft Windows Networking, OS/2 Warp Server, Banyan Vines, and others
Client Platforms Tested:	DOS, Microsoft Windows 3.11, Microsoft Windows for Workgroups, Microsoft Windows 95, Microsoft Windows 98, Microsoft Windows NT 3.51 and 4
BIOS Fix Available for:	DOS, Microsoft Windows 3.11, Microsoft Windows for Workgroups, Microsoft Windows 95, OS/2
Languages:	English International, November 1998: German, Italian, French, January 1999: Japanese, Portuguese
Service:	Greenwich Mean Time provides Year 2000 PC software. "My one stop shop for a single walk up solution," says Cliff Evans, Y2K Project Manager, Qantas.
Company:	Group West Systems Ltd.
Address:	Suite 200, 6400 Roberts Street Burnaby, BC V5G 4C9
Exchange:	VSE: GPW.V
Web site:	www3.stockgroup.com/gpw/
E-mail:	ddeath@groupwest.ca
Phone:	604-473-2118
Languages:	RPG, CL, OCL, COBOL(II), COBOL (for MVS), VSE, OS/VS COBOL PL/1, Assembler, TELON, CSP, Natural, C++, VB, OS/390 OS/400, VSE, MVS, VM, PC (various)
Description:	Group West is a Year 2000 conversion services provider with a fully tooled and staffed conversion factory. It uses a combination of state-of-the-art tools, multiple mainframe and PC platforms, experienced personnel, and dedicated testing platforms. The factory has technical capacity to support the analysis/testing in excess of 300 million lines of code per year. Group West also offers other services which include migration planning, software conversion, and review.
Company:	Hendela System Consultants, Inc.
Address:	P.O. Box 766 Lyndhurst, NJ 07071-0766

Web site:	www.scany2k.com
E-mail:	info@scany2k.com
Phone:	201-460-1253 or 888-SCANY2K
Platforms:	IBM PCs and compatibles
Languages:	Foxpro, Clipper, Dbase, and other text-based languages such as M204, NOMAD, C/C++, COBOL, RPG, FORTRAN, Pascal, BASIC, REXX, JCL Windows 3.1x, 95, NT
Description:	SCANALYZER Y2K Solution Software sizes, finds, and helps fix problems in xBase and other languages. It comes with 1,200+ date text strings to get you started fast. PowerOrder browser allows fast remediation of similar lines of code across all applications and files. Results stored in standard DBF format for easy reporting. Hendela System Consultants has been serving the software needs of Fortune 500 companies and government agencies since 1988.

Company:	Infinium Software
Address:	25 Communications Way Hyannis, MA 02601
Exchange:	NASDAQ: INFM
Phone:	508-778-2000
Web site:	www.infinium.com
E-mail:	webteam@infinium.com
Platforms:	IBM AS/400 and Microsoft Windows NT platforms
Description:	Since 1981, Infinium Software has provided Year 2000–enabled business applications for midsized organizations. Infinium offers a full range of client/server financial, human resources, materials management, and process manufacturing business applications that can be rapidly implemented for the twenty-first century. All Infinium products are certified by the ITAA as Year 2000–enabled. Infinium has over 1,400 customers worldwide such as 3M, Coca-Cola, Benjamin Moore, and Harley-Davidson. Infinium Software was recognized by *Business Week* as one of the Top 100 Growth Companies of 1997.

Company:	INFORMISSION GROUP INC.
Address:	1260 Lebourgneuf Boulevard, Suite 250 Quebec, P. Quebec G2K 2G2
Exchange:	MSE: IFN

Phone:	418-627-2001
Web site:	www.informission.ca
E-mail:	quebec@informission.ca
Platforms:	IBM, BULL, DIGITAL
Languages:	COBOL, PL/1, CA-IDEAL, CA-ADS-O, MVS, VMS, VSE
Services:	Informission provides the economical, fast, and proven conversion solution for extending the life of your computer systems well beyond the year 2000.
Description:	Informission Group is a public information technology company providing innovative and cost-effective solutions for the conversion, development, and migration of information systems.

Company:	International Software Finance Corporation
Address:	45 Danbury Road Wilton, CT 06897
Phone:	203-762-1666
Web site:	www.isfnet.com
E-mail:	isf@isfnet.com
Description:	Software Finance ISF is a leading provider of financial solutions for software acquisitions. Its Y2K offering, Financing 2000, empowers corporations to fix the Y2K bug without exhausting budgets by spreading the costs of software and services out over time. Financing 2000 is a single-source financial solution for all Y2K-related costs, including software, consulting, training, and implementation.

Company:	INTO 2000, Inc.
Address:	453 Big Canoe Jasper, GA 30142
Phone:	888-TRY-IN2K
Web site:	www.INTO2000.com
E-mail:	info@INTO2000.com
Platforms:	IBM AS/400 only; Operating systems: OS/400
Languages:	RPG II, III, COBOL/400, CL
Services:	The INTO 2000 products are the only complete Y2K toolset for the AS/400 environment; it includes inventory, methodology, analysis tools, and seven conversion techniques.

Description: INTO 2000 distributes INTO2000 in the Americas. To date, over 1 billion lines of RPG have been processed at nearly 1,000 AS/400 sites.

Company: Keane, Inc.

Address: Ten City Square
Boston, MA 02129

Exchange: AMEX: KEA

Phone: 617-241-9200

Web site: www.keane.com

Description: Keane, a $1 billion software services company, helps clients plan, build, and manage high-performance IT organizations. Having helped more than 350 clients address Y2K, Keane was named one of the top three Y2K service providers by Gartner Group. On each of these initiatives, Keane has deployed its Resolve 2000 solution, which leverages rigorous migration and project management methodologies together with best-in-class analysis and migration tools. Keane's Resolve 2000 services address the full life cycle, from planning and analysis to migration and testing.

Company: Legacy Solutions Corporation

Address: 12025 Gibbons Lane
Setenino, WA 98589

Phone: 888-676-5673

Web site: www.legacy-sol.com

E-mail: sales@legacy-sol.com

Company: LGS Group Inc.

Address: 4110 Yonge Street, Suite 606
North York, Ontario
Canada M2P 2B7

Phone: 416-222-3003

Web site: www.lgs.ca

E-mail: Bill_Steele@lgs.ca

Services: Legacy's RTtool software automates large-scale batch regression testing in the MVS OS 390 environment, allowing individuals with no prior application knowledge to fully test a large-scale batch process, while at the same time establishing a new best practice within their organization's QA area.

Description: LGS is a full-service provider for all aspects of Year 2000 renovation in mainframe and client/server environments. Established in 1995, LGS's Year 2000 practice offers risk assessments, project management, awareness seminars, analysis and planning, third-party S/W product planning, conversion services, infrastructure upgrading, testing, and implementation. As a corporation with a national focus, LGS has developed experienced Year 2000 teams in Toronto, Montreal, Quebec City, Ottawa, Winnipeg, Regina, Calgary, Edmonton, Vancouver, and Victoria.

Company: McCabe & Associates Inc.

Address: 5501 Twin Knolls Road Suite 111
Columbia, MD 21045

Phone: 800-638-6316

Web site: www.mccabe.com

E-mail: info@mccabe.com

Platforms: PC, UNIX (source code platform: any); Operating systems supported: Windows 95/NT

Languages: Cobol, C, C++, FORTRAN, Ada, Visual Basic, Solaris 2.5+

Services: McCabe Visual 2000 assists in Year 2000 testing by visually highlighting the problem areas, providing a comprehensive and objective test plan, and monitoring the testing progress. The tool eliminates unnecessary testing and focuses testing efforts where they will be the most effective, resulting in a more thorough test effort and a significant reduction in testing time and cost.

Description: McCabe & Associates is a leading provider of software products and related services for the analysis, reengineering, and testing of software systems. Over the company's 20-year history, McCabe & Associates' solutions have been used by Fortune 1000 and other major international companies and government organizations to test, reengineer, and verify the quality of mission-critical code.

Company: Mercury Interactive

Address: 1325 Borregas Avenue
Sunnyvale, CA 94089

Exchange: NASDAQ: MERQ

Web site: www.merc-int.com/

E-mail: info@merc-int.com

Platforms: Mainframe, AS/400, client/server, UNIX, Operating Systems: (for tools) Windows NT, 95, and 3.1X

Languages: Language-independent

Service: Mercury Interactive's Year 2000 integrated products help IS organizations gain confidence in solving the Year 2000 problem by offering a complete set of software tools for test management, automated regression testing, test data generation, and load/performance testing.

Description: Mercury Interactive is the world's leading provider of automated client/server testing tools. The company offers a comprehensive line of automated enterprise testing tools that address the full range of quality needs for testing Y2K, client/server, e-business, and packaged applications. Its testing solutions enable corporations, system integrators, and independent software vendors to identify software errors more quickly and efficiently than traditional methods allow.

Company: Micro Focus

Address: 701 East Middlefield Road
Mountain View, CA 94043

Exchange: NASDAQ: MIFGY. London Stock Exchange: MICF

Phone: 650-938-3700

Web site: www.microfocus.com

Platforms: Operating systems: Windows NT, Windows 95

Languages: MVS COBOL, Unisys COBOL

Services: SoftFactory/2000 is an integrated family of products and services that takes users through each phase of their Year 2000 life cycle—from find to fix and test. SoftFactory/2000 enables users to bring their applications to compliance quickly, while saving time and work effort at each stage of the project.

Description: As a long-standing leader in the COBOL industry, with more than 20 years experience in providing the technology that helps companies maintain COBOL systems more effectively, Micro Focus has a true understanding of Year 2000 issues and challenges.

Company: MigraTEC, Inc.

Address: 12801 Stemmons Freeway, Suite 710
Dallas, TX 75234

Exchange:	OCT: MIGR
Phone:	972-969-0300
Web site:	www.migratec.com
E-mail:	gbrantley@migratec.com or info@migratec.com
Platforms:	Desktop and C/S: Windows 95/98/NT; OS/2; UNIX; DOS C
Languages:	C++; Visual Basic; FoxPro; Clipper; Delphi; PowerBuilder; Pascal; Access; dBase III, IV, V
Services:	MigraTEC 2000 is a tool for automating project inventory, Y2K analysis, and remediation. Y2K Impact Assessment. MigraTEC 2000 is best in class for true C, C++ parsing and data flow tracing. MigraTEC 2000 efficiently analyzes source, selects remediation method(s), and generates corrected source code.

Company:	Milan Data Services
Address:	P.O. Box 122069 Chula Vista, CA 91912
Phone:	(+52)-61-74-73-96
Web site:	www.milandata.com
E-mail:	milanes@telnor.net
Platforms:	ScanXL; Operating systems: Windows 95 and 3.1
Languages:	Fifteen versions of ScanXL accurately scan for dates in mainframe versions of Assembler, COBOL, Dyl-280, Easytrieve, Focus, FORTRAN, Mark IV, Model 204, Natural, PL/1, RPG, SAS, Telon, Generic Text, Visual Basic (PC).
Description:	First sold in 1993, ScanXL is easy to use and the search criteria is fully configurable. Free evaluation copies of ScanXL are available from Milan Data Services, which is a software-development company specializing in multilanguage date-scanning software and systemwide analysis services and software.

Company:	Millennia III
Address:	400 Nyala Farm Road Westport, CT 06880 Rousemount Avenue, West Byfleet Surrey KT14 6LB
Phone:	203-221-1121 (United States)
Phone:	+44 (0) 1932339100 (United Kingdom)

Web site:	www.millennia3.com
E-mail:	sales@millennia3.com
Description:	A global professional services company offering cross-platform and language-independent Y2K solutions. CONVERSION2000 provides risk assessment, inventory analysis, resource planning, conversion, testing, redeployment, and contingency planning. ALTER2000 automates IBM Assembler code conversion. TEST2000 includes testing readiness assessments, management, planning, and execution. AUDIT2000 provides an enterprise-level evaluation of Y2K risks, including value-chain assessments. INFORM2000 assesses, creates, and distributes critical Y2K information to targeted audiences for compliancy communications.

Company:	NeoMedia Technologies, Inc.
Address:	1025 Reed Hartman Highway Cincinnati, OH 45242
Phone:	513-984-1822
Web site:	www.neom.com/y2k
E-mail:	y2kinfo@neom.com
Platforms:	Mainframe, midrange, PCs, DOS, OS/390, VM, MVS, VSE, UNIX/AIX/HPUX. Operating systems: Solaris, OS/400, VAX/VMS, Windows NT, Windows, Unisys, NCR
Services:	NeoMedia provides tandem Year 2000 software and service products and consulting services. ADAPT/Enterprise, the company's Year 2000 and mass change tool suite, provides centralized Y2K data and source code analysis, tracking and risk management across the entire enterprise—PC to mainframe. The ADAPT/Enterprise suite consists of ADAPT/2000 and ADAPT/PC-2000.

Company:	New Art Technologies, Inc.
Address:	200 West 79 Street, Suite 8H New York, NY 10024
Phone:	800-276-1118
Web site:	www.newarttech.com
E-mail:	info@newarttech.com
Platform:	Operating systems: Windows 3.1, Windows 95, Windows NT
Languages:	Language-independent

Descriptions: NA-Series is a low-cost but powerful set of utilities which can be used to assess the impact of Year 2000 modification. Tools consist of NA2000 and NAIMPACT, which are impact analyzers with include, exclude, ignore, Boolean, and fuzzy matching capabilities. NATRACE is a propagation tracing tool for COBOL and C. NA-Excel for Spreadsheets is available, and NA-Word is for search, replace, and compare.

Company: Pinnacle Decision Systems, Inc.

Address: 100 Roscommon Drive, Suite 310
Middletown, CT 06457

Phone: 860-632-7766

Web site: www.pinndec.com

E-mail: y2k@pinndec.com

Platforms: FOCUS, Operating systems: MVS/TSO, VMS, VM/CMS, UNIX, PC

Description: Pinnacle Decision Systems offers an on-site assessment and Year 2000 white paper, conversion/consulting services, FOCUS on 2000 Training and PinnPoint+ Automation software. PinnPoint+ is the Year 2000 tool for Focus. It is the only complete tool that finds the obvious and the hidden date references and allows you to automate the change. Plus, it drills down to indicate where each reference exists across the application. See the Web site to request a CD demo or to download a Y2K countdown clock.

Company: PRINCE Software Inc.

Address: 3 Pearl Court
Allendale, NJ 07401

Phone: 800-934-2022

Web site: www.PRINCEsoftware.com

E-mail: PORTAL2000@PRINCEsoftware.com

Platform: IBM and compatible mainframe

Languages: COBOL, BAL, PL/1, and other languages varying by product MVS/XX Y2K; Products/services for COBOL application analysis (SURVEY 2000), renovation (TRANSLATE 2000), testing (SIMULATE 2000)

Descriptions: With over 1,000 customers, PRINCE Software has 25 years of proven experience in COBOL program translation and renovation.

Company:	Princeton Softech, Inc.
Address:	1060 State Road Princeton, NJ 08540
Phone:	609-497-0205 or 800-457-7060
Web site:	www.PrincetonSoftech.com
E-mail:	info@PrincetonSoftech.com
Platform:	MVS/Windows 95, 98, NT; the database server can be on any platform
Language:	Not language-dependent
Descriptions:	Princeton Softech provides software tools for IT professionals who develop and maintain critical business applications. Princeton Softech's tools for Year 2000 testing tackle some of the most time-consuming, difficult, and unique aspects of the Year 2000 effort: simulating Year 2000 conditions more accurately in tests by aging test data and managing the system date, creating truly realistic test databases that help you find the defects before you turn programs over to production, quickly pinpointing changes to test data so that you don't get bogged down evaluating test results, and managing multiple program versions so that Year 2000 changes can be merged into production without loss of functionality.
Company:	Progestic International Inc.
Address:	Ottawa, Toronto, Montreal, Winnipeg, Florida 401 Provencher Boulevard Winnipeg, Manitoba, Canada, R2H 0G9
Phone:	204-925-7616
Web site:	www.progestic.com
E-mail:	jules.selymes@progestic.com
Platforms:	Midrange and PC
Languages:	Cobol, SAS, PL/1, C, C++, VB, Basic, PRO-C, PowerBuilder, Progress, Oracle2000 (Forms & Reports) DBMS, ADABAS, DB2, IDMS, IMS, Oracle, Sybase, MS SQL Server, RDB, MS Access, dBase, Clipper, FoxPro, Lotus 1-2-3, MS Excel, Lotus Approach
Services:	Progestic International offers the following services: management, review, audit, information management, systems development, technology support, and Year 2000 assessment and renovation services.

Company:	Ravel Software, Inc. (also known as Turnkey 2000)
Address:	150 River Oaks Parkway, 2nd Floor San Jose, CA 95134
Phone:	408-955-1990
Web site:	www.unravel.com
E-mail:	sales@unravel.com
Platforms:	Software runs under Windows NT or 95
Language:	COBOL tools: MVS, VAX, Hewlett-Packard, Unisys, ICL. Tools for other languages are not sensitive to the platform on which the code runs. Oracle Forms, Oracle Reports, PL/SQL, Transact-SQL, FoxPro, Perl, JAM, C/C++, Visual Basic, PowerBuilder, UNIX Shell Scripts, COBOL Source code may be from one of five COBOL platforms or from any environment for the other products.
Services:	Ravel offers Y2K and euro assessment and remediation tools and application maintenance and migration tools and services. Ravel also offers multivendor, multiplatform Y2K, euro, and other tools and services, from shrink-wrapped up to enterprise license. Oracle Corporation Y2K tools of choice.
Company:	Reasoning, Inc.
Address:	700 East El Camino Real Mountain View, CA 94040
Phone:	650-429-0350
Web site:	www.reasoning.com
E-mail:	info@reasoning.com
Languages:	ANSI COBOL 68, 74, and 85; IBM dialects: OS/VS COBOL, VS COBOL II, DOS/VSE COBOL, COBOL for MVS & VM, AS/4000, Tandem COBOL; UNISYS COBOL; DEC VMS COBOL, Sun UltraSPARC ws with Solaris 2.5.1 & X11 Window Systems, Sun Ultra Enterprise servers with Solaris 2.5.1 & X11 Window System clients, and support for PC clients with compatible versions of X Window System
Services:	Reasoning/2000 for Inspection is an accurate and automated Y2K inspection tool and process for COBOL. It reduces the risk and cost of Y2K compliance. The product is fast and easy to use, eliminating the tedious and error-prone process of inspecting code manually.

Description: Reasoning is a leading provider of transformation software technology and services including code-base management systems, application mining tools, and second-generation solutions for the Year 2000 problem. Reasoning/2000 for Inspection is an accurate and automated Y2K inspection tool and process for COBOL. It reduces the risk and cost of Y2K compliance. Its design and graphical user interface make it fast and easy to use, eliminating the tedious and error-prone process of inspecting code manually.

Company: RICOMM Systems, Inc.

Address: 108E Centre Boulevard
Marlton, NJ 08053

Phone: 888-983-1818

Web site: www.ricommsystems.com

E-mail: b2kweb@ricommsystems.com

Platforms: All platforms

Languages: All versions of COBOL, JCL, SQL, DB2, IMS, IDMS, DL/1, CICS, DATACOM, NOMAD, APS, RPG, CL, C, C++, FORTRAN, Assembler UNIX, MVS, VSE, VM, DEC VAX, VMS

Services: RICOMM offers inventory, assessment, impact analysis, remediation, testing, tools, implementation, project management, verification and validation, and consulting. Beyond 2000 is a proven Y2K solution. Using artificial intelligence discovery techniques, RICOMM has reduced labor dependency and achieved highest accuracy at the lowest cost.

Company: SAS Institute Inc.

Address: SAS Campus Drive
Cary, NC 27513

Phone: 919-677-8000

Web site: www.sas.com

E-mail: software@sas.com

Platforms: MVS, CMS, VSE; OpenVMS for VAX and AXP; UNIX; Windows 95, Mac, OS/2, Windows NT, Windows 3.X

Description: SAS Institute is devoted to the development, support, and maintenance of SAS software—an integrated suite of data warehousing and decision support software—and its related services. Founded in 1976, SAS Institute is one of the top 10 largest software vendors in the world and is the largest privately held software company.

Company:	The Source Recovery Company
Address:	1080 Holcomb Bridge Road, Bldg. 200, Suite 200 Roswell, GA 30076
Phone:	770-650-1090
Web site:	www.source-recovery.com
E-mail:	sales@source-recovery.com
Platforms:	MVS, VM, VSE
Language:	COBOL, Assembler
Descriptions:	The Source Recovery Company recovers missing or out-of-sync source code from MVS, VM, or VSE executable modules. The recovered source code is guaranteed to be 100 percent functionally equivalent to the original executable module. Renaming and reconciliation services are also offered. "How can you fix the problem, if you don't have the Source?"
Company:	Standardware Inc.
Address:	424 Pelham Manor Road Pelham Manor, NY 10803
Phone:	914-738-6382
Web site:	www.standardware.com
E-mail:	cope@standardware.com
Description:	Standardware's COPE product answers the Year 2000 need to provide multiple independent IMS or DBCTL test systems without changing application source code or purchasing additional hardware. The creation of independent test environments avoids conflicts and corruption. Multiple independent logical copies of an IMS or DBCTL application run in a single physical region. Each logical copy has its own system date which is independent from the dates in other logical copies. Each logical copy accesses its own DL/I databases, DB2 tables, and program load libraries.
Company:	Strategia Corporation
Address:	P.O. Box 37144 Louisville, KY 40233-7144
Exchange:	AMEX: SAA
Phone:	800-325-3977
Web site:	www.strategiacorp.com
Platforms:	IBM, BULL, UNIX, AIX, NT, Novell, PC Access, MVS/ESA, OS2200, VSE/SP 3.2, VSE/ESA 2.2, Unisys 2200, OS390, UNIX SCO 2.x, 3.x, SCO Open Server, OS400, AIX, HPIX, OS2 Server,

Windows NT Server, Digital UNIX, Novell 2.x, 3.x, 4.x, KER-MIT, OS2, Windows 3.1, 95, 97, Windows/wgrps, Windows NT 2.x, 3.x, 4.x

Languages: Assembler, Clipper, Cobol, Easytrieve, Mantis, C, C++, VS COBOL, Natural, CA-IDMS ADS, Cobofli, Easytrieve Plus, FORTRAN, Power Builder, Power Building 5.0, Oracle/Forms, Oracle, RPG, COBOL 74, PL/1, REXX, UNIX Scripts, Visual Basic 3 or 4, Visual Fox Pro, Basic

Services: Strategia offers the following services: Year 2000 services (end-to-end solutions), compliance testing centers, business continuity services, and outsourcing. Strategia is a data vaulting end-to-end solutions provider including embedded chips, PCs and biomedical devices. Computer Associates Designated Year 2000 Testing Services Provider.

Company: Systemic Solutions, Inc.

Address: 1218 Third Avenue
Seattle, WA 98101

Phone: 206-344-4477

Web site: www.systemicsolutions.com

E-mail: info@systemicsolutions.com

Services: Systemic Solutions, a privately owned company, headquartered in Seattle, Washington, is a technology management company specializing in Year 2000 business solutions for the high-growth middle market. Systemic's broad range of consulting and problem management services assists companies in strategically managing their technology portfolios and enterprisewide business operations. READINESS 2000, the company's suite of scalable Y2K products, identifies potential Y2K exposures, delivers comprehensive project plans to abate the risk, and provides ongoing project management and updated metrics on a company's progress toward becoming millennium viable. Timothy Carlsen and Richard Bergeon founded the company in 1997. Bergeon is also the coauthor with Peter de Jager of one of the world's widest-selling books on the Y2K problem, *Managing 00: Surviving the Year 2000 Crisis,* published by Wiley Computer Publishing.

Company: TAVA Technologies, Inc.

Address: 7887 E. Belleview Avenue, Suite 820
Englewood, CO 80111

Exchange: NASDAQ: TAVA

Phone: 1-800-TAVAY2K

Web site: www.tavatech.com

E-mail: planty2kone@tavatech.com

Descriptions: For more than 24 years, TAVA Technologies has been providing companies with superior manufacturing solutions—intelligent, integrated hardware and software solutions, from PLC/DCS to SCADA to high-speed data acquisition. TAVA Technologies has the breadth and depth of experience to cover every aspect of plant automation—production management, quality assurance, inventory control, process optimization, engineering maintenance, and environmental control. TAVA provides full vertical market integration—from corporate and plant mainframes to manufacturing systems to field devices, vision systems, and bar-code readers. Located in 11 regional offices throughout the United States, TAVA has a staff of more than 400 employees.

Company: Titan Software Systems

Address: 1115 Elkton Drive, Suite 200
Colorado Springs, CO 80907-3535

Exchange: NYSE: TTN

Phone: 719-528-1800

Web site: www.cst.titan.com

E-mail: cst.marketing@titan.com

Platforms: PC, UNIX, IBM RS6000, HP 9000, HP 3000,

Languages: Sun, DEC Alpha C/C++, COBOL, COBOL II, Assembly 390, JCL, DB2, Adabas/Natural, Informix, Oracle, FoxPro, MS Access, Visual C++ Windows 95, Windows NT, Windows 3.1, HPUX, UNIX, AIX, Solaris, MVS, Novell Netware

Description: Titan offers a full range of assessment, analysis, testing, and conversion services for Year 2000 compliance. Using Titan 2000—its formal Web-based process—Titan Software has helped some of the largest U.S. companies remain competitive.

Company: TKS-TEKNOSOFT SA

Address: Chemin du Jura CH 1270
Trélex, Switzerland
(TKS is an associate company of
Tata Consultancy Services, India)

Phone:	41 22 363 62 00
Web site:	teknosft.marketing@tks.ch
Platforms:	Vaccine 2000 supports IBM AS/400, Native-S/36 and S/38; OS/400 versions: V2R3, V3R1, V3R2, V3R6, V3R7 RPG, COBOL, CL, and OCL
Services:	TEKNOSOFT offers physical and logical files, display and printer files, menus and embedded SQL. The Y2kit/400 effects a comprehensive and controlled Year 2000 conversion of applications running on AS/400: it is proactive and proposes solutions to Year 2000–related problems. It keeps the process under total control and helps users to manage the conversion. It provides multiple conversion options, expansion, or windowing, and supports flexible strategies based on user-specific options. It is user-friendly with the standard AS/400 look and feel and provides a configurable environment with the flexibility to manage the conversion of multiple applications effectively. TKS/TCS in an international company employing over 9,500 engineers, among whom 2,500 are fully dedicated to Year 2000 projects. More than 50 Y2K projects have already been completed including those for major names: Credit Suisse, American Express, Post Bank, and Royal Bank of Scotland, to name a few.
Company:	TRANSCEND 2000 PROJECT MANAGEMENT
Address:	7655 Sunset Boulevard Los Angeles, CA 90046
Phone:	800-999-9395
Web site:	www.transcend2000.com
E-mail:	alist@transcend2000.com
Platforms:	IBM 309x, ES9xxx, 43xxx; Amdahl 59xxx; HDS 6xxx, 8xxx; IBM AS400, RS6000; Hewlett-Packard HP3000, HP9000; DEC VAX all models; Intel-based PCs; MacIntosh
Languages:	COBOL, Assembler, PL/1, C, C++, Basic, Visual Basic, Access, DL/1, CICS, IMS-DC, DB2, IMS-DB, Oracle, Sybase, Adabase MVS, OS/390, VSES, VM, DOS, Windows, MPE, VMS, UNIX, MAC/OS
Services:	Assessment, planning, remediation, testing, project review, and DocuTrail.
Descriptions:	Transcend 2000 is an amalgam of senior project managers, programmers, and analysts with a range of skill sets that cover the spectrum of information technology.

Company: Transformation Processing Inc. (TPI)

Address: 2121 Argentia Road, Suite 200
Mississauga, Ontario L5N 2X4

Exchange: OTC: tpii

Phone: 905-812-7907 or toll-free: 888-222-5967

Web site: www.tpii.com

E-mail: mburfield@tpii.com

Platform: Mainframe, Midrange, AS/400, Desktops; Operating Systems: MVS, OS/400, UNIX

Languages: EMBEDDED COBOL, C++, RPG, VB, Java, C, Assembler, PL/1

Services: Client/server migration, y2k it, y2k non-it, embedded system, emu (euro) conversion.

Description: Transformation Processing is an information technology company that develops and markets software and services enabling companies to automatically migrate their application programs and data from legacy systems to open systems and client/server environments. TPI has four lines of business: client/server migration, Year 2000 solutions, groupware, and support services. In addition, the company's ability to scan code to diagnose Year 2000 problems, as well as perform similar diagnostic procedures on embedded chips, positions it as an industry leader in this area.

Company: TRW Systems & Information Technology Group

Address: 1501 BDM Way
Commercial IT Group
McLean, VA 22102

Phone: 800-565-0162

Web site: www.bdm.com

E-mail: Year2000@bdm.com

Description: TRW Systems & Information Technology Group, the fusion of BDM International and TRW Systems Integration Group, helps customers leverage information technology to meet strategic business goals. The company offers controlled, focused Year 2000 solutions based on its ITAA-certified SMART/2000+SM methodology. SMART/2000+ is an end-to-end solution that effectively addresses technical and business issues across the enterprise. The company also offers focused services including BDM SMART ManagerSM for program management; BDM SMART 2000 TestSM for independent Year 2000 testing; BDM

SMART ValidatorSM for enterprisewide compliance management and documentation of IT and non-IT systems; and SMART EvaluatorSM for standardized, objective evaluation of Year 2000 programs and timely, strategic recommendations to improve performance.

Company:	Ultra 2000 Software
Address:	P.O. Box 1214 Lynnwood, WA 98046-1214
Phone:	425-744-1897
Web site:	www.computersoftware2000.com
E-mail:	y2k@computersoftware2000.com
Platforms:	Software runs on Windows 3.1, 95, and NT; scans COBOL source from any platform
Services:	Date-scanning tool to assist managers and programmers with the task of converting legacy COBOL programs to be Y2K–compliant.
Description:	The date-scanning software allows customized searches to be run. Results may be printed or displayed. Upgrades are free until January 1, 2000. A free demo is available at the Web site. Ultra 2000 Software is located north of Seattle, Washington.
Company:	Unisys Corporation
Address:	Township Line and Union Meeting Roads Blue Bell, PA 19424-0000
Exchange:	NYSE: UIS
Phone:	215-986-4011
Web site:	www.unisys.com
Platforms:	All platforms supported: emphasis on Unisys A Series, 2200; all operating systems supported
Languages:	All languages supported
Description:	Through TEAM2000, Unisys offers one of the industry's most comprehensive suites of services to address millennium business issues. Recently, Unisys TEAM2000 introduced Fast Cycle to Year 2000. This service radically reduces time required to address the range of risks related to Year 2000 migration and get clients into production as rapidly as possible. Unisys is an information technology solutions provider.
Company:	Unitech Systems, Inc.
Address:	1240 East Diehl Road Naperville, IL 60563-1439

Web site:	www.unitechsys.com
E-mail:	year2000@unitechsys.com
Phone:	800-950-5225
Description:	INSPECT/2000 is a new testing tool suite designed specifically for Y2K testing of batch application programs on MVS operating systems. The product suite was developed to fill gaps in the testing process left by traditional test tools and consists of UNITEST/2000 for Smart File Comparison and BASETEST/2000 for automated systemwide acceptance testing. INSPECT/2000 is particularly powerful for compliance testing because output comparisons with the baseline can be performed directly with aged data without an extra aging step. INSPECT/2000 also provides comprehensive end-to-end test results documentation to protect from future litigation.

Company:	Veronex Technologies Inc.
Address:	1508 Brookhollow Drive, Suite 363 Santa Ana, CA 92705
Exchange:	OCT: VXTK
Phone:	714-668-0680
Web site:	www.veronex.com
E-mail:	tgoodbody@veronex.com
Platform:	Mainframe; Operating systems: MVS
Language:	COBOL
Services:	Y2K Software
Description:	Veronex Technologies I/Nova System is a fully automated methodology that performs an end-to-end solution for the Y2K problem. Most importantly, it provides a return on the investment.

Company:	Viasoft, Inc.
Address:	3033 N. 44th Street Phoenix, AZ 85018
Exchange:	NASDAQ: VIAS
Phone:	888-VIASOFT
Web site:	www.viasoft.com
E-mail:	info@viasoft.com
Platforms:	IBM mainframes and the IT desktop
Mainframe:	COBOL/370, OS/VS COBOL, VS COBOL II, PL/1

Desktop: C/C++ IBM MVS/XA, MVS/ESA and OS/390 for Batch, CICS, IMS and IDMS environments, Windows 3.x, Windows 95, and Windows NT 3.51, 4.0

Services: Integrated software tools and professional services for the IT enterprise.

Description: Viasoft is a leading provider of business solutions, consisting of integrated technology and specialized professional services.

Company: Wincap Software, Inc.

Address: 235 Littleton Road, Suite 4
Westford, MA 01742

Phone: 888-722-6885

Web site: www.wincap-na.com

E-mail: info@wincap-usa.com

Platforms: MVS, AS400, VSE, VMS & GCOS7/8

Languages: COBOL, Assembler, Natural, PL/1, CL, DCL, JCL, RPG, AS400 Objects, DB2, IMS, and many schedulers

Services: Software runs on Oracle Server and 32-bit Windows clients; Year 2000/Euro and any legacy management issues (tools and consulting)

Description: Wincap Software is a leading provider of tools for the Global 5000 that enable the understanding, control, and management of legacy systems.

Company: Wipro Infotech—Enterprise Solutions Division

Address: 40/1A, Lavelle Road
Bangalore 560-001
India

Exchange: Wipro Limited at the Bombay Stock Exchange

Phone: +91 80 2210818 or 221 5010

Web site: www.wipro.com

E-mail: mktg@wipsys.soft.net

Platforms: IBM mainframes, digital VAX, AS400, client/server (UNIX, NT, DOS); Operating systems: MVS, VAX/VMS, UNIX, NT, DOS

Languages: COBOL, TEBOL, PL/1, Assembler, Mantis, Easytrieve, PDLs, Viewprints, C, C++, VB, PowerBuilder

Services: Flexible yet full Y2K services provided from assessment to impact analysis to conversion to testing to implementation support.

Description: Wipro Infotech is India's number one IT company, providing a complete range of IT solutions to customers worldwide. Service offerings range from application software to middleware to systems software.

Company: WRQ, Inc.

Address: 1500 Dexter Avenue North
Seattle, WA 98109

Phone: 800-872-2829 or 206-217-7100

Web site: www.wrq.com

E-mail: info@wrq.com

Platforms: DOS 4.0 or later, Windows 3.1x, Windows NT, Windows 95

Description: The WRQ Express 2000 Suite includes everything IT managers need to discover, prioritize, and control desktop Year 2000 problems. It's a complete compliance solution that runs on nearly any network. WRQ is a leading provider of connectivity and management solutions to enterprises worldwide. WRQ Express software management tools ensure intelligent IT decisions with clear information about software assets across the enterprise. WRQ is the sixteenth largest PC software company in the United States. It has offices throughout the world and distributes products in more than 50 countries through a worldwide distribution network.

Company: Xinotech Research, Inc.

Address: 1313 5th Street SE, Suite 213
Minneapolis, MN 55414

Phone: 612-379-3844

Web site: www.xinotech.com

E-mail: info@xinotech.com

Platforms and languages: IBM mainframes, HP 3000, HP 9000, DEC VAX, Bull COBOL (all dialects), PL/I MVS, OS360, HP UX, UNIX, VAX, Bull GCOS

Description: Xinotech's metalanguage technology supports type inference and transformation to solve Year 2000, Euro, and other domain-specific and architectural reengineering problems, such as the standardization under the International Securities Identification Standards (ISIN) and the decimalization of fractional values in stock pricing. 2001 supports automatic enterprisewide software model extraction and partitioning, semantic (impact) analysis and reporting, automated transformation of heterogeneous components (programs, JCLs, data definitions, screens, reports), and automatic transformation of data (databases and datafiles). 2001 allows user-level customization to combine multiple solutions such as expansion, compression, windowing, (e.g., temporary type coercion and signature replacement, functional replacement, in-memory expansion), and data bridging.

Company:	Year 2000 Inventory Management Ltd.
Address:	Draycott House Hawley Road, Camberley, GU17 9ES England
Phone:	+44 1923 446995
Web site:	www.y2kiml.com
E-mail:	queries@y2kiml.com
Platforms and languages:	PC, Windows 3.x, 95, NT
Description:	Year 2000 Inventory Manager is a database application designed specifically for managing Year 2000 inventories. It allows you to store all inventory information in one place, track key dates and dependencies, and much more. Available for free download.
Company:	Zitel Corporation
Address:	47211 Bayside Parkway Fremont, CA 94538
Phone:	510-440-9600
Web site:	www.zitel.com
E-mail:	Y2K@zitel.com
Platforms and languages:	IBM COBOL (ANSI '68 '72 '85), VSAM, CICS, IMS, and DB2 MVS
Description:	Accelerated Automated Factory Y2K Code Conversion. Zitel offers full Y2K services including project management, planning, analysis, code conversion, and testing. Zitel's primary code-conversion methodology for IBM mainframe COBOL code is based on MatriDigm's MAP2000sm factory for Y2K code conversion and MARC2000sm for analysis of code that has already

been converted. Code is processed either at the central factory in California or on a portable version of MAP2000sm for on-site conversion in sensitive environments. The key features of MAP2000sm factory conversion are high speed and accurate code remediation, 100 percent testing of all converted date fragments, fast turnaround time, which significantly lowers overall project cost and reduces the complexity of the system test.

Year 2000 Web Sites

ADDRESS	DESCRIPTION
www.2000.jbaworld.com/index.asp	General information.
www.2k-times.com	A collection of articles about legal issues.
www.aiag.org/	Automotive Industry Action Group.
www.bog.frb.fed.us/y2k/video_index.htm#19980602	Videos.
www.cbn.org/news/stories/y2k-links.asp	CBN News Y2K resource center.
www.cio.com/forums/y2k/index.htm	General reference.
www.comlinks.com	Alan Simpson's Y2K site.
www.data-dimensions.com	*Millennium Journal.*
www.erols.com/steve451/main_y2k.htm	Good site with diverse topics/links.
www.erols.com/steve451/main_y2k.htm	General information.
www.esofta.com/pdfs/Y2KEmb.pdf	Embedded systems guidance.
www.euy2k.com/bookstor.htm	Books on Y2K.

www.euy2k.com/links.htm	This is a decent place to find information based on industry.
www.ft.uni-erlangen.de/~mskuhn/iso-time.html	International date and time representations.
www.gao.gov/special.pubs/bcpguide.pdf	U.S. Government Accounting Office's Business Continuity and Contingency Planning.
www.gao.gov/special.pubs/y2kguide.pdf	U.S. Government Accounting Office's Year 2000 Assessment Guide.
www.gao.gov/y2k.htm	U.S. Government Accounting Office advice and guidance.
www.gsa.gov/gsacio/bpfedgud.htm	Government guidance.
www.hewm.com	A review of selected litigation issues.
www.iee.org.uk/2000risk	Institute of Electrical Engineers.
www.implement.co.uk/faqs.htm	A good place to go in order to get answers on the impact of Y2K on a PC.
www.it2000.com	Year 2000 bulletin board.
www.itaa.org/year2000.htm	Decent vendor list. Also, under Y2K Publications, the Y2K Software Conversion is good.
www.itpolicy.gsa.gov/mks/yr2000/cioy2k.htm	U.S. General Services Agency advice and guidance.
www.llgm.com/FIRM/article5.htm	Legal assertions with background data.
www.marketplace.unisys.com/year2000/rmapcase/rmapcase.htm	Unisys Year 2000 case studies.
www.microsoft.com/year2000/	Product status. More appearing all the time.
www.millennia-bcs.com/SUMMARY.htm	Cassandra Project.
www.mitre.org/research/cots/COMPLIANT_BIOS.html	Personal PC date handling.
www.mitre.org/research/cots/Y2K_SOLUTIONS.html	Explanation of the Y2K issues.

www.mitre.org/research/y2k/docs/ CONTINGENCY_PLAN.html	Contingency planning discussion.
www.mitre/research/y2k/docs/ VENDORS	Good vendor list.
www.nrc.gov/NRC/NEWS/ year2000.html	Nuclear Regulatory Commission statement.
www.ourworld.compuserve.com/ homepages/roleigh_martin	Convincing article for the technically minded.
www.rx2000.org	Medical industry help site.
www.senate.gov/~bennett/y2k.html	U.S. Senate Year 2000 Technology Committee.
www.software.ibm.com/year2000/	IBM's information center.
www.software.org/y2k/index.html	Software certification guidelines.
www.spr.com	Capers Jones' Software Productivity Research company site.
www.state.mn.us/ebranch/admin/ ipo/2000/2000.html	State of Minnesota's Year 2000 clearinghouse.
www.support2000.com/ indexcrp.htm	General support.
www.systemicsolutions.com	Rich Bergeon's views and opinions.
www.techweb.com/wire/technews/ year2000.html	News clippings.
www.tmjb.com	Thelan, Merrin, Johnson and Bridges Year 2000 law center.
www.tycho.usno.navy.mil/time.html	U.S. Naval Observatory.
www.wa.gov/dis/2000/y2000.htm	State of Washington's resource center.
www.watch.org	Bill Koenig's news site.
www.wsrcg.com/	Warren Reid's legal Web site.
www.y2kjournal.com	News articles.
www.y2klinks.com	Year 2000 resource links database.
www.y2ktimebomb.com/Industry/ index.htm	Westergaard's site for opinions and commentary.
www.y2ktimes.com	Y2K news clippings.
www.yardeni.com	Financial projections.

www.year2000.com — Peter de Jager's Web site with most complete offerings of information, news, products, legal issues, and more.

www.year2000.com/archive/audit.html — Perspective on auditing.

www.yourdon.com/books/fallback/fallbackhome.html — Ed Yourdon's Timebomb 2000 site.

Recommended Reading

The Mythical Man-Month

Frederick P. Brooks, Jr.

Must reading classic for project managers faced with the dilemma of not enough time, too much to do, and desperate to meet a deadline. The twentieth anniversary edition includes four chapters not in the original work. These new chapters include a condensation of the propositions made in the earlier work, an up-to-date review of those propositions, a reprint of Brooks's classic paper, "No Silver Bullet," and a refreshing look at the topic that asserts, "There will be no silver bullet within ten years."

To order: Available through on-line and local bookstores. 292 pages, $26.75, Addison-Wesley Publishing Company, 1995.

The Year 2000 Computing Crisis: A Millennium Date Conversion Plan

Jerome T. Murray, Marilyn Murray

At the dawn of a new millennium, computer systems all over the world will begin generating bad data because of the way software has been written to interpret years. This urgently needed handbook offers solutions to the problem. This book provides a concrete plan for IS developers and consultants scrambling to beat the clock before their systems collapse. The work in this book will endear itself to hard-core assembly language programmers. Over half of the book lists assembly language programs for solving a host of Year 2000 problems. Two introductory chapters contain basic information about

Year 2000 issues and document the notational conventions used in the assembly language programs. The remaining seven chapters of the book are each dedicated to explaining a Year 2000 problem, mapping out a solution, and implementing the solution in the form of a fully documented program. The book includes all of the source code on floppy disk.

To order: Available through on-line and local bookstores. 321 pages, $39.95, Computing McGraw-Hill, 1996.

The Millennium Bomb

Simon Reeve, Colin McGhee

The book is the first in the world to examine the so-called Year 2000 problem, whereby computers fail when clocks tick past midnight on December 31, 1999. Authors Simon Reeve, a former journalist for *The Sunday Times*, and Colin McGhee, a journalist and technology expert, warn that the problem is much more serious than currently acknowledged. Figures now show that remedying the glitch will cost more than $400 billion. However, even if enough money can be found, there are not enough technical experts to solve the problem in the three years left.

To order: Go to www.implement.co.uk/millbomb.htm, or, for a direct line, 0171-460-4684, fax is 0171-460-4679, $14.95, Vision Paperbacks, 1996.

The Year 2000 Problem Solver: A Five-Step Disaster Prevention Plan

Bruce Ragland

As the year 2000 approaches, computer systems in place throughout the world are starting to go haywire because they treat the year as two digits instead of four. It's been estimated that businesses and governments worldwide will spend at least $300 million to correct this. For all the system administrators and managers scurrying to meet the millennium deadline, this crucial guide will be a problem solver and a lifesaver.

To order: Available through on-line and local bookstores. 300 pages, $29.95, Computing McGraw-Hill, 1996.

Embedded Systems and the Year 2000 Problem Guidance Notes

Institution of Electrical Engineers

Don't let the title mislead you. This book covers the technology domain with sections about hardware, software, applications, and vendors. A nontechnical book aimed at the IT director looking for a good understanding. Published in Great Britain.

To order: Available from IEE; P.O. Box 96, Stevenage, Herts, United Kingdom, SG1 2SD or www.iee.org.uk/. 159 pages, Institution of Electrical Engineers, 1997.

The Year 2000 Software Problem: Quantifying the Costs and Assessing the Consequences

Capers Jones

Capers Jones, acknowledged expert on the economic impact of the Year 2000 software problem and leading author and speaker, offers a framework for examining the effect that the Year 2000 problem will have on your company, placing this timely issue into a practical business perspective. This book explains what it will cost to address this impending issue, quantifying the expenses by country, industry, programming language, and application. It further examines the expected results of not achieving Year 2000 compliance and estimates what the damages and recovery costs will be. The author's pragmatic approach allows you to assess the scope of the problem, identify the appropriate solution strategy, and test and measure the effectiveness of your solution implementation.

To order: Available through on-line and local bookstores. 352 pages, $29.95, Addison-Wesley Publishing Company, 1997.

Year 2000 Solutions for Dummies

Kelly C. Bourne

A late arriver to the Year 2000 genre, like others in the popular *Dummies* series, it summarizes much of the more technical aspects of the problem, concentrating on techniques for programmers and analysts looking for a primer in Year 2000 solutions.

To order: Available through on-line and local bookstores. 400 pages, $24.99, IDG Books Worldwide, 1997.

Meltdown 2000: 25 Things You Must Know to Protect Yourself and Your Computer

Lawrence Cleenewerck, Pamela D. Jacobs

A guide to the Year 2000 crisis for nontechnical readers, this book provides a simple and objective explanation of the problem and its potential consequences. It also offers advice on how to protect yourself, your family, your computer, and your business—before it's too late.

To order: Available through on-line and local bookstores. $4.95, Robert D. Reed Publication, 1997.

Year 2000 Problem: Strategies and Solutions from the Fortune 100 (Software Engineering Series)

Leon A. Kappelman, Ph.D

This book has a practical approach to solving the Year 2000 problem and applying its methods to your own enterprise, business, or organization with a ready-to-use guide. An accompanying CD-ROM includes a vendor risk assessment strategy, a business risk assessment database, a project management database tool, PC test software, and a file conversion utility.

To order: Available through on-line and local bookstores. 300 pages, $29.95, International Thomson Publishing, 1997.

Solving the Year 2000 Problem

James Edward Keough, Stephen C. Ruten, Jim Keough

Although the book is aimed at business executives, IT managers, information systems managers, it is also relevant to anyone using computers—it is "everyone's problem." If educational institutions run critical applications, such as birth dates for staff and students, when fees are due, pay schedules for staff, property management, and others, they, too, may run into problems. The impact may vary according to applications and hardware employed within these institutions. The significance of the Year 2000 problem dawns when you realize that computers that track your personal details, details used to make critical decisions about you, may not recognize the year 2000.

To order: Available through on-line and local bookstores or go to www.exam-ta.ac.uk/year2000.htm. 264 pages, $27.95, AP Professional Publication, 1997.

Year 2000 Software Crisis: Solutions for IBM Legacy Systems (Software Engineering Series)

Keith A. Jones (drkajones@aol.com)

Now, with off-the-shelf software solutions—both diagnostic and planning—here is everything you need to quickly identify the best Year 2000 automated methods and tools for your needs. Get advice on simulating time and cost for each category of Year 2000 software date changes. Learn how to assess risks in order to prioritize Year 2000 efforts and help avoid losses and liabilities. Determine what to scan to measure source code and to inventory software portfolios at the program level. Get automated methods and technologies in the top 10 classes of Year 2000 tools, estimate costs of Year 2000 conversion with expert information for assessing costs, and learn about Year 2000 pilot projects using innovative new technology and tools.

To order: Available through on-line and local bookstores. 483 pages, International Thomson Publication, 1997.

The Year 2000 Software Systems Crisis: Challenge of the Century

William M. Ulrich, Ian S. Hayes, Ian Hays

The impact of the impending year 2000 on computer software is gaining tremendous attention in the media. According to analysts, the cost of this problem worldwide is likely to exceed half a trillion dollars over the next four years. This book discusses the global implications of this problem on government and private industry—along with various solutions.

To order: Available through on-line and local bookstores. 340 pages, $39.95, Yourdon Press Computing Series, 1997.

The Deadline

Tom DeMarco

Tom DeMarco is a management consultant widely known for his wit and wisdom on project management and people issues. This book is not about the Year 2000 project, it's about project management in general. In particular, it's about the absurdities, paradoxical behaviors, and lunacy that surrounds and confounds projects both large and small. In a time when many management books expound theory, DeMarco illustrates simple management concepts describing situations many of us will find all too familiar; we might even see ourselves as participants in his carefully selected vignettes. The strength of this book lies in DeMarco's ability to focus our attention on what is important during project management.

To order: Available through on-line and local bookstores. 300 pages, $29.70, Dorset House Publishing, 1997.

Calendrical Calculations

Nachum Dershowitz, Edward M. Reingold

Any programmer who becomes embroiled in Year 2000 programming might also become afflicted with an abnormal interest in calendars; this book will help scratch that itch.

When you first run across the Gregorian calendar rule that states years evenly divisible by 4 are leap years, unless they are evenly divisible by 100, unless they are evenly divisible by 400, you begin to suspect that calendars are a bit more complex than counting your knuckles to see how many days are in the month.

This is an exploration of calendars, in particular the Gregorian, ISO Commercial, Julian, Coptic and Ethiopic, Islamic, Solar and Jewish, Mayan, French Revolutionary, Chinese, Hindu (mean and true) and a few others less well known! It is a fascinating tour of the many ways in which we mark our meager time on earth. Recommended for the curious and the obsessed and, of course, those required to translate from one dating system to another.

To order: Write to Cambridge University Press, 40 West 20th Street, New York, NY 10011-4211. 306 pages, $22.95, Cambridge University Press, 1997.

Time Bomb 2000: What the Year 2000 Computing Crisis Means to You!

Edward Yourdon, Jennifer Yourdon

Edward and Jennifer Yourdon address how the Y2K problem will affect the lives of average people and everyday systems. They present a collection of scenarios ranging from the best we can hope for to the worst cases. Each chapter investigates a different area of computing and possible effects of this disaster on each. From PCs to world financial networks, this book explores a variety of domino effects that January 1, 2000, could trigger and the necessary time, effort, and cost to fix the aftermath.

To order: Available through on-line and local bookstores. 415 pages, $19.95, Prentice Hall Computer Books, 1998.

Finding and Fixing Your Year 2000 Problem: A Guide for Small Business and Organizations

Jesse Feiler

A hands-on approach is offered for addressing and solving the Year 2000 problem in the small enterprise (small businesses, schools, medical offices, home offices, and so forth). The authors have created a comprehensive guide to ensuring the Year 2000 problem is fixed for good by providing a general overview, details on specific categories of problems, types of technologies available, and how to test and modify solutions.

To order: Available through on-line and local bookstores. 446 pages, $39.95, AP Professional Publishing, 1998.

Software Runaways

Robert L. Glass

For IT executives, project managers, and developers, this book provides 16 documented software failures that demonstrate why government and large business Year 2000–problem remediation efforts are most likely already doomed to fail. Glass does provide some guidelines that may help to minimize the impact of failure including risk and issue management.

To order: Available through on-line and local bookstores. 251 pages, $28.88, Prentice Hall PTR, 1998.

How to 2000

Raytheon E-Systems

For the enterprise faced with proprietary code requiring remediation and hardware and software vendors, here is an inexpensive methodology covering awareness, planning, inventory, triage, assessment, resolution, testing, deployment, and fallout. This book comes with a CD-ROM containing a project plan, Web links, and an electronic version of the book so that it can be copied and modified to fit the needs of your enterprise. It is a must-have for any IT project manager no matter how many other books you have on the topic.

To order: Available through on-line and local bookstores. 589 pages, $49.99, IDG Books Worldwide, 1998.

Teaching Chipmunks to Dance: The Business Leaders' Guide to Making Distributed Enterprise Year 2000 Compliant

Chris Jesse

Weaving together humor, personal anecdotes, and proven corporate experience, the author exposes the distributed Year 2000 problem and shows you how to defuse this time bomb with a simple, six-step process. Learn how to plan, implement, and manage your compliance effort—before disaster strikes. With your distributed assets under control, you can safely ring in the New Year and swiftly dance your way through the millennium celebration.

To order: Call Kendall/Hunt Customer Service at 1-800-228-0810 (in the United States) or go to www.assettracking.com/chipmunk/order-c.htm. $24.95, 1998.

The Year 2000 Computer Crisis: Law, Business, Technology

Michael D. Scott, Warren Reid

Michael Scott is a practicing lawyer and his coauthor, Warren Reid, is a litigation and technology management consultant. Their goal is to scope out the legal landscape surrounding the year 2000, and they succeed without resorting to legal jargon. They rely heavily on the expertise of those in the Year 2000 field and on skilled attorneys practicing in such areas as computer systems failures, project management, license agreements, and high-tech intellectual property disputes.

The main benefit of the book is that it neatly compiles a vast number of scenarios, which could create legal exposures for any company. It also drives home the important concept that this is no longer a technical problem, that it has become a business problem with legal ramifications, which reach all the way up to the board of directors. This book, or one like it, should be mandatory reading for the primary Year 2000 project leader, legal counsel for your company, and all executives and directors of the board.

To order: Go to www.legalwks.com or call 1-800-308-1700. 400+ pages, $125.00, Glasser Legalworks, 1998.

The Millennium Bug

Mark Ludwig

In less than two years, computers around the world will fail when they cannot interpret the year 2000 correctly in their databases. What nobody is telling you is that this computer glitch, known as the millennium bug, will probably cause bank runs in late 1999. Those bank runs will lead to government intervention and the establishment of the cashless society—a world in which every financial transaction is monitored and controlled by government, and freedom is a bygone dream. Everything is in place to make this happen. The historical precedents are clear. The laws and executive orders are on the books, just waiting to be used. A media-generated scare is already in the works. The architects of the new world order are salivating at the prospects. If you find the cashless society noxious for any reason, read this book today! We can still avoid it, but soon it will be too late. Time is running out. . . .

To order: Go to www.logoplex.com/resources/ameagle/milbug.html.

Electric Utilities and Y2K

Rick Cowles (rcowles@waterw.com)

This book offers expanded coverage not offered in the euy2 Web site of Y2K issues and strategies for the electric industry and personal preparedness tips for the individual. This is an easy-to-read, complete guide for understanding the dependency problem in this industry.

To order: Go to www.accsyst.com/writers/book.htm.

Practical Methods for Your Year 2000 Problem: The Lowest Cost Solution

Robert B. Chapman

This book gives the Year 2000 project team a comprehensive, cost-effective, step-by-step methodology for addressing the Year 2000 problem. The book is geared toward (1) helping the in-house personnel understand, scope, and execute their project while (2) removing the need to spend large amounts of money on professional consulting firms. The goal of the book is to minimize the amount of work to be performed, and thus maximize the probability of having a successful Year 2000 project. It offers practical advice on all aspects of the Year 2000 problem, from inventorying software and hardware through to implementing large numbers of interrelated programs, files, and tables.

To order: Go to www.manning.com/Chapman/index.html. 236 pages, $55, Manning, 1998.

Evaluating Success of a Y2000 Project

Howard Rubin, Brian Robbins

Howard Rubin is chair of the department of computer science at Hunter College of the City University of New York. In a field dreadfully short of hard statistics, he has been one of a handful of researchers attempting to turn anecdotes into hard evidence. His coauthor is the senior vice president at Chase Manhattan Bank and is responsible for managing its Enterprise Year 2000 program. His first-hand experiences of the complexities of the problem are evident throughout this book in the form of piercing, uncompromising questions.

Rubin and Robbins have attempted and succeeded in providing an instrument for self-assessment. They provide a series of questions to be asked not of your year 2000 manager, but of the entire organization. Answered honestly with the goal of uncovering the true status of your project, this book could be a large first step toward reducing unnecessary risk. A copy in the hands of a competent objective auditor would provide the best insurance possible against failure.

To order: Go to www.bookmasters.com/markplc.htm or call 1-800-800-0448. 74 pages, The Information Economics Press, 1998.

The Year 2000 and 2-Digit Dates: A Guide for Planning and Implementation

IBM, GC28-1251-04

On October 30, 1995, IBM held a press conference to announce that the Year 2000 problem was real, that it affected not only mainframe products, but PCs as well, that it needed to be addressed as soon as possible. As part of this teleconference, it announced the availability of a Year 2000 guide which it made freely available to anyone interested in obtaining it.

The guide is comprehensive. It describes the problem in detail, the various solutions used to fix it, the necessity for good management, and, in particular, how it affects various IBM products. It also makes available information on when specific IBM problems will be made Year 2000–compatible and the upgrade paths from noncompatible product lines. For any IBM customer, this is an invaluable resource; it certainly provides the foundation for the discussions you will need to have with IBM if you are a heavy user of its products. If you are not an IBM customer, it still provides a very good overview of the problem and the outlines for a successful project.

To order: Go to ftp://lscftp.pok.ibm.com/pub/year2000/y2kpaper.txt or www.s390.ibm.com. 250 pages, free, IBM, 1995.

Computer Related Risks

Peter G. Neumann

"We live in the Computer Age." Everyone has heard that phrase, few seem to understand what it implies. Peter Neumann's book details the inevitable consequences of being dependent upon technology in general and computers in particular. His book is primarily a compendium of technologically based mishaps combined with insights as to why we continue to suffer these failures and what we might do to avoid them. His flashlight shines only momentarily on the Year 2000 problem, so this cannot rightly be classed as a

Y2K book; nevertheless, it is necessary reading for anyone who would like to better understand the potential consequences of endemic Y2K failures.

To order: Available through on-line and local bookstores. 367 pages, $26.75, Addison-Wesley Publishing Company, 1994.

The Year 2000 Computer Crisis: An Investor's Survival Guide

Tony Keyes

We admit upfront to a negative bias toward certain approaches to the Year 2000 issue, in particular, "Run for the hills, we're all doomed" and "How you can profit from failure." Both strategies strike us as nonconstructive approaches to the problem. Tony Keyes's book appears to straddle both these perspectives using both *survival* and *investor's* in the title. While some parts of the book do indeed rely on the old standbys of "buy gold in troubled times," it is mostly a reasoned wake-up call to the reality of the problem. He has collected a slew of clippings, quotes, and congressional testimonies and woven them into a compelling argument for personal action. How good is the financial advice? Like all advice, we'll have to wait until after the event to draw fair conclusions.

To order: Available through on-line and local bookstores. 314 pages, $29.95, The Y2K Investor, 1998.

Death March

Ed Yourdon

Before offering any review of this book, it is necessary to define *death march*. A death march is any project which has been allocated less than 50 percent of the necessary resources, whether the shortfall be in the area of funding, staff, time, or computer resources. (The reviewer adds another possible area of shortfall to consider: less than 50 percent of the common sense necessary to succeed.)

By this definition, practically every single Year 2000 project is a death march, making Yourdon's book mandatory reading for all team members and management.

The book offers advice on how to survive death marches with your sanity, health, and personal relationships intact. As advice goes, it seems reasonable, logical, well thought out, so it makes sense to at least find out what the advice is and how it might help you.

The book, however, is built upon a single, shaky premise, which, to his credit, Yourdon does not side-step even if he can't provide a viable answer.

If we're so stupid as to get ourselves involved with death marches, what will make us smart enough to follow advice on how to survive the experience? Even with this glaring shortfall, the book is required reading.

To order: Available through on-line and local bookstores. 218 pages, $24.95, Prentice Hall, 1997.

Le Syndrome de L'an 2000

Daniel Giraudeau

The most distinctive aspects of this book are the date of publication, 1996, and the location, France. This was published long before any books were published in English on the subject and it highlights the anomaly that Europe appears, despite early awareness, as evidenced by this publication, to lag far behind North America in project plans.

Giraudeau offers a comprehensive overview of the problem and a list of then-available vendors and descriptions of their services.

To order: Write to 61 bd Saint-Germain, 75005, Paris, Cedex 05 or call (1) 44 41 11 55 or fax (1) 44 41 11 85. 1996.

How Bad Will It Be?

So? When all is said and done, how bad will it be? The honest answer is, nobody knows. There are too many programs, too many systems, too many organizations, too many countries, and too many interactions between all of these to predict how things might fail. In addition, not all the consequences will be immediately visible; many will lie hidden for days, weeks, even months before they make themselves known.

Yes but . . . how bad will it be? No matter how unreasonable the question is, it's compelling, thought-consuming, and persistent; it won't vanish in the face of rational arguments, cautious qualifications, and a reluctance to make predictions. The question doesn't go away, it begs an answer. . . . How bad will it be?

Before we offer our foolhardy attempt to do the impossible—to predict a future event—let's take a look at some past events. They'll allow us to make some reasonable observations about how people have reacted to adversity in the past. If we're lucky and cautious in our generalizations, we might be able to predict how we'll react in the future.

The Nature of Disasters

At 5:16 P.M. on November 9, 1965, eastern Canada and northeastern America were hit by the Great Blackout. Thirty million people populating some 80,000 square miles were plunged into darkness at the height of rush hour for periods lasting up to 13 hours. This huge, all-encompassing event was caused not by a vast number of failures, but by a single, solitary power switch doing exactly what it was programmed to do, but with devastating consequences.

The first lesson from this bit of history is that our society is vulnerable to what are called *single points of failure.* The costs in lost business in New York City alone was estimated to be more than $100 million. Imagine your incredulity if you had been touring the Sir Adam Beck Station #2 on November 2, 1965, and the tour guide, pointing to a single power switch, stated, "30 million people depend on that switch doing its job correctly. If it were to fail, all those people would be without power. Its failure would cost New York City $100 million in lost business. Its my responsibility to make sure that never happens." Your first thought would be, "He's exaggerating. There's no way that single device is that important." A few days later, you would be proven 100 percent wrong.

Here's the question we're forced to ask ourselves. How many other single, seemingly unimportant devices do we unknowingly depend upon? Some obvious examples come to mind, such as the O-ring that malfunctioned on the ill-fated *Challenger* shuttle. Or the *Galaxy 4*, the single satellite that, when it went on an unplanned vacation, turned off 50 million pagers throughout North America on May 20, 1998.

How did people react to the power outage? Did they panic? Did they riot and run wild in the streets of New York? Were there hordes of looters taking advantage of the situation? The answer to all of these is an unqualified *no*. There was no panic. No rioting. No looting. There was instead, by all accounts, a festive mood. A party atmosphere, admittedly tinged with a growing sense of anxiety as time passed, but which lasted the duration of the event.

People came together as they usually do in times of adversity. Here's a quote from "Disaster" by R. K. Merton and R. A. Nisbet, published in *Contemporary Social Problems* (Harcourt, Brace, and World, 1976) describing *convergence behavior*.

> . . . Contrary to the popular image of behavior in disasters, movement toward the disaster area is usually quantitatively and qualitatively more significant than flight or evacuation from it. Within minutes after most domestic disasters, thousands of persons begin to converge on the disaster area and on first aid stations, hospitals, relief centers, and communication centers near the area. Along with this physical movement of persons, incoming messages of anxious inquiry and offers of help from all parts of the nation and from foreign countries begin to overload existing telephone, telegraph, and other communication and information facilities. Shortly afterward, tons of unsolicited equipment and supplies of clothing, food, bedding, and other material begin arriving in the disaster area or in nearby relief centers.

Despite all reports and rumors to the contrary, the skin of civilization is not a "thin veneer." Instead, it is a rather thick skin, and it reacts positively to temporary inconveniences. We may even be more *civilized* when civilization is threatened.

Another recent event is the Great Ice Storm of 1998. Between January 6th and 11th, the same region, eastern Canada and northeastern America, was assaulted by the worst ice storm in recorded history. Ice 60 to 100 millimeters thick covered every exposed surface; trees and electrical wires sagged and snapped under the weight; roads and buildings glistened in the glare of icy reflections. A dreadful beauty brought society to a halt.

In Montreal alone, more than 3 million were without power. In 1965, the power outage lasted only 13 hours; in this instance, some people were without power for more than 3 weeks. Unlike the Great Blackout, people lost their lives to the Great Ice Storm. They fired up generators and succumbed to carbon monoxide poisoning; they died in houses burnt to the ground in attempts to stay warm; they were laid low by hypothermia. Ultimately, the death toll of 20 was due to the lack of a continued supply of a mission-critical service—electricity.

Part of the solution deployed to overcome the challenge of restoring service was a series of priorities set by Hydro Quebec. Due to limited resources and the size, complexity, and nature of its task, it could not bring back electrical services to everybody at the same time. It had to make a conscious decision as to what was most important, what was less important, what could wait. Following is the priority list set by Hydro Quebec:

1. Hospitals
2. Seniors' residences
3. Hydro Quebec offices
4. Accommodation centers for electrical system repair crews
5. Street lighting
6. Suppliers of essential materials to Hydro Quebec
7. Selected commercial customers: shopping centers, dairies, and food wholesalers
8. Residences
9. Farms
10. Industries
11. Commercial establishments
12. Other clients

The *convergence behavior* mentioned earlier was evident again during the Great Ice Storm disaster. Companies across Canada shipped in supplies, volunteer people, and services. Canada saw the largest peace-time mobilization of military personnel. Electrical engineers and plumbers were flown in from all over Canada. Society rose to its own defense once again.

A question often asked after a natural disaster is, "How did it affect the economy?" It is obvious to even the most casual of observers that the economy must be negatively affected in the short term. But in the long term? Does the affected area recoup what it lost?

It turns out in the long term that natural disasters sometimes generate a small positive impact. This effect has even been given a label, the *economic paradox of natural disasters.* The Commerce Board of Canada describes it as follows:

Incremental investments required for reconstruction will have a positive impact on the economy, which often outweighs the initial loss in output caused by the disaster itself. However this result disguises the real loss to society. Changes in wealth are not part of the GDP calculation. In the current context, the capital losses experienced by Hydro-Quebec, Ontario Hydro and the insurance companies do not appear. The human suffering and pain associated with any disaster are also not measured, the economic analysis is limited to only one aspect of the impact of a disaster. Therefore, in no way does the net positive GDP impact of the Ice Storm, from the subsequent reconstruction, suggest that such catastrophes are socially beneficial.

So far, we've learned several things including the following:

1. Small events can have large consequences.
2. Convergence behavior occurs when disaster strikes.
3. When you can't do everything at once, identify what you'll do first and next.
4. In the long term, things get better, but in the short term, people suffer.

Another example also deals with power supply, but this time it takes place in a much more hospitable and civilized climate. At 3:30 P.M. on February 19, 1998, Auckland, New Zealand, was plunged into darkness. This blackout lasted longer than the soon-to-be-renamed Great Blackout; it even lasted longer than the Great Ice Storm blackouts of three weeks. It lasted a total of six weeks.

The reasons for the Auckland blackout are still being hotly debated by the many parties involved. The technical details are that the four electrical cables supplying power to the central business district failed. At first glance, you might say to yourself, "What a coincidence that all four cables failed at the same time. What are the chances of that happening?"

The chances are pretty good, when you consider that the cables are not independent of each other. They are part of the same system. Let's assume they each carry the same load, and that they operate at about 80 percent of their full capacity. If one cable breaks, the 80 percent load it was carrying is now distributed across the remaining three cables, increasing their load to 80 percent plus 0.33×80 percent, to a total of 106 percent. This overload could break either none, all, or one of the remaining three cables. If one fails, then that 106 percent load is now spread across the remaining two cables. This is similar in concept to what happened during the Great Blackout and the Great Ice Storm as power companies attempted to return power to the affected areas.

In Auckland, the problems were more bearable than those in the ice storm. The affected area was smaller, so it was a relatively simple matter for some businesses to move out of the "dark zone" and seek power elsewhere.

In Montreal, there was the added need for plumbers because the water in pipes froze, adding flooding to the list of problems. Auckland didn't have the same ripple effect.

In Montreal, several hundred shelters were needed for warmth and the basic necessities of life. In Auckland, again, this was not necessary.

The Auckland problem was not as severe the Great Ice Storm, even though it lasted significantly longer. Nor was it, in the opinion of many of those in Auckland, a true natural disaster. There are many who share the opinion that the disaster was due more to bad management than an act of God. When one considers the fact that the company in charge of supplying power to Auckland was advised to replace the cables 10 years prior to their failure, then this argument has some merit.

Natural or not, it still exhibited some of the attributes of other disaster events. People came to help from as far away as Australia, an example of convergence behavior. The disaster recovery used the strategy of prioritizing to fix the power outage, and there is growing evidence that the economic paradox of natural disasters is playing itself out in the blackout area of Auckland.

A significant difference is the lower impact of the longer (6-week) outage. If Montreal or New York had been without power for 6 weeks, the effects would have been more severe for obvious reasons. The lesson here, lesson number 5, is that luck plays a role in determining the severity of consequences stemming from a particular failure.

The Problem at Hand

So, how do the power outage stories relate to the problem at hand?

The first question to answer is, "Will we experience failures due to Year 2000?" The answer, despite any reluctance to predict the future, is an unqualified *yes.* Even if we all do everything we can to avoid the problem, we will still miss some existing problems and will unavoidably introduce new errors as we attempt to fix the old ones. The question is, how many problems will still exist in our systems as we move forward?

To answer this question we need to compare the Year 2000 problem to similar problems from the past. Once we have a benchmark, we can ask the question, "Do we expect to have fewer or more problems than we had in the past disaster?" To find a number, we must ask enough people with adequate knowledge of the problem. The estimate resulting won't necessarily be accurate, but it'll be in the ballpark.

We've repeatedly asked this question of audiences with some technical savvy. We've asked them to compare the Year 2000 problem to five prominent computer-related leap year problems (each costing about $1 million in either physical damages or in lost earnings) experienced in 1996. They zeroed in on 50,000 equivalent Year 2000–related computer problems as being a reasonable number of failures to expect.

In actuality, the number ranged from between 5,000 and 500,000, but the vast majority of responses were around 50,000. As far as predictions go, this one has a wide margin of error. Nevertheless, in the language of statisticians, we're 90 percent confident that the actual number of errors will be in this range. Errors will not all occur on January 1, 2000, but will start in January of 1999 and go on until about mid-2000—a total of 18 months of failures of varying degrees of impact.

Part of the issue, of course, is that many of the problems will be relatively trivial, merely costing about $1 million to fix, which in the greater scheme of things is of no consequence, fixable on the fly in mere hours, perhaps days. However, in the mix of problems, there could be several important *single points of failure*—applications that, like the electrical switch at the Sir Beck Power Station #2, make their importance known only after they fail in some spectacular fashion.

You could, of course, ignore the example of the single power switch, or the four cables leading into Auckland, or the O-ring, or Galaxy 4, and claim there is no way any of these 50,000 failures will have a similar effect. You may believe that somehow 50,000 failures (if that number is anywhere near accurate) will not create consequences that the proverbial "man in the street" will notice. Personally, we prefer to expect the worst, plan for it within reason, and then be pleasantly surprised when our fears are proven groundless.

If we draw on nothing more than a common cliché, and optimistically assume that really bad problems are 1 in 1000, then we have about 50 significant events to anticipate. This is not the same as stating that 50 of these failures will be equivalent to single switches or O-rings. It's merely a guess as to how many of these problems will be *significant*.

Fifty problems, even problems that last six weeks, will not be an end of the world scenario. It will, however, be a severe blow to the economy worldwide. The economy will be even more adversely affected if Year 2000 problems interact with each other to create compounding effects.

In convergence behavior, we all get on the phone lines to coordinate our attempts to solve the problem. What if, while we're trying to fix a power outage, we also discover the phone system doesn't work because the communications satellites are also affected by the problem? In addition to this mess, the train-scheduling systems are unreliable, or the applications that schedule crews for commercial airlines are not getting the right crew to the right plane on time? Combine all these problems, and the situation gets ugly.

It doesn't get so ugly that everything falls apart. We have an ace in the hole. The one thing, which disaster after disaster has demonstrated, is that when we are pushed into desperate situations, we somehow always find ways to overcome the difficulties facing us. This is not a Pollyanna-ish view of the world. The workarounds are inefficient, costly, temporary, dangerous, and avenues of last resort. Somehow they will be enough to bring us through to the other side.

We've already spent a great deal of time and money trying to fix problems we were lucky enough to identify before they occurred. What remains will be the unexpected problems. If we've done our job to the best of our abilities, with a bit of luck, these remaining problems will be manageable. Yes, it all boils down to faith in our own competence, and a dash of luck, but it's only a technical problem, not an asteroid from space. This too shall pass.